# Landmarks in American Literature

## History in the Making

DEDICATED
WITH GRATITUDE
TO

PROFESSOR ISAAC SEQUEIRA
(1930-2006)

# Landmarks in American Literature

## History in the Making

*Edited by*

MANJU JAIDKA
ANIL RAINA

Prestige
*an international publishing house*

**PRESTIGE BOOKS**
3/28, East Patel Nagar
New Delhi 110 008
email: prestigebooks@gmail.com
Mobile: 9818755529

ISBN: 81-7551-199-0



Printed at Chaman Offset Press, New Delhi 110 002

# Contents

## FOR PROFESSOR ISAAC SEQUEIRA

## A TRIBUTE

### DEDICATION

Professor Isaac Sequeira (5 January 1930-7 September 2006)

His life was gentle, and the elements
So mixed in him that Nature might stand up
And say to all the world, "This was a man!"

One of the founder members and Patron of MELUS-India, Isaac Sequeira is no longer in our midst but monuments of his selfless service to education and to society at large are scattered everywhere. Take his undeniable dedication to the American Studies and to MELUS-India and MELOW, in particular. When the American Studies Research Centre in Hyderabad was totally abandoned by the powers that be, it was he who held the fort, not for any personal gain but for a deep conviction that institutions are to be nurtured; they cannot and should not be abandoned callously. ASRC would have perished many years ago, had Isaac Sequeira not been at the helm to keep it going. There are many other milestones, many landmarks associated with Isaac, scattered across the country. Take a look at any university department in the country, and one may easily find several senior professors whose lives have been touched and careers have been shaped, in one way or another, by Isaac Sequeira.

As members of MELUS-India and MELOW, we owe him a debt of gratitude. About a decade ago, when we floated MELUS-India, a society dedicated to the study of multi-ethnic literatures of the U.S., he was one of our strongest pillars. In 2005, when we wanted to float a parallel academic organization, he was equally enthusiastic and MELOW (the Society for the Study of the Multi-Ethnic Literatures of the World) was born. He was a Patron and attended ALL of our conferences. The two organizations, under his guidance, have been thriving and now have an established international network (website www.melus-melow.org).

We are grateful to Professor Sequeira for showing us the way, for being our guiding light and steering our organization from its earliest teething troubles to its present position in the international arena when it commands respect and authority for its academic endeavors from year to year. He will remain a role model for us to emulate. May his light continue to guide us in the years to come!

This volume of essays, selected from the papers presented at the MELUS-India 2005 Conference on "Landmarks on the American Scene" is dedicated to him with gratitude and love.

THE EDITORS

# Presidential Address

**M.G. Ramanan**
**University of Hyderabad**

This is my fourth address to this body. In my earlier addresses I attempted to chalk out a prolegomena to studying American literature in the Universities in India, spoke of the governing motifs of American literature, focused on the paradigm shift in studying America in a multi-cultural context, elaborated on the implications of American multiculturalism for an Indian audience, and in my very last address last year asked the question "Where shall we go from here?" Yes indeed where are we to go and today I propose reflecting on this question and to suggest some answers, answers which I believe to be somewhat different from the ones I suggested last time. Things have changed a lot in English Studies in India and I use the term to include what in most English departments is a part of English Studies—American literature. The recent events in Iraq have not gone down well with academicians in India and certainly in spite of détente among Governments, there is a suspicion of America and things American even in the bureaucracy. This clearly was one reason why that venerable Institution which all of us love—the ASRC lost out in the whole business of finding funds which would protect its fundamental character. No doubt the UGC has now stepped in but it is an open question if the ASRC will be the Institution we all cared for, not least because it provided a refuge for the beleaguered Humanities in our country. It was one place where Humanists could actually go freely, because they had some award or the other to support their research. It was a place where we met our peers, formed friendships and made our careers. It was a place where one could do research in areas other than American literature because of the kind of journals we got there and many of us made discoveries of books and materials we never imagined the ASRC would possess, in subjects quite remote from the concerns of the ASRC. In short there was no other Institution in India which could match the facilities and the ambience of the ASRC. It was our pride until the Americans abandoned the Institution. The disaster was coming and if the people who managed the ASRC had been a little more prudent in financial arrangements it would not have come to this pass. I had a small role to play in the difficult days before the UGC finally decided to take over the ASRC and I know the frustrations Professor Isaac Sequeira, Professor Richard Cohen, and I experienced. There were humiliating moments too and we tried everything we could to save the ASRC in the form in which we had known it. Time alone will tell us what is to happen to the place, whether it will retain its character as the prime American Studies Institution of the country, the best outside America, save for Berlin's Kennedy Center.

The suspicion with which the American bureaucracy viewed Indian scholars was indeed painful. In Washington, I am told, we were suspected of being Commies! In India we were the stooges of American Imperialism. Between these perceptions we fell and what has suffered are the Humanities. The Humanities are under siege in this country as never before. American outsourcing, business machinations, multinational trade, an increasing demand for IT professionals—these and a Technologico-Benthamite value system have ensured that the Humanities will get more and more marginalized. Clearly this is not something we at MELUS-India can contemplate with equanimity. Our business is with the Humanities, and American Studies as we have practised it is a marker of the interdisciplinary culture of the Humanities. American Studies was holistic in its tendencies because it made interdisciplinarity a way of life. The demise of the ASRC as we knew it is a threat to the Humanities and it is a challenge proffered to us to affirm the relevance of our work in this big bad world. I believe that we might need to foreground

Humanistic concerns in MELUS-India in a more self conscious way than before. We have for a time abandoned the study of the classics in our quest for the margins and the periphery. Thus while we might have been brought up on a diet of Emerson, Whitman, Dickinson and Melville, our present interest in the ethnic minorities and in pluralistic cultures compels us to read Momaday, Kingston, Bharati Mukherjee. This was of course necessary but it does look as if the pendulum has moved to the other extreme and we are now guilt ridden if we are found reading *Self Reliance* or *Walden* or *The Turning of the Screw*. The study of the literature of the Asian Americans, the Hispanics, the Indigenous American or that of the African American certainly enriched us but it is time now, I believe, to make some strategic mental adjustments. In our quest for the new we have missed out on the old and it is time to reassert a reformed Humanism by bringing back to centrestage the best that has been thought and said in the world. In the context of this meeting of MELUS-India this would mean a healthy respect for the American classics. But this is not easy given the experience of multiculturalism in the last twenty five years. It calls for a deliberate effort to see American literature as a rich and varied tapestry made up of several strands but all leading to a sense of unity. I must distinguish the idea of unity from uniformity. The two are different and in American Literature, I see diversity held together by some basic and core patterns. In an unfashionable manner and against the grain of present modes of thinking I am arguing that in MELUS-India we should transcend our fixation with multiculturalism and seek certain kinds of unities in the literary tradition which we are involved with. I would like to draw your attention to the master narratives of America and their dependence on certain tropes and figures and symbols. I am thinking of the idea of America viewed as the Just City on the hill, the idea of the Westward movement and the related ideas of seeing America as a Virgin Land, as a Frontier, as unexplored territory, as representing the world of the unknown and the untested for mankind. I would like to seek connections between these governing motifs and the fresh set of metaphors which a multicultural society has generated—ideas of Home and Exile, ideas of Hybridity, of the Self as essentially constructed through narrative, of lives being lived in the interstices and of identity being determined by the condition of wandering and adventure. In this context it would appear that ruptures and apertures constitute the sufficient and necessary condition of existence.

Let me spend a few moments with only two of many possible texts for illustration. My first is Thoreau, whose relevance for Indians is so obvious. In *Walden* he has the finest evocation of loss and the quest for wholeness which is not peculiarly or quintessentially American. Like all good literature anywhere in the world Thoreau's text is about loss and recovery. It is a critique of the present and it evokes a vision of possibilities, not unlike T.S. Eliot invoking Krishna or the Upanishads so that modern man can experience the peace that passes all understanding. Hear Thoreau's haunting words:

> I long ago lost a hound, a bay horse, and a turtle-dove, and am still on their trail. Many are the travelers I have spoken to concerning them, describing their tracks and what calls they answered to. I have met one or two who had heard the hound, and the tramp of the horse, and even seen the dove disappear behind a cloud, and they seemed as anxious to recover them as if they had lost them themselves.

What is this if it is not at one level an evocation of man's existential dilemma, of the loss of Innocence, of Home, of values, and the desperate cry for recovery, for wholeness and for Home and the stabilities of Tradition. Now my point is that Thoreau is not speaking only for America, or for WASPS or for an elite set of Transcendentalists. He is giving expression to the existential state of all human beings—and that would include a James Welch, a Momaday, a Vikram Chandra and surely women writers like Bharati Mukherjee or Meena Alexander or Maxine Hong Kingston. I am in other words arguing for a reformed humanism, a humanism under correction if you like, but a humanism nevertheless. The humanism I have in mind has no truck with racism, imperialism, colonialism, or white male ascendancy. It will also have no truck with reverse racism, minority celebration at the cost of basic human solidarity and with gender-specific talk which refuses the common humanity of us all. Thoreau is in this special sense of the term a universalist and I use the expression fully aware of the pejorative implications of the term for many post-modern scholars who celebrate difference at the cost of human oneness.

My second example is from the work of Tennessee Williams. For me he remains the greatest American playwright of our times and I say this because unlike many other distinguished writers contemporaneous to him, Williams has that exquisite quality of tenderness. It is a value he propagated all his life and at crucial moments in his writing it is this yearning for human connection, this tenderness, this desire to love to distraction that gives that extra value to what William writes. Whether it is the youngman who has a wound, whether it is the vulnerable Laura, whether it is Blanche asking to be treated with dignity, it is this human quality which gives Williams's plays the excellence they have. Again my point is that of mainstream writers, if we want to use such an expression at all, Williams is the one dealing with women, freaks, homosexuals, colored people, and the marginalized. He had sympathy for the homeless and the exiled and his plays are a cry for compassion and tenderness. In this respect he compares favorably with the author of *Color Purple* or the novelist who wrote *Wife* or a poet like Agha Shahid Ali. Williams, like Thoreau has an appeal which goes beyond America or the WASPS, and he speaks of concerns which one associates with the multiculturalists. Surely it should be possible for us in MELUS-India to include him in our schemes of things.

Salman Rushdie speaks of chutneyfication of not only language but of history. His example in *Fury* should show how the experimental verve of his earlier novels is magnified in this tale of Brooklyn violence and the fantastic experiences of Malik Solanka, a Professor of Indian origin. The language Rushdie uses is a chutney, a hybrid, a proper expression of the hybrid lives of exiles and migrants. Agha Shahid Ali, who I have referred to earlier, carries Rushdie's culinary metaphor forward by speaking of the Biryanification of English by which I suppose he means that the language should be an adequate expression of his own Kashmiri-Urdu provenance fused with English. In a multicultural society like the US it is impossible to speak of a Standard English and it would appear that the Chutneyfication and Biryanification are a condition of linguistic existence in the Americas. Ali who wants his Kashmiri Urdu to mix with English, to produce not the Rushdiean chutney, but the Indian Biryani is therefore at the cutting edge of contemporary American experience. The Biryanification of English is what I believe Mark Twain indulged in when he wrote *Huckleberry Finn.* Indeed American English which got its distinctive character around the 1820s when the American literary Renaissance got underway is a Biryanification of the Standard English of the Mother Country. Mencken gives enough proof of the way the new language through a process of hybridization and creative ingenuity gave itself a new character. Look at the way in which American Language and Literature have evolved. Mencken's great book shows the influences at work and the hybrid nature of the American language which becomes American only because it distinguishes itself from English. When Twain wrote *Huckleberry Finn* it is said that he was particularly focusing on questions of language. There are several strains of American speech and Mississippi speech in the novel and what we hear in India is only a small part of that provenance. And yet the fluent rhythms and the colorful tropes that Huck uses endear us to the American hero and his creator. Huck Finn is a practitioner of a free speech and in its Creolish way it set the tone for American Literature. No wonder Hemingway said that all American Literature had its origins in *Huckleberry Finn.* With that novel the great endeavor to create a distinctive literature in English came about and we have as some one put it two literatures in one language because American is English, but an English which is heavily burdened with the weight of American experience. What I am suggesting is that multiculturalism is only one more phase in the progress of the English language in America, from its colonial imitativeness, to its postcolonial distinctiveness. I should think that African-American rhythms, Chicano sounds, Red Indian chants, Asian metaphors are all part of the wonderful tapestry which is American literature and American language. In the name of ethnicity we should not forget the nature of America and her linguistic triumph. What we are witnessing today is only one more strand being added to that palimpsest which American language is. If we use terms like Chutneyfication or Biryanification it is only a measure of the richness that has overcome America. Multiculturalism is the final triumph of American pluralism and democracy.

And thus the question arises as to what the relevance of this culture is to us here in this part of the world. The relevance cannot be overstated. It is in many ways a parallel to the Indian context. It is after all the reality of the only global power in the world today. Much as we resent American hegemonic intentions, the fact is that its soul is not with its politicians. It is with the people who have time and again demonstrated their solidarity with the people of the world. It is that America which we should hold dear and study in India. Not to study America is to cop out or opt out of an important aspect of contemporary reality. To study her we can build our own paradigms and our own methods. We need no instruction from Washington or the MLA or any one else. We are our own center. MELUS-India is moving on and from this year we will also be merging our concerns with the larger concerns of studying World literature. This is the only logical and correct step to take and it is necessitated by the realities of our experience in academia and by the threat to the Humanities I have outlined. If we are to survive, if the civilized world of academic endeavor is to mean anything I can't see how we can refuse to read America as part of the larger world and American literature whether mainstream, or multicultural as part of the emerging world order of literary franchise.

# Diaspora Blues:
# A Poetics of Home and Displacement

**Susan Stanford Friedman**
**University of Wisconsin, Madison**

Landmarks on the American Scene—a provocative title for a conference and a richly suggestive conference call on the multiple meanings of the term *landmark*. I wonder how the land marks the body, how land marks the spirit of people in motion from one locality to another, from one state of being to another. What are the landmarks of liminality for the heart, for the intimacies of everyday life?

I begin with a common American story, a tale of migration. full of contradictions. Noreen is my daughter's friend, her roommate during their first year of law school in New York City. Noreen is the eldest of three children born in the United States to parents from an elite family in Pakistan. Her father is a surgeon, and the family goes back and forth "home" to Pakistan at the drop of a hat. Noreen is vibrant, full of infectious laughter and whimsy, warm and endlessly generous. Irreverent with her friends, she is also ever the dutiful daughter, to her family, religion, and homeland. Three years ago, Noreen's father arranged a marriage for her with a young man she had never met. Amazed, my daughter watched Noreen's initial shock fade and then turn into eagerness as she and the young man fell in love. A year later, her father abruptly cancelled the engagement after a serious disagreement with the young man's family. Noreen was devastated, but accepted her father's decision. After a while, Noreen announced to my daughter with some pride of independence that she would not select a mate of her own, but she also would not accept an arranged marriage. She would remain single—a space in between having her father choose and choosing for herself. In this space between worlds, Noreen allowed herself to become "just friends" with a fellow law student, a Jewish man so different on the surface of things but so alike in their laughter and dreams. Inseparable as "just friends," they became in the eyes of their classmates clearly an "item." Over winter break, Noreen goes back "home," as usual, to Pakistan. She returns with a bombshell. Her father has announced a new engagement—she is to be married in June to a young man in Pakistan she has only just met. She speaks to my daughter of her anguish and confusion, her sense of duty, the competing loves she feels for her boyfriend and her family. To defy her father would mean to lose her family. What to do? My daughter, the product of a mixed marriage, in an interracial relationship herself, does not know what to say.

I don't know the end of this story. But I wonder, what happens to the human spirit between worlds, to desire and longing as they cross and re-cross geographical and cultural borders, to the domains of intimacy and family in migration, dislocation, and relocation? Will Noreen's laughter be silenced?

For some Asian Americans, Meena Alexander writes in her essay/poem "Alphabets of Flesh," "assimilation translates into doing well, very well, not just making do. But the streets lined with gold are hard to walk and what happens with the heart can give one pause" (149) In her poem "Estrangement Becomes the Mark of the Eagle," lovers "lie in a white room, on a bed with many pillows":

> you whisper: exile is hard
> let me into your mouth, let me blossom. (89)

Whether or not "the streets are lined with gold"—and for most migrants, they are not—diaspora is hard on intimacy.

Intimacy begins in the body, needs the body—the body of touch, the body of sensation and feeling, the body of speech. What Homi Bhabha calls the *affective body*—the body that feels—can be the site of pleasure, but also of pain; the place of resistance, but also of mutilation and abjection (271). "One is marked by one's body," Alexander observes, "but how is one marked?" ("Alphabets" 149). As the Lebanese expatriate writer Etel Adnan notes, "The problem is that the heart can never be separated from the flesh" (61).

The body is the home of the heart. Flesh is the body of home. But what is home? Who feels at home while at home? "I had to leave home so I could find myself," writes Gloria Anzaldúa in *Borderlands/La Frontera*. "But I didn't leave all parts of me: I kept the ground of my own being" She is rooted in a sense of home as a place she can never be at home and from which she must escape to feel at home with herself. "I am a turtle, wherever I go I carry 'home' on my back" (21).[1]

* * *

***Longing for Home: Adages***

Longing for home is the body's desire—a feeling of homesickness experienced viscerally in the flesh, in the "affective body." But *homesickness* too is a cryptogram: the word opens up into opposites: sick *for* home and sick *of* home.[2]

Dorothy in *The Wizard of Oz* is doubly homesick. First, she's sick *of* home, her rage surrealistically embodied in the whirling tornado that transports her away from Kansas. Then, she's sick *for* home, pining for the Kansas homestead intensified with each fantastical scene on the journey to Oz. She longs for home—but only after she fulfills her wish to leave it. The lesson she learns in the far away of fantasy land is that she can get home simply by reciting a mantra: *There's no place like home. There's no place like home. There's no place like home.* Once said and repeated, the words transport her back home in a flash, undoing the displacement from home brought about by her home-sick-ness, her anger at home.[3]

The magical phrase—*there's no place like home*—is also doubly cryptic. "There's no *place* like home" means home is *the* best, the ideal, everything that elsewhere is not. Places elsewhere can never bring the same happiness as home. Alternately inflected, the phrase turns into its opposite. "There's *no* place like home" also means that no place, anywhere, is like home. Nowhere is there a place like home. Home is a never never land of dreams and desire. Home is utopia—a no place, a nowhere, an imaginary space longed for, always already lost in the very formation of the idea of home.

*Home is where the heart is.* Born in the Punjab, migrating to Britain at age nine, the sociologist Madan Sarup reflects on the adage. "*Home is where the heart is.*" He muses:

> But what makes a place home? Is it wherever your family is, where you have been brought up? The children of many migrants do not know where they belong. Where is home? Is it where your parents are buried? Is home the place from where you have been displaced, or where you are now? Is home where your mother lives? ("Home and Identity" 94)

If *home* for the migrant, the exile, the refugee, is the place of *tradition*, he writes, then what is lost in the need for security is how that homeland is ever-changing. "Tradition is fluid," he writes, "it is always being reconstituted. Tradition *is* about change—change that is not being acknowledged" (97).

Aisha Ravindran, a friend and Fulbright scholar from Kerala, India, explains to me that people far from home often reconstitute the traditions of home as unchanging, frozen in time. Noreen, she tells me, might have more freedom to choose her own mate in Pakistan, where marriage traditions are changing for some, than she has as part of a diasporic family in the United States.

Another adage: *You can't go home again.* From Thomas Wolfe, a migrant from the southern hills of North Carolina to New York City, an itinerant wanderer across the Atlantic, in Europe, and on the North American Continent, Wolfe moves from *Look Homeward, Angel* in 1929 to *You Can't Go Home Again* in 1940. *Again*? Does this mean *once* you COULD go home, and now you can't? That once upon a time in fairyland you could go home? You can have *one* return, but no more, never again?

*To market, to market to buy a fat hog. Home again, Home again, jiggedy jog.* But you can't go home again. *This little piggy went to market, this little piggy stayed home. This little piggy had roast beef. This little piggy had none. And this little piggy went weeweewee aaaallll the way home.* But you *can't* go home again.

*He* can't go home again. But some men can. *An Englishman's home is his castle. A man's home is his castle.* You've heard the sayings before. A castle is a fortress, a retreat behind moat and walls to make one safe, a place to ride out a siege—a haven in a heartless world. Castles are safest for the men who rule them. If the world chews him up and spits him out, at least a man can be a man within the walls of his castle-home. Inside the walls, he can lord it over others. His home is no one else's castle. It's for him to decide if the walls will protect the others from the outside. Inside the castle, what walls protect people from him?

The nation too is home—the *homeland* as *fatherland* or *motherland* to be defended by *Homeland Defense* and *Patriot Acts*. Domestic politics is national politics, the government within, at home.[4] The nation is family, the imagined community of Us against Them. Whoever *Them* is, we know they are not *US*. Not the U dot S dot of A dot. But if Them is Us, a part of US, everywhere in U.S.A., doesn't the defense of the homeland become an attack on US, all of US in the U dot S dot? Do you feel more secure now that the Acts of Patriots are trained against some of us, all of us? Jailing the stranger within, who can't join the motherland, the fatherland, the homeland, can't ever be one of us because of the home he left behind? Have you figured out how to protect yourself from Homeland Defense? Have you bought your duct tape to cover up your mouth, your eyes, your ears: Say no evil, See no evil, Hear no evil? Just let the Acts of Patriots do it all for you! While you retreat to a sealed up room.

*Once upon a time, there were three little pigs who were all afraid of the Big Bad Wolf.* One built a house of straw. One built a house of sticks. And one built a house of bricks. When the Big Bad Wolf huffed and puffed and blew down the house of straw and blew down the house of sticks, the pig inside the brick house locked the door so nobody could get in. Yes, a man's home is his castle. A man's nation is his home. *The king was in his castle, counting out his money.*

And where was the queen? *She was in the parlour eating bread and honey.* Oh yes. The Queen was eating. The Queen was swelling, queen bee of the home as hive. She's the hub of *Mamaland*, the *omphalos* of universe. She's the body of desire, the body as food, the body as blanket of comfort. The navel of love. The nipple of suck. She is the apple pie she makes. She is the chicken soup of soul. *Home Sweet Home*. She is the sweets of home, to be licked in need, to be lapped in desire, to be suckled for unconditional love. She is *homeland security* of a different sort. *The sky is falling, the sky is falling* cries Chicken Little. *Run to Mamaland.*

The Queen is also the Mother/Other, the Other Mother, the wicked evil stepqueen who would eat you up. She is the (m)other, m/other as womb/tomb: the imaginary origin and end of life. *Motherlove* can be *smotherlove*. Think of Paul Morel, the budding artist in D.H. Lawrence's autobiographical *Sons and Lovers*. Cancer is eating his mother alive, the mother who is eating him alive. So he smothers the mother who is smothering him.

Or Joan in Margaret Atwood's *Lady Oracle*. She becomes the trickster queen of harlequin escape once she wins the battle of the body with her mother. *Mirror mirror on the wall, who's the fairest of them all?* "In the image of her that I carried for years hanging from my neck like an iron locket," Joan reflects, "she was sitting in front of her vanity table, painting her fingernails a murderous red" (71). Eating—eating always, eating anything—is Joan's weapon of choice: "The war between my mother and myself was one in earnest; the disputed territory was my body. . . . I swelled visibly, relentlessly, before her very eyes. I rose like dough, my body advanced inch by inch towards her across the dining-room table, in this at least I was undefeated" (73).

And the mother of *Mamaland*? Is she safe at home? So busy *homemaking* that no one notices how the home makes her. As everybody's *homebody*, Mama turns to stone as fast as Lot's wife.

*There's no place like home. Home Sweet Home.*

* * *

***Home away from Home***

Is home a place? A memory? An ideal? An imagined space? The black hole of desire? Born of displacement, diasporas spawn the creation of an imaginary homeland, a place of fixed location and identity. "Home is an idea," Janet Zandy writes, "an inner geography where the ache to belong finally quits, where there is no sense of 'otherness,' where there is, at last, a community" (1). Being away from home engenders fictionalizing memories of the past and dreams of the future. In Sandra Cisneros's *The House on Mango Street,* home is the hope of a writer-to-be for Esperanza, the young protagonist of the story collection. Esperanza indigenizes Woolf's famous trope of "a room of one's own" in longing for home as a form of independence: "A House of My Own. Not a flat. Not an apartment in back. Not a man's house. Not a daddy's. A house all my own . . . a house quiet as snow, a space for myself to go, clear as paper before the poem." (108)[5]

And what is home for people on the move? Chandra Talpade Mohanty grew up in Bombay and came to the U.S. as a student and has stayed, with her Indian passport and green card, to live and teach. She reflects,

> What is home? The place I was born? Where I grew up? Where my parents live? Where I live and work as an adult? Where I locate my community, my people? Who are 'my people'? Is home a geographical space, a historical space, an emotional, sensory space? . . . I am convinced that this question—how one understands and defines home—is a profoundly political one. (497)

Dr. Marianne Ferrara, a retired physician and friend, tells me simply, "Home is where I am." She was a Jewish child in France hidden in the early days of the Nazi occupation with a Catholic family to whom she expressed her gratitude by becoming and remaining a devout Catholic. Hating France, she fled to the United States for college, practised medicine in the Northeast, and retired to Dallas to be near her five American sons. She doesn't even like to visit France, let alone think of it as her home. But things French continue to exert their hold, however ambivalently, and not only in the trace of an accent. As perfect recapitulation of her multiple dislocations, she fell in love again with an old college flame, a woman with whom she had acted in a French play at Bryn Mawr College, a secular Jew who had become a famous professor of French, a Francophile *par excellence* who nonetheless articulated with brilliance the meanings of phallogocentrism and anti-Semitism in French tradition: Elaine Marks. That Elaine should die suddenly of cancer one year after their reunion brings home the ironies of human existence in the face of which Marianne states complexly, "Home is where I am."

For filmmaker Mira Nair (*Missippi Masala, Monsoon Wedding, Vanity Fair*), home is paradoxically in flight:

> I used to have a joke when people asked where I live. . . . I'd say, 'I live on Air India.' But the other side is that you live between your ears. You carry your home within yourself. That's a nice-sounding cerebral concept, but the truth is that you're torn. (qtd. Bumiller 12)

Nair comes from a Punjabi family that fled to New Delhi at Partition in 1947. She grew up in eastern India, went to college in Delhi and Cambridge, Massachusetts, and married an African Indian from Uganda, who teaches at Columbia University. New York, New Delhi, and Kampala are all "home" for Nair. For her home is everywhere and always elsewhere. Her "Home" resides in the eyes that film the existence of being "torn." Her cinematic muse is the spirit of identity in motion—motion pictures for identities located through repeated dislocations. Bodies in motion too. The bodies of intimacy and sometimes hunger.

The hunger to come may be the desire to go home, feel at home in the body. To her lover in "The Floating Poem,

Unnumbered," Adrienne Rich plays with metaphors of travel, of coming and going, to taste the sweet, natural home: "Your traveled, generous thighs/ between which my whole face has come and come—/ . . ./ reaching where I had been waiting years for you/ in my rose-wet cave." (32) How far must I travel, Rich asks in "Sibling Mysteries," to recover the "woman's flesh . . . made taboo to us" (49). "Remind me," she muses, "how we loved our mother's body/ our mouths drawing the first/ thin sweetness from her nipples. . . .// The daughters never were/ true brides of the father// the daughters were to begin with/ brides of the mother// then brides of each other/ under a different law// Let me hold and tell you" (48, 56). For Rich, home is the long lost, forever gone—maternal body, motherland. To live is to be away from home.

* * *

### *Stranger Bodies*

Fostering the dream of home is the experience of being alien, of being forever marked as the stranger who doesn't belong. The body as a sight of cultural determination first marks someone as "the stranger"—it might be the skin, the eyes, the hair, the shape, the sex; it might be the walk, the posture, the angles of movement; it might be the clothes, the jewelry, the shoes, the decorations, adornments, and accoutrements of the body; it might be the sounds that come out of the mouth, off the pen or keyboard—the cultural materiality of speech, accent, rhythm, style, writing.

"In Europe today," Sarup writes, "it is largely black migrants who perform the function of marking the boundary." Sarup's Europe is home to the demographic implosions of past empires, and the U.S. has its own history of the color line as demarcation of strangeness. I wonder. . . . Who is the stranger in India? In China? South Africa, Morocco, Australia, Argentina? Each location creates its own strangers. Perhaps the measure of any society is how it treats the ones it marks as strangers. Can strangers ever become homebodies? *Landsmen*? *Homies? Bros?*

Must bodies remain ever the trace—the sign, the symptom—of foreignness? And thereby the justification for exclusions and violations?

"I do not know the face of this country," writes poet Janice Mirkitani of the United States. "It is inhabited by strangers/ who call me obscene names.// Jap. Go home./ Where is home?" (qtd. Bow 12)

To a nation that imagines itself homogeneous, the alien is an uncanny reminder of repressed difference, a ghostly presence that must be expunged to restore the sense of oneness. (Bhabha, DissemiNation 294-95)[6] Those who feel at home in the world need strangers to remind them of who they are not.

* * *

***Violence on the Home Body***

To inhabit the body of the stranger is to be never at home. But what if home itself is the site of violence to the body? Home may in fact be constituted upon an act of violence against the body, even as that body travels, migrates, or goes into exile. Safety might reside neither in home nor homeland, but only in flight. Diasporic narratives often tell the story of travel to a new land where memory and desire produce an idealized image of the homeland. But violence done to the body in *both* old and new homes disrupts this familiar pattern.

Think of Edwidge Danticat's novel *Breath, Eyes, Memory*, on the face of it, the typical *Bildungsroman* of immigration, the "coming to America" for the adolescent Sophie, a journey that produces generational strain, conflict with her mother, and the limbo of between worlds existence. A closer look, however, reveals a complex interrogation of home and homeland as overlapping sites for violence against the female body—in both Haiti and the United States. The novel revolves around the Haitian custom of "testing"—that is, mothers regularly inserting a finger into the vaginas of their teenage daughters, feeling for the hymen that will insure the family's honor until marriage.[7] Virginity as prize and badge of masculine honor is common to many cultures, but the regular testing for it in this way is not. Danticat likens the custom to rape by setting up an uncanny parallel between the politics of the Haitian state and the politics of the Haitian home, wherever that home may be.

Sophie's initiation into adulthood is not the flowering of womanhood, but rather its deflowering. She comes to understand the random fragments of her life: how the violence of the state and the home echo each other, how the violence passes down through the generations of women who serve and service the needs of men. Once upon a time, Sophie learns, her mother got relief from her grandmother's probing finger only after she is raped by a soldier, not a foreign soldier, but one of the vicious *ton ton* macoutes in Haiti. She is disgraced, half-crazed with nightmares, pregnant. She leaves her baby with her unmarried sister, migrates to the States, and 12 years later abruptly calls her daughter north. Torn from her home, Sophie finds the repetition of home elsewhere, when her mother tests her nubile body nightly, to ensure the family honor, in an act of bodily invasion that imitates the rape that produced her.

Where can the daughter go to feel safe? She flees to Providence with a man of her own choosing, but she cannot escape the effects of violence on her body. How can she break the cycle of bodily invasions in Haiti and New York when her own baby daughter grows up? She goes back to Haiti to bury her mother, to find a way out of the maze in which at every turn mothers rape their daughters in the service of men. Does she find her answer?

*You can't go home again and anyway, do you want to?*

The Partition of India in 1947 forced millions from their homes and unleashed massive communal bloodletting. The mutilated body of Mother India found its avatar in the violated bodies of its women. "*Partition,*" writes Ritu Menon in her oral history collection, "is *a metaphor for irreparable loss.*" And yet, she also found that some women "saw in this rupture a moment of unexpected liberation for themselves *as women*" (19).[8] For some, the violence on the body at home *before* Partition was worse than *after*, when Partition's chaos opened pathways formerly closed. This is the story the American writer Shauna Singh Baldwin tells in her recent Partition novel, *What the Body Remembers* (2001).[9] The novel is about the two wives of a prominent Sikh engineer in the Punjab in the 30s and 40s: one, Satya, the lover and soulmate who bears no children; and the other, the fecund child-bride Roop, who leaps at the chance to escape the purdah of home without understanding her fate as a breeder destined to lose her children to the barren wife. Paradoxically, Roop comes the closest to feeling at home only in the midst of Partition's violence, the dispersal of millions, and her own family's exile. Satya dead, her husband destroyed, Roop thrives on dislocation, becoming the backbone of the family's survival. *Home is where the heart is*, but the body's heart can be riven. A Partition of the heart.

Riven too in the *Heartland*, the *American Heartland*, Alice in the Wonderland of Dairyland. Think of Jane Smiley's *A Thousand Acres*. The novel revisits Shakespeare's story of dutiful and undutiful daughters. Right there in the wholesome acres of cornland. America's breadbasket, feeder of the nation, hub of the national imaginary. The midwestern farm family, descendants of pioneers in Conestoga wagons who broke the virgin sod of the prairie and tamed it to produce a cornucopia of dreams. People tied to the land. Good people. People who live the ethic of hard work and clean living. But what is the deep dark secret the family refuses to remember? The father's violence upon the bodies of his daughters. The daughters riven, split: the bad daughter who remembers and insists on telling; the good daughter who forgets and keeps the faith of innocence. Partition within the family.

* * *

### *Home Lost*

Home comes into being most powerfully when it is gone, lost, left behind, desired and imagined. As the daughter of Holocaust survivors, Grace Feuerverger calls her first language,

Yiddish, her *Mamaloshen*, her mothertongue and her lost home" to which she "cannot ever return because it was razed to the ground" (11, 19).[10]

The story of home making is often the history of home razing—that is, the razing of some one else's home to clear the way for one's own settlement. The end of one people's wandering can be the beginning of another's diaspora. "My feet are lacerated, homelessness has exhausted me," wrote the Palestinian poet Taufiq Sayigh in 1960.[11] Home making built upon the unmaking of the homes of others: it's history's return of the repressed. It happens again and again—the uncanny repetitions of a territorial species, of peoples' yearning for home and making others homeless out of the force of their own desire and suffering.

America's heartland was once other peoples' homelands—stolen, now lost, now shrunk to a fraction of its early range. Oh, Dorothy, Dorothy, what history of loss does your Kansas home-sweet-home plow under? For Diane Glancy, the farmlands of her German-Irish lineage fester atop her Cherokee ancestors, the "old tribes disc-harrowed/into the ground."[12] Oh, Dorothy, Dorothy, in that Home, Home on the Raaaaange, where the deer and the antelope roam, the prairies were once the range of Indians, the homeland as a range for patterned movements with the seasons. There's no place like home on the Rez.

The lullaby of an old Navajo woman in Leslie Marmon Silko's *Storyteller* comforts a dying man by singing of the earth as homeland never lost, always there:

> The earth is your mother,
> she holds you.
> The sky is your father,
> he protects you.
> Sleep,
> sleep.
> Rainbow is your sister,
> she loves you.
> The winds are your brothers,
> they sing to you.

Sleep,
sleep.
We are together always
We are together always
There was never a time
when this
was not so.

* * *

## *Writing Home*

Travel, migration, exile—these are the itineraries of being as becoming, identity in motion. Fragments of each place remain as locations to which memories are attached, out of which identities are formed. In each, the body as marked and read is catalyst for reflection. The body in motion is the muse.

"For some writers," Carole Boyce Davies reflects, "exile is a desired location out of which they can create. . . . Migration creates the desire for home, which in turn produces the rewriting of home." (112-13). Writing identity in motion fills the gap with sign symbols of homes lost and new homes in the making.

Homes lost and found through writing is no walk in the park. There's blood on the ground of being. Hear Gloria Anzaldúa: "Living in a state of psychic unrest, in a Borderland is what makes poets write and artists create. It is like a cactus needle in the flesh" (73).

Virginia Woolf's needle in the flesh is the sensation of shock, of dislocation, of unmooring to which writing is the curative response. "And so I go on to suppose that the shock-receiving capacity is what makes me a writer," she reflects in *A Sketch of the Past*.[13] For Woolf, writing induces "rapture" as she enters into the body of words, of the Word. The rapture of writing rupture.

It is the "shock of arrival," of multiple arrivals, that compels the writing of Alexander's memoir: *The Shock of Arrival.* Growing up in India and the Sudan, educated in Britain, and living in New York city, she has learned "that even as time and localities shift, there is very little we can take for granted as we etch ourselves in complex palimpsests of knowledge and desire" (68-69). She emphasizes the linguistic mediation of bodies on the move: the self as tabula upon which the meanings of location and dislocation are etched, the self as etcher upon layers of being across space and through time.

The poetics of shock—of rupture, dislocation—involves emotional, spiritual, and often physical partition—a severing from "home." Writing about the loss of home brings one home again. *You can't go home again*—except in *writing home.*

The rapture of writing rupture.

*  *  *

***And Noreen?***

What about Noreen's unfinished story—Noreen marrying the stranger in June? In the domains of intimacy, dislocation can be at its most painful. She is living between worlds without the compensatory pleasures of poetry and fiction. The cactus of the Borderland needles her flesh too. Sometimes pain is just pain and not a poem.

On the other hand, Noreen has her laughter. She has her family, her culture, her religion. Maybe she'll do just fine. Maybe she won't feel lost at home, homeless at home. After all, choosing one's own mate has not always produced *Home Sweet Home*. Then again, the families we are born into and the homelands to which we belong don't always make us feel at home either.

# NOTES

1. Gloria Anzaldúa, *Borderlands/ La Frontera: The New Mestiza Consciousness* (San Francisco: Spinsters/Aunt Lute Press, 1987), pp. 16, 20. For recent cultural theory on the meanings of home, see for example, Sarup, "Home and Identity"; Bammer, *Displacements*, esp. pp. 57-202; Roberston et al., ed., *Travellers' Tales*; Avtar Brah, *Cartographies of Diaspora: Contesting Identities* (London: Routledge, 1994); Minnie Bruce Pratt, "Identity: Skin Blood Heart," in Elly Bulkin, Minnie Bruce Pratt, and Barbara Smith, *Yours in Struggle: Three Feminist Perspectives on Anti-Semitism and Racism* (Brooklyn, NY: Long Haul Press,

1984), pp. 9-64; Biddy Martin and Chandra Talpade Mohanty, "Feminist Politics: What's Home Got to Do with It?," in *Feminist Studies/ Critical Studies*, ed. Teresa de Lauretis (Bloomington: Indiana U P), pp. 191-212; bell hooks, "Homeplace: A Site of Resistance," in *Yearning: Race, Gender, and Cultural Politics* (Boston: South End Press, 1990), pp. 41-51; Roberta Rubenstein, *Home Matters: Longing and Belonging: Nostalgia and Mourning in Women's Fiction* (New York: Palgrave, 2001); Rosemary Marangoly George, *The Politics of Home: Postcolonial Relocations and Twentieth-Century Fiction* (Cambridge: Cambridge U P, 1996); Catherine Wiley and Fiona R. Barnes, ed., *Homemaking: Women Writers and the Politics of Home* (New York: Garland, 1996); Carol Boyce Davies, *Black Women, Writing and Identity: Migrations of the Subject* (London: Routledge, 1994), esp. pp. 113-30; Iain Chambers, *Migrancy, Culture, Identity* (London: Routledge, 1994); Linda McDowell, *Gender, Identity, and Place: Understanding Feminist Geographies* (Minneapolis: University of Minnesota Press, 1999), esp. pp. 71-95; R. Thomas Foster, "Homelessness at Home: Oppositional Practices and Modern Women's Writing," Diss., University of Wisconsin-Madison, 1990; Susan Stanford Friedman, *Mappings: Feminism and the Cultural Geographies of Encounter* (Princeton: Princeton University Press, 1998), esp. pp. 107-31, 151-78.

2. Thanks to Roberta Rubenstein, who reads "homesickness" two ways in *Home Matters* (2). She argues that the dismissal of homesickness as nostalgic as well as the feminist critical emphasis on home as confining ignores the way women writers deploy tropes of home and homesickness for "imaginative repair" in the face of displacement (5).

3. I am indebted to feminist sociologist Audrey Springer, whose class I observed in 2000, for stimulating me to think about the contradictions of home in *The Wizard of Oz.* See also Virginia Woolf's extensive play with "*There's no place like Home*" and "'Ome, Sweet 'Ome" in *Between the Acts* (New York: Harcourt Brace Jovanovich, 1941), 172-73. After drafting this essay, I discovered that Roberta Rubenstein also references *The Wizard of Oz*, Thomas Wolfe's *You Can't Go Home Again*, and Homer's *Odyssey*, but for somewhat different purposes than mine in her defense of nostalgia for home (*Home Matters* 2).

4. Rosemary Marangoly George asks, "When is the word 'home' shrunk to denote the private, domestic sphere and when is the

'domestic' enlarged to denote 'the affairs of the nation'?" (*The Politics of Home* 13). The rhetorical link between home and nation is widespread; see Linda McDowell's overview, "Unsettling Naturalisms," in the Forum on Interdisciplinary Perspectives on Home and Garden, *Signs* 27.3 (Spring 2002): 815-23; Nira Yuval-Davis, *Gender & Nation* (London: Sage, 1997).

5. See also Juta Ittner's "My Self, My Body, My World: Homemaking in the Fiction of Brigitte Kronauer," which opens with the query of what and where is "home": "Is it a fortress to be guarded against invasions by outsiders? Is it a woman's workshop, walled in and commodified, a place filled with icons and consumer goods, the house beautiful? A shelter for day-dreams, or private family utopia? A mirror of myself and my longs—for stability in an alienating world, for a space that is safe, for a retreat where I can finally be myself all by myself, 'chez moi'?," in Wiley and Barnes, *Homemaking* 53.
6. For other invocations of Freud's "The Uncanny" (1919) for discussions of migrancy, identity, difference, and national identity, see Sarup, 94-95; Iain Chambers, *Border Dialogues: Journeys in Postmodernity* (London: Routledge, 1990), 103-4; and Lars Engle, "The Political Uncanny: The Novels of Nadine Gordimer," *Yale Journal of Criticism* 2.2 (1989), 101-27.
7. Edwidge Danticat, *Breath, Eyes, Memory* (New York: Vintage, 1994); for references to "testing" and its relation to rape, see especially pp. 151, 154-56, 170.
8. Ritu Menon, Preface, in Ritu Memon and Kamla Bhasin, *Borders & Boundaries: Women in India's Partition* (New Brunswick, NJ: Rutgers University Press, 1998), p. xi. See also Urvashi Butalia, *The Other Side of Silence: Voices from the Partition of India* (New York: Viking, 1998).
9. Baldwin was born in Montreal and now lives in Milwaukee.
10. Grace Feuerverger, "My Yiddish Voice," *Journal of Curriculum Theorizing* 16.4 (Winter 2000), pp. 19, 11. See also Maerra Y. Shrebier's discussion of Yiddish as the language of "linguistic homemaking" in the work of Holocaust survivor Irena Klepfisz in "The End of Exile: Jewish Identity and Its Diasporic Poetics," *PMLA* 113.2 (March 1998), pp. 273-87.
11. Taufiq Sayigh, *al-Qasida*; qtd. Mona Takieddine Amyuni, Introduction. *Season of Migration to the North: A Casebook*, ed. Mona Takieddine Amyuni (Beirut, Lebanon: American University of Beirut, 1985), p. 21.

12. Diane Glancy, "Portrait of Spring," in *Lone Dog's Winter Count* (Albuquerque, New Mexico: West End Press, 1991), p. 71. Thanks to Hsinya Huang for pointing out that L. Frank Baum wrote *The Wizard of Oz* out of the Dakota territories and that some critics read his Oz fantasy as a rural populist as an allegory for the extermination of Indians.
13. Virginia Woolf, *A Sketch of the Past*, in *Moments of Being: Unpublished Autobiographical Writings,* ed. Jeanne Schulkind (New York: Harcourt Brace and Jovanovich, 1972), p. 72.

## Other Works Cited and Consulted

Adnan, Etel. *Of Cities and Women* (*Letters to Fawwaz).* Sausalito, CA: Post-Apollo Press, 1993.

Alexander, Meena. "Alphabets of Flesh." *Talking Visions: Multicultural Feminism in a Transnational Age.* Ed. Ella Shohat. Cambridge, MA: MIT Press, 1998.

_____. "Estrangement becomes the Mark of the Eagle." *The Shock of Arrival: Reflections on Postcolonial Experience.* Boston: South End Press, 1996.

Atwood, Margaret. *Lady Oracle.* New York: Avon, 1976.

Baldwin, Shauna Singh. *What the Body Remembers.* New York: Anchor, 2001.

Bhabha, Homi K. "DissemiNation: time, narrative, and the margins of the modern nation." *Nation and Narration*, ed. Homi K. Bhabha. London: Routledge, 1990.

_____. "Frontlines/Borderposts." *Displacements: Cultural Identities in Question.* Bloomington: Indiana University Press, 1994.

Bumiller, Elisabeth. "Of a Big Punjabi Family, By a Big Punjabi Family." *The New York Times*. 17 February 2002.

Mirkitani, Janice. *Shedding Silence.* Berkeley: Celestial Arts, 1997.

Mohanty, Chandra Talpade. "Crafting Feminist Genealogies: On the Geography and Politics of Home, Nation, and Community." *Talking Visions: Multicultural Feminism in a Transnational Age*, ed. Ella Shohat. Cambridge, MA: MIT Press, 1998.

Rich, Adrienne. *The Dream of a Common Language, Poems 1974-1977.* New York: Norton, 1978.

Smiley, Jane. *A Thousand Acres.* New York: Ballantine, 1991.

Woolf, Virginia. *A Sketch of the Pas. Moments of Being: Unpublished Autobiographical Writings*, ed. Jeanne Schulkind. New York: Harcourt Brace and Jovanovich, 1972.

Zandy, Janet. *Calling Home: Working-Class Women's Writings.* New Brunswick, NJ: Rutgers University Press, 1990.

# Space as Landmark in American Literature

**Mukesh Williams**
**Soka University, Japan**

> I take SPACE to be the central fact to man born in America, from Folsom Cave to now. I spell it large because it comes large here. Large and without mercy. It is geography at bottom, a hell of a wide land from the beginning.[1]

Most literary landmarks, like geographical and territorial landmarks, are imagined, coerced, and manipulated based on cultural concepts, ideology or belief. In due course literary landmarks become the focal points that create a national literary web. The American literature that we receive today also has similar origins though it has gone through some transformation in the latter half of the twentieth century because of minority politics and development in the methodology of American literary studies itself. In this paper I have attempted to highlight certain ideological concepts that have shaped the course of American literature and created various literary landmarks around it. These concepts are:

a) Writing as historical representation,
b) Transforming America as a sacred place,
c) Eugenics and fitter families,
d) Possessing America,
e) Changes in literary studies,
f) Culture wars or multiculturalism, and
g) The American Empire.

Since 'writing as historical representation' and 'transforming America as a sacred place' are interconnected I would like to explain how European writing appropriated the New World and then talk about 'eugenics' and 'culture wars.' Since much has been said about culture wars or multiculturalism I quickly go over it and get into the neo-conservative politics of today that has a strong bearing on American literature.

## a) Writing as Historical Representation

Right from the start, American literature had to encounter the spellbinding and harsh presence of the New World—to reckon with the space—and if possible to transform it into a place.[2] The attempt to transform took different and diverse forms, which now represents the diversity of American literature from the European conquest of the continent to the present. Courses in American literature select representative texts from six different cultural traditions—White, Latino/a, American Indian, African American, American Jewish, and Asian American—and understand what connects them to and differentiates them from each other. Why are the texts by American writers such as Mark Twain, Cabeza de Vaca, Zitkala-Sa, Harriet Jacobs, Emma Lazarus, Langston Hughes, Saul Bellow, Maxine Hong Kingston, Leslie Marmon Silko, and Ana Castillo American?[3] And why are they celebrated as literary-cultural landmarks? Apart from other issues represented in the texts, they are about exploration, appropriation, topology, space and relating that space with the self.

When we talk of American literature we talk of the exploration narratives of white Europeans from the sixteenth century that included imagined and prejudiced histories of the land and its people, in the process erasing the oral literatures of Native Americans. The Italian explorer Amerigo Vespucci's expeditions in 1499 and 1500 were published in 1505 and the German cartographer Martin Waldseemuller published the *Cosmographiae Introductio*, which contained documents and letter from Christopher Columbus to King Ferdinand and Queen Isabella of Spain, in 1507. The English writers like Sir Walter Raleigh, Richard Hakluyt, Thomas Harriot, and John White documented the Americas in great detail before the 1600. Though Raleigh wrote about Venezuela, he also founded the first English colony in America in 1585 called the Roanoke Colony,

North Carolina. In 1616 Captain John Smith wrote a historical account of his observation of American colonial life in *A Description of New England.* By and large, tales of exploration concentrated on the difficulties of travel, while historical accounts narrated the actual experience of settled life. Governors William Bradford of Plymouth Colony and John Winthrop of Massachusetts Bay Colony wrote histories—*History of Plymouth Plantation (1630-1647)* and *History of New England from 1630 to 1649*) respectively—though both were published centuries later. Since most histories gave religious explanation for events, religious writings of John Cotton, Thomas Hooker, Roger Williams, and Cotton Mather dominated literature in the seventeenth century. The indigenous people were mostly ignored except in the work of Roger Williams, *Key into the Language of America* (1643) that tried to understand the language and cultures of the Native Americans.

The word landmark originally meant an "object set up to mark the boundaries of a kingdom, estate etc.," and was therefore used as a physical marker of the topography of a land. Its figurative meaning of an "event considered as high point in history" emerged around 1859. So before the mid-nineteenth century the word "landmark" was not commonly used to refer to a "high point" or watershed in history. Before Christopher Columbus set sail to seek an empire he wrote the *Diario*, a narrative of global exploration that established a strong link between writing and colonization; a link that helped Europeans appropriate the New World and expropriate "millions of prior inhabitants."[4] Through the fifteenth century and until the nineteenth century, writing was seen as personal representation creating texts that wrote the history of Europe's discovery of America (Jehlen 13).[5] Most early nineteenth century American writers, like Henry David Thoreau and Ralph Waldo Emerson, saw landmark as geographical space to be identified and appropriated through language.[6] The literary discourse as it developed in America signified how lived experience and subjectivity can create an inexorable image of power and at the same time leave the center nebulous without the certainty of closure (Bhabha 297-98).[7] Throughout the colonial and early post-colonial period European/American writers felt that since the Indians lacked a system of writing they did not possess the right to the land. This helped the Europeans to identify themselves with the continent. In this way the "word" was made the "land (Jehlen 14)."[8]

## b) Transforming America as a Sacred Place

The early beginnings of American literature attempted to create a sense of place, which could be used as a location to enact the human drama of exploration, settlement and appropriation. Before the mid-nineteenth century America lacked the literary tradition of appropriating place though much of the works by William Bartram and H. Hector St., John de Crevecoeur were place-centered works. Henry David Thoreau is perhaps the first writer who directed his literary abilities to assimilate the wilderness within the boundary of human habitation. In creating Concord, Thoreau brought together the diverse resources of sociological fieldwork, autobiographical observation, environmental history and European land ethic.[9] Most nature writing either falls in the category of describing travel through a region or residence in a particular place.[10] It is the second category, which acquires significance both in creating a sense of place in literature and providing emotional attachment to a place. Thoreau's heightened awareness of the wilderness as home gives a special meaning to its topography, and historical and cultural significance by wresting it away from the mythic dimensions of Native American narrative into the domains of English language.

Dwelling in a place creates a space within which, according to Martin Heidegger, "something comes into its own and flourishes." Obviously settlers come to cherish the wilderness they call home and endeavor to preserve its pristine simplicity by introducing their exemplary living in symbiosis with nature. Both in *Walden* and his *Journals* (1837-1862), Thoreau provides us with detailed accounts of understanding human life through a study of home topography. By doing this Thoreau not only explored American wilderness as an intimate phenomenon but also transformed the geographical exploration of Massachusetts into a psychic exploration of the self. In other words, by identifying the nineteenth century landscape of Massachusetts as home, and developing a strong emotional attachment with the place, Thoreau transformed the alien American landscape into a sacred place, both Europeanizing and appropriating it—creating a new concord (Scheese 141).[11] According to his *Journal* entries Thoreau walked anytime of day or night. He took nocturnal walks to observe moonlit wilderness or conducted "fluvial walks" naked in the Concord River. On December 1860 he caught a cold while examining tree stumps, which led to his demise.[12]

Thoreau's *Journal* reveals how human beings can make a strong resolution when their objective becomes clear. In one of his entries, Thoreau announces that he will go to Beck Stow's Swamp about a mile northeast of Concord to study a small species of European cranberry (9:35) but his resolution dissipates. Quickly he resolves again in the hope of gathering some fresh information or learning a moral. This ability to transform a near defeat into total victory follows an ideal of self-transformation. According to Joseph Campbell, Thoreau's walks establish an archetypal pattern in American nature writing—separation, transformation, and return.[13] The separation from society allows Thoreau to forget the sordid debate about slavery raging at the time or the economic benefits of farming. Disgusted by the "restless, nervous, bustling, trivial Nineteenth Century" Thoreau feels a superior sense of rejoice in ascertaining "the flavor of a cranberry" (9:37).[14] This prepares the way for his philosophical assertion that the American wilderness in its transcendental and pure simplicity can be a worthy corollary to human civilization. Thoreau writes: "I see that all is not garden and cultivated field and crops, that there are square rods in Middlesex County as purely primitive and wild as they were a thousand years ago, which have escaped the plow and the axe and the scythe and the cranberry-rake, little oases of wildness in the desert of our civilization" (9:44). Many environmental historians believe that the development of national parks in America can be attributed to Thoreau's exhortation to preserve the wilderness in order to reinvigorate rural community life. In *Walden* he makes this claim rather boldly: "Our village life would stagnate if it were not for the unexplored forests and meadows which surround it. We need the tonic of wilderness."[15] This "tonic of the wilderness" can be extracted from anywhere, even from plots of lands as small as 16.5 square feet and even from lands that have been commercially cultivated. The only thing we need is to transform or recreate the place by our own imaginative awakening. Thoreau harnesses the typical nineteenth century homesteading attitude of living against the land and transforms it with his transcendental version of coexisting with the land. By recasting the greedy pioneer as an unworldly transcendentalist, Thoreau introduced the moral and spiritual content in American literature.

A new worldview required the ability to see the world from a new perspective. Perception was a phenomenon "of deep perplexity to the nineteenth century romantic mind" (Peck 104).[16] Thoreau realized, as he sojourned in the wilderness that it was impossible to find the wilderness outside unless it already existed within. Thoreau argued: "It is vain to dream of a wildness distant from ourselves. There is none such. It is the bog in our brain and bowels, the primitive vigor of Nature in us, that inspires that dream. I shall never find in the wilds of Labrador any greater wildness than in some recess in Concord, i.e., than I import into it" (9:43). By implication Thoreau extends the boundaries of American physical space, the terra cognita, to the psychological and linguistic space, the terra incognita thereby expanding the canon of American literature to include not only place but the perception that went along with it. While describing the wildness of Concord Thoreau dehistoricizes it; he argues that the swamp of Concord lacks apparent human history and therefore possesses only a natural history. He inquires "Has any white man ever settled on it? Does any now frequent it? Not even the Indian comes here now" (9:42). This superb quality to destroy time transforms the place into "other places" (Scheese

146).[17] The attempt to imagine a new place not only erases the past literature and history of Native Indians but also the Anglo-Americans and cranberry traders who were present in the country around Concord.

Thoreau will not rest here. The wilderness and the swampland is transformed under the pressure of Thoreau's imagination into a sacred place where man can recreate himself upon entry: "When I would recreate myself, I seek the darkest wood, the thickest and most interminable and, to the citizen, most dismal swamp. I enter the swamp as a sacred place, a sanctum sanctotum. There is the strength, the marrow of Nature" (9:45).[18] Apart from other things Thoreau was fascinated by Emerson's belief to discover the marvelous in the commonplace, something that American literary anthologies incorporated as part of early classics or nature writing.[19]

**c) Eugenics and Fitter Families**

It has been amply illustrated through the writings of Edward Said that works of literature signify "concepts of nation, nationality, and even race" (169).[20] By the nineteenth century as the American nation space is clearly established the difference is turned from the "boundary outside" to the "finitude within." As Homi Bhabha points out the "threat of cultural difference is no longer a problem of 'other' people. It becomes a question of the otherness of the people-as-one" (301).[21] Since exploitation has been the hallmark of the history of the West, most European and American cultural practices are colored by imperialism. But imperialism is one thing and nationalism is another. Within the domain of nationalism certain discursive and representational practices are employed that valorize specific individuals as ideal members of the nation state (During 138).[22] In the early twentieth century eugenics attempted to create an ideal Anglo-Saxon America and the construction of American literature dominated by white writers reflected this tendency.[23]

Eugenics developed as early as 1850 and was a covert attempt to apply Mendelian pea-plant genetics to improve the human race. American eugenicists like Charles Davenport—

funded by Rockefeller and Carnegie dollars—argued that society should be scientifically engineered to bring out the best genetic traits among its citizenry.[24] With this view in mind they divided eugenics into two broad categories—positive eugenics that encouraged breeding desirable traits and negative eugenics that prevented undesirable traits. Obviously researches in eugenics were backed by a racist ideology and the "science" was both anti-Black and anti-immigrant. Though primarily right-wingers and conservatives like Lucien Howe supported it, social radicals and progressive thinkers such as Teddy Roosevelt, Franklin Delano Roosevelt, Oliver Wendell Holmes, Jr., Woodrow Wilson, H.G. Wells, Emma Goldman, and Margaret Sanger (the founder of Planned Parenthood) and English psychologist Havelock Ellis were no less enthusiastic about the science. Both Sanger and Ellis felt that the widespread use of eugenics would promote birth control and hence liberate women. Socialists felt that eugenics prevailed the interests of society over those of the individual and therefore was good.

Eugenics-inspired rhetoric of improving the human race was reflected in the popular literature from the late 1800s to the 1930s. State-sponsored sterilization was an effective weapon to improve American genes, but it was the underclass, poor, immigrants, criminals and mentally ill who suffered eugenics sponsored sterilizations.[25] Inspired by the U.S. eugenics movement, Hitler introduced the Nuremberg Laws in 1935, a national program to sterilize the undesirables. Hitler beat the Americans at their own game. And by the end of World War II, as the horror of the holocaust unfolded, support and funding for the eugenics movement was gone.[26]

**d) Possessing America**

Upon reading Columbus's writings, it is possible to conclude that his essential motives in discovering the new world were to tell "unheard of stories, like Ulysses," spread Christianity and to become rich. And one or all of these motives in varying shades have also guided many who came after him (Todorov 8-13).[27] In 1939 Williams Carlos Williams wrote that from his "earliest childhood" he felt it was his "first business" to "possess" America in order to know where he "stood."[28] Williams' claim to appropriate America within his poetic sensibility was in line with Ralph Waldo Emerson's belief that the poet is the "true land-lord" of the American landscape whereas "others are only tenants and boarders."[29] Emerson was suggesting more than self-reliance; he was advocating "economic self-interest."[30] Thoreau translates Emersòn's self-reliance into a real estate usurper when he asserted in *Walden*: "Wherever I sat, there I might live, and the landscape radiated from me accordingly."

Both the eighteenth and nineteenth century American writers realized with regret that they have arrived late in America when the project of appropriation was already over; they nevertheless appropriated the emotional territory through figurative language paralleling the physical expansionism of Euro-American settlement into Native Indian territory. In his long poem *Paterson*, Williams not only attempts to repossesses America as a part of a belated Columbian experience but also wishes to mark the landscape for "proprietorship" (Meyer 153).[31] During a startling revelation in *Paterson* he confesses:

> Language
> Is not a vague province. There is a poetry
> Of the movements of cost, known or unknown.[32]

Like Walt Whitman in *Song of Myself*, Williams in *Paterson* seeks the center of American experience by creating a strong self; but unlike Whitman loses the centrality of self by acknowledging the historical past of appropriation and control. Unable to possess America, Paterson "stammers in his speech" when he discovers that language itself "stutters" (Book I, ii.22) As language lacks the ability to allow the poet to achieve"radiance" independent of "symbols" he can only gain a "partial victory" (Book III, i.10B and Book I iii.30). Williams tries to bring the individual and the world together but somehow fails to reconcile the two:

> The rock
> Married to the river

Makes
No sound

And the river
Passes—but I remain
Clamant
Calling out ceaselessly
to the birds
and clouds
(listening)
Who am I? (Book III, i.107)

In a comment on Poe's works Williams remarks: "Either the New World must be mine as I will have it, or it is a worthless bog. There can be no concession. His attack was from the center out. . . . It was a wish to HAVE the world or leave it" (Williams 219-20).[33]

Even if Williams fails in his attempt to figuratively claim America, most twentieth century American writers continue to make the material and symbolic acquisition of America their "first business." Obviously the business of representation in Christian and egalitarian terms on the one hand and the injustice of the American conquest per se on the other plague the twentieth century writer more than his predecessors. Both Jay Gatsby and Ike McCaslin fail in their endeavor to restore the "fresh, green breast of the new world" as they ignore their historical responsibility. As the twentieth century writer mutes the images of virgin land and the rhetoric of Manifest Destiny and other expansionist ideas, it nevertheless resurfaces either as eternally available whore or eternally unavailable virgin.[34] As recent ethnographic studies like that of Johannes Fabian deconstruct the hegemonic or imperialistic epistemology of representation, we have come to understand better the process of transforming and creating the other according to the power the American writer wields (Fabian 753-73).[35]

**e) Changes in Literary Studies**

In the 1930s and 1940s American literature had to reckon with many problems simultaneously. It had to de-link itself from imperial British literature, create its own national landmarks in literature and then establish its distinctive identity in the Anglophone culture. F.R. Leavis's conservative literary canon defined what was "normally and robustly human" by doing away with writers like E.M. Forster, Virginia Woolf, W.H. Auden and James Joyce as being abnormal in one way or the other.[36] Leavis and his conservative literary journal *Scrutiny* were both comfortable in dealing with "native literatures" that originated in different languages from their home ground such as English, French, German, Italian but not the hybrid colonial forms.[37] American writing in English was more of a vernacular, hard for conservative critics like Leavis to incorporate in *The Great Tradition*. The influence of Leavis and *Scrutiny* had a baneful effect on the consolidation of American literature. While American scholars were trying to establish the "essential Americanism" of writers like Henry James, Leavis was trying to do the very opposite. Though British imperialism had established the dominance of English as the lingua franca of the colonial world, most of the English speakers were "not ethnically English." In the United States, Ireland, Australia, India and the Caribbean, English was a "foreign literary vernacular" though for *Scrutiny* the United States and Ireland were quite important.[38] American literature itself was a nonentity in the 1940s and 1950s. In India the strong influence of English literature and the Leavisian discourse in Indian universities did not allow the dissemination of American literature, except a few texts by writers like Mark Twain, Ernest Hemingway, Arthur Miller and Walt Whitman.

During the 1950s the representation of both Afro-American and women writing in American literature was almost negligible. Some graduate schools occasionally introduced minority writers like Richard Wright, Ralph Ellison and James Baldwin and women writers like Emily Dickinson to complete the canon (Lauter xxx).[39] In the 1960s minority scholars from ethnic backgrounds began to question the narrowness of the American canon and researched to restore "lost, forgotten, or suppressed literary texts" to show the "diversity" that always existed in

American literature (Lauter xxxi).[40] And as Michael Foucault affected the methodology of literary studies in the 1970s, literary scholarship developed greater awareness towards issues of race, gender and class in the making of literature. But literary anthologies were rather slow to respond to these radical changes in the construction of American literature. From 1979 to 1982 many American scholars including Paul Lauter of Trinity College met at Yale University under the project "Reconstructing American Literature" supported by The Feminist Press to review both theory and content of American literature. Their efforts published under the title *Reconstructing American Literature* not only provided the faculty with "models" for changing their courses but also highlighted the "limitations" of existing texts—there were no Latino or Asian-American writers included in anthologies at all (Lauter xxxi).[41]

The restructuring of American literature project also resulted in the publication of *The Health Anthology of American Literature* in 1990, which published not only canonical writers but also non-canonical Native American, Black, Asian-American and women writers.[42] This not only expanded the literary canon but "fundamentally redefine[d]" the literature produced in the United States (Lauter xxxii).[43] The new scholarship dealing with race, women, minorities and ethnicity not only energized the classroom but also altered the context in which American literature was placed and studied.

**f) Culture Wars or Multiculturalism**

Feeling the overpowering dominance of white America in the twentieth century, ethnic minorities and women introduced identity politics in the 1960s to create a cultural and political space for themselves.[44] Identity politics coincided with the development of Afro-American Studies that focused attention on the socio-economic plight of the Afro-American community, which subsequently gave a new "urgency" to literary studies in America introducing multicultural writing as a new landmark in American literature.[45] In many cases multiculturalism involved the problem of identity politics, a phenomenon affecting capitalistic societies, something unheard of in peasant communities of the past.[46] In the 1980s and 1990s the canon of American literature was expanded to include ethnic writings of different hyphenated Americans, such as Afro-American, Native Americans, Chicano/a, Chinese Americans and Japanese Americans. In other words ethnic groups competed for space with the hitherto white hegemonic texts for recognition.

Right wing liberals such as Robert Bellah, Arthur Schlesinger, Jr., and Michael Sandel and left wing liberals such as Henry Louis Gates, Jr., and Michael Walzer found it rather frustrating to bring together issues raised by multiculturalism and a new democratic ideal. Indeed, central to multiculturalism was the notion of otherness that liberals found hard to incorporate within the notion of either an assimilationist ethic or more significantly American solidarity.[47] Though the strong appeal of liberalism had weakened in the early 1990s, it still remained "a historical modality, a way of life" in which we may construct our "political existence" and enjoy our rights and liberty. However, the problem lies in the way liberalism constructs the other or the enemy, its role as a heroic global protector of liberal siblings, and the development of an awesome military power.[48] It is an undeniable fact that American society has become fragmented "by ethnicity, class and gender," and this society would undoubtedly disintegrate without the twin values of "cultural tolerance" and cultural understanding." America faces the challenge of building a common "public culture" and responding to the "long-silenced cultures of color." Gates, Jr., emphatically concludes: "If we relinquish the ideal of America as a plural nation, we've abandoned the very experiment that American represents."[49]

**g) The American Empire**

Multiculturalism, or 'culture wars' as it was called then, has been replaced in recent years by the war on terror. Since the 1990s evident notions of American supremacy in world affairs has made the word 'empire' together with the phrase 'homeland security' more acceptable, contradicting the metaphors of melting pot and boundless mobility.[50]

America has always been an "empire in denial" and this denial has been the ideological cornerstone of American imperialism and an important aspect of American exceptionalism.[51] American scholars no longer see the notion of the American Empire as just a "left-wing polemic." It is an assertive imperial identity of the neo-conservatives celebrating American manifest destiny on a global scale, declaring a war against terror, against the Muslim world in self-righteous terms. Amy Kaplan sees this new American narrative encompassing the perennial notions of time and space as the immortality and global invincibility of the empire.[52] Now within the discipline of American Studies scholars feel a sense of urgency to expose the "racism of empire" and understand the method by which the Arabs and Islam are "racialized" within the U.S. and outside in Guantanamo and Abu Gharib detention centers (Kaplan 5, 12-16).[53]

## NOTES

1. Charles Olson, *Call Me Ishmael* (San Francisco: City Lights, 1947), pp. 11-12.
2. Commenting on the term the "New World," Jose Rabasa writes: "The term *New World* should be understood, not solely as that imaginary geographic space that emerged in the European wish-horizon of ideal landscapes in the sixteenth and seventeenth centuries, but also as the constitution of the modern conception of the world that results from the exploration of the globe—and, by extension, the metaphorical use of 'new world' among such philosophers and painters as Francis Bacon and Jan Vermeer to speak of new fields of vision and inquiry." *Inventing America: Spanish Historiography and the Formation of Eurocentrism* (Norman and London: University of Oklahoma Press, 1993), p. 3.
3. Mark Twain, *Pudd'nhead Wilson;* Álvar Núñez Cabeza de Vaca, *Adventures in the Unknown Interior of America;* Zitkala-Sa, *American Indian Stories, Legends, and Other Writings;* Harriet Jacobs, *Incidents in the Life of a Slave Girl;* Emma Lazarus,

*Selected Poems and Other Writings;* Langston Hughes, *Selected Poems;* Saul Bellow, *The Adventures of Augie March;* Maxine Hong Kingston, *Tripmaster Monkey;* Leslie Marmon Silko, *Ceremony;* Ana Castillo, *My Father Was a Toltec, and Selected Poems.*

4. Myra Jehlen, "The Literature of Colonization: The Papers of Empire," *The Cambridge History of American Literature Volume One: 1590-1820* (1994; Cambridge University Press, 1997), p. 13. Also see Christopher Columbus, *Diario of Christopher Columbus's First Voyage to America*,
5. Myra Jehlen establishes a link between personal representation and the literature of the New World: "Columbus's *Diario* thus represents writing as a kind of action, and action as a form of personal representation. The literature of the New World—the literature of discovery, exploration, and colonization—is composed of just such books. The literary history of Europe's discovery of America is the story of a literature that sought to shape history. The texts depicting the first European landings and early settlements in the Americas are almost always self-conscious participants in the events they represent." *Ibid.*, p. 19.
6. Claude Lefort, *The Political Forms of Modern Society*, (Cambridge: Polity, 1986). Claude Lefort calls this complex process—"The enigma of language—namely that it is both internal and external to the speaking subject, that there is an articulation of the self with others which marks the emergence of the self and which the self does not control—is concealed by the representation of a place outside—language from which it could be generated." pp. 212-14.
7. See Homi K. Bhabha, "DissemiNation: time, narrative, and the margins of the modern nation," *Nation and Narration* (London: Routledge, 1990, rpt. 2000), pp. 297-98.
8. See Jehlen, p. 14. Also see Richard R. Bernstein, *The New Constellation* (MIT Press Ingram pubnet, 1992). Bernstein places the problem of "otherness" as central to a theory of knowledge. He argues that self must willingly risk its assumptions and convictions in order to encounter something new and different. Our knowledge and, therefore, our understanding are always possible when we encounter the alien, the other. The only problem in this encounter, as Emmanuel Levinas points out, is that the alterity of the other gets incorporated through understanding into "sameness." The

other is always at risk of losing his identity that he so diligently wants to preserve. Furthermore, Levinas argues that since self is ethically formed it is difficult to understand how the "other" in an encounter manages to retain his alterity. Jacques Derrida has the answer to this question. He believes that the other preserves his alterity by acting as an alter ego. In other words Levinas develops the narrative of self and other as a reciprocal trope capable of functioning through themes of enmity, estrangement, abjection and violence. Mikhail Bakhtin sees self and other interacting from different positions and areas of reference; their interaction is never transparent. The other can never be completely understood as understanding takes place from the locus standi of the self. Bernstein, unlike Isaiah Berlin, believes that when self invokes an ethical obligation to the other, it can either understand the "other" or understand self in relation to the "other."

9. It is rather difficult to slot the different methodologies employed by Thoreau in creating the sense of place in American literature as no clear definition of his method is available. For more details see Don Scheese, "Thoreau's Journal: The Creation of a Sacred Place," *Mapping American Culture*, ed. Wayne Franklin and Michael Steiner (Iowa City: University of Iowa Press, 1992) pp. 139-151; Philip Marshall Hicks, *The Development of the Natural History Essay in American Literature* (Philadelphia: University of Pennsylvania Press, 1924); Joseph Wood Krutch, introduction to *The Best Nature Writing of Joseph Wood Krutch* (New York: Williams Morrow, 1969), pp. 13-27; Ann Ronald, introduction to *Words for the Wild: Sierra Club Trailside Reader* (San Francisco: Sierra Club Books, 1987), pp. xi-xviii; Thomas J. Lyon, introduction to *This Incomparable Land: A Book of American Nature Writing* (Boston: Houghton Mifflin, 1989), pp. 3-91; Don Scheese, "Nature Writing: A Wilderness of Books," *Forest and Conservation History* 34 (1990), pp. 204-8.
10. Both Gilbert White in *The Natural History of Selbourne* and Annie Dillard in *Pilgrim at Tinker Creek* describe in detail the place they inhabit.
11. Don Scheese, "Thoreau's Journal: The Creation of a Sacred Place," *Mapping American Culture*, ed. Wayne Franklin and Michael Steiner, p. 141.
12. For Thoreau's night walks, see Walter Harding, introduction to the *Journal of Henry David Thoreau*, 2: vii, and the *Journal*, 2:234-39,

2:248-61. On his fluvial walks see Harding, introduction to the *Journal*, 4: vi, and the *Journal*, 4:211-15, 3:7-9, and 4:320-21. For events related to Thoreau's death see Walter Harding, *The Days of Henry Thoreau* (New York: Dover, 1982), p. 441.

13. Joseph Campbell, *The Hero with a Thousand Faces* (Princeton: Princeton University Press, 1949). Campbell suggests that Thoreau's walk to Beck Stow's Swamp takes him away from society to the wilderness where he experiences an awakening or a transformation. And when he returns to Concord he is a different person. Thoreau's daily walks are a quest for the transforming encounter with self and nature.
14. Henry David Thoreau, *The Illustrated "Walden,"* ed. J. Lyndon Shanley, (Princeton: Princeton University Press, 1971), p. 329. Looking for European cranberry, which is hard to find, and not the American variety, which is ubiquitous, Thoreau underscores the sharp eye of the naturalist that looks for minute details in obscure things and places. Also his heroic self-concept forged in alienation from society that criticized him for not finding a proper occupation and ridiculed him as a "woodsburner" for accidentally setting fire to large tract of local wilderness. For more details see Henry Harding, *The Days of Henry Thoreau* (New York: Dover, 1982), pp. 160-62. To understand Thoreau's alienation from Concord see Leon Edel, *Stuff of Sleep and Dreams: Experiments in Literary Psychology* (New York: Harper and Row, 1982), pp. 47-65.
15. Henry David Thoreau, *The Illustrated "A Week on the Concord and Merrimack Rivers,"* ed. Carl F. Hovde, William L. Howarth and Elizabeth Hall Witherell (Princeton: Princeton University Press, 1980), p. 54; *The Illustrated 'Walden'*, p. 317. In his essay "Walking" he makes the famous proclamation: "In wildness is the preservation of the World." See "Walking" in *The Natural History Essays*, ed. Robert Sattelmeyer (Salt Lake City: Peregrine Smith, 1980), p. 112.
16. H. Daniel Peck, Thoreau's *Morning Work: Memory and Perception in "A Week on the Concord and Merrimack Rivers," The Journal and "Walden"* (New Haven: Yale University Press, 1990), p. 104
17. Don Scheese, "Thoreau's Journal: The Creation of a Sacred Place," *Mapping American Culture*, ed. Wayne Franklin and Michael Steiner, p. 146.

18. The quotation is from his lecture "The Wild" later combined with another entitled "Walking" and published posthumously in the *Atlantic Monthly*, 1862. See Harding, *The Days*, pp. 315 and 469.
19. See Ralph Waldo Emerson, *Emerson's "Nature": Origin, Growth, Meaning*, ed. Merton M. Sealts, Jr., and Alfred R. Ferguson (Carbondale: University of Southern Illinois Press, 2nd Ed., 1979), p. 15. Looking for the marvelous in the commonplace Thoreau writes, "When we are lifted out of the slime and film of our habitual life, we see the whole globe to be an aerolite (meteor), and reverence it as such, and make pilgrimages to it" (9: 45).
20. Edward Said, "Reflections on American 'Left' literary criticism," *The World, the Text, the Critic* (London: Faber, 1982), p. 169. Some modern critics like Simon During beg to disagree with this view and believe that "literary criticism canonizes those texts which do not simply legitimate nationhood" (p. 138). See Simon During, "Literature—Nationalism's other? The Case for revision," *Nation and Narration*, pp. 138-153.
21. See Bhabha, "DissemiNation," p. 301.
22. Simon During writes, "Nationalism attaches to the modern state, revealing itself fully in subjects whose being is saturated by their nationality" (p. 138).
23. Annual state fairs in the US in the early twentieth century for example in Kansas city (1928) showed not only a Ferris wheel, corn dogs, cotton candy, horses, cattle and hogs but also a blue-eyed blonde family of four or five on elevated platforms under the banner Fitter Families Contest. This was an attempt to identify Aryan facial characteristics as models of godly living, something that the burgeoning eugenics movement was doing surreptitiously.
24. Charles Davenport spearheaded the American eugenics movement under the aegis of the Eugenics Record Office, a consortium funded largely with Rockefeller and Carnegie dollars. He advocated the prevention of birth amongst genetic undesirables such as the "feebleminded," paupers, alcoholics, criminals, epileptics, the insane, the constitutionally weak, people predisposed to specific diseases, deformed persons, and those born deaf, blind, or mute. Davenport's negative eugenics found widespread acceptance amongst middle and upper class Americans.
25. The U.S. Department of Agriculture was closely aligned with the American Breeders Association, a prominent supporter of

eugenics. And in 1907, states began sterilizing citizens they considered a problem. Indiana was first, followed by Washington, Connecticut, Virginia, and California.

26. Daniel Kevles published what may be the best history of eugenics to date in 1985, *In the Name of Eugenics* (Harvard University Press). Kevles is also the author of *The Physicists: The History of a Scientific Community in Modern America* (Harvard), *The Baltimore Case: A Trial of Politics, Science, and Character* (W.W. Norton); and co-author of *The Code of Codes: Scientific and Social Issues in the Human Genome Project* (Harvard) and *Inventing America: A History of the United States* (W.W. Norton). In addition, Kevles has written for *The New Yorker*, *The New York Review of Books*, *The New York Times*, and the *Los Angeles Times*, among other publications.
27. Tzvestan Todorov, *The Conquest of America: The Question of the Other* (Norman: Univerity of Oklahoma Press, 1999), pp. 8-13.
28. William Carlos Williams's letter to Horace Gregory dated 22nd July 1939 in *The Selected Letters of William Carlos Williams*, ed. John C. Thirlwall (New York: McDowell, Obolensky, 1957), p. 185. Williams wrote, "I felt from earliest childhood that America was the only home I could possibly call my own. I felt that it was expressly founded for me, personally, and that it must be my first business in life to possess it, that only by making it my own from the beginning to my own day, in detail, should I ever have a basis for knowing where I stood."
29. Ralph Waldo Emerson, "The Poet" in the *Health Anthology of American Literature*, p. 1581. In the same essay Emerson writes, "The poet is the sayer, the namer, and represents beauty. He is sovereign, and stands on the centre. For the world is not painted, or adorned, but is from the beginning beautiful; and God has not made some beautiful things, but Beauty is the creator of the universe. Therefore the poet is not any permissive potentate, but is emperor in his own right" (p. 1568).
30. Kinereth Meyer, "Possessing America: William Carlos Williams's Paterson and the Poetics of Appropriation," *Mapping American Culture*, p. 153. Myra Jehlen posits that the American self-reliant individualist was not just a poet but also a capitalist, as he believed that "a man's value manifests itself in material possession." See Myra Jehlen, *American Incarnation: the Individual, the Nation,*

*and the Continent* (Cambridge, Mass.: Harvard University Press, 1986), p. 4.

31. Kinereth Meyer, "Possessing America," *ibid.*, p. 153.
32. William Carlos Williams, *Paterson* (New York: New Directions, 1963), III.i.109.
33. William Carlos Williams, *In the American Grain* (London: MacGibbon and Kee, 1925, rpt 1933, 1966), pp. 219-20.
34. Kinereth Meyer, "Possessing America," p. 154. Meyer draws attention to speeches of Teddy Roosevelt especially before the 1898 war against Spain where Roosevelt connected the "queer lack of imperial instinct" in the American people with notions of "manliness" (pp. 165-66). Also see Alfred Kazin, *A Writer's America: Landscape and Literature* (New York: Knopf, 1988), p. 101. Meyer points out that landscape poems written by American women writers do not make any attempt to "possess" the landscape. See Annette Kolodny, *The Land Before Her* (Chapel Hill: University of North Carolina Press, 1984).
35. Johannes Fabian, "Presence and Representation: The Other and Anthropological Writing," *Critical Inquiry* 16 (1990), pp. 753-73.
36. *Scrutiny*, volume 7, number 2 (September 1938) and volume 13 number 2 (September 1945). Also see "'Joyce and 'the revolution of the word.'" *Scrutiny*, Volume 2, number 2 (September 1933), pp. 193-201. Also see Francis Mulhern, "English reading," *ibid.*, pp. 258 and 260.
37. F.R. Leavis, *For Continuity* (Cambridge: Cambridge University Press, 1933), Leavis qualified his criticism of Spengler by observing, "More and more dos human life depart from the natural rhythms, the cultures have mingled, and the forms have dissolved into chaos" (p. 139). Mulhern believes that this was an attempt by Leavis to restore "integrity and order." See Mulhern, "English reading," ibid., p. 260.
38. Francis Mulhern, "English reading," *Nation and Narration*, Homi K. Bhabha, ed., p. 260. Mulhern points out that Marius Bewley tried to show the "essential Americanism" of Henry James by showing that the novel begins in Jane Austen and returns to England in the person of Henry James—the American line of the Great tradition. F.R. Leavis had already rejected James Joyce as a product of colonial Ireland who wrote in the mother language as another language. Leavis was favorable to James and Conrad for their Englishness and not of their foreignness. To see English

writing in America as part of the Great Tradition and admit its Americanness would be quite paradoxical for Leavis.

39. Paul Lauter, "Preface to the First Edition," *The Health Anthology of American Literature*, Volume I (Lexington, Massachusetts: D. C. Heath, 1994), p. xxx.
40. *Ibid.*, p. xxxi.
41. *Loc. cit.* Also see *Reconstructing American Literature* (Old Westbury: Feminist Press, 1983).
42. Along with canonical works from antebellum fiction writers like Poe, Hawthorne and Melville but also non-canonical works by prose writers like William Wells Brown, Alice Cary, Rebecca Harding Davis, Caroline Kirkland, Harriet Prescott Stoddard, Elizabeth Drew Stoddard and Harriet Wilson apart from many others were also published.
43. Paul Lauter, p. xxxii.
44. Henry Louis Gates, Jr., sums up the controversy underlying multiculturalism thus: "Ours is a late-twentieth-century world profoundly fissured by nationality, ethnicity, race, class, and gender. And the only way to transcend those divisions—to forge, for once, a civic culture that respects both differences and commonalties—is thought education that seeks to comprehend the diversity of human culture. Beyond the hype and the high-flown rhetoric is a pretty homely truth: There is no tolerance without respect—and no respect without knowledge. Any human being sufficiently curious and motivated can fully possess another culture, no matter how 'alien' it may appear to be." Gates, Jr., believes ours is a multicultural world and Afro-American writers sensitive to this new development have already "blended forms of Western literature and African-American vernacular and written traditions." This "cultural impulse" can revitalize American culture in the new century. See Henry Louis Gates, Jr., *Loose Canons: Notes on the Culture Wars* (New York: Oxford University Press, 1992), pp. xv-xvii and 176.
45. Henry Louis Gates, Jr., *Loose Canon*, p. xiii. Multiculturalism may be defined as the existence and occasionally the coexistence of diverse interdisciplinary practices to identify, understand, and separate cultural uniqueness of ethnic and marginalized or non-ethnic or dominant groups
46. Capitalism, as Marx pointed out in his *Manifesto*, gives rise to a highly developed economic society, forcibly bringing nations and

groups together through slave trade, white settlements and Third World immigrant workers. In such situations as Alex Callinicos points out, "identity becomes an issue." But together with the formation of identities the process of assimilation also starts giving rise to "eclectic cultures." See Alex Callinicos, *Theories and Narratives: Reflections on the Philosophy of History* (Cambridge: Polity Press, 1995), p. 200.

47. A recent sociological study by John J. Miller argued that multiculturalism has prevented the Americanization of immigrants. Miller, vice president of the Center for Equal opportunity in Washington, sees the multicultural agenda responsible for this. Since the ideology campaigns for affirmative action and bilingual education in public schools in order to preserve its cultural it finds the idea of Americanization somewhat disturbing. Miller's strongly conservative position, flaunted as liberal, makes him see multiculturalists as "global village people" and prompts him to link them with gay and Communists with the phrase "fellow travelers." Therefore Miller advocates for a return to the coercive process of Americanization that prevailed at the turn of the 20th century in public policy issues. John J. Miller, *The Unmaking of America: How Multiculturalism has Undermined the Assimilation Ethic* (New York: Free Press, 1998). Multiculturalism also faced the problem of ideological positioning in a post-communist world mythologized by the supposed triumph of the free world. Western liberalism still remained an intellectually viable proposition despite its failures in Vietnam and Guatemala, "stemming from," what Robert Latham calls, "its overzealousness and its greed due to its grounding in capitalism." See Robert Latham, "Liberalism's Order/ Liberalism's Other: A Genealogy of Threat," *Alternatives: Social Transformation and Humane Governance*, Vol. 20, No. 1 (Jan.-Mar. 1995), p. 111.

48. Latham, *ibid.* Liberal heroes have entered into global struggles arguing that they wish to protect their liberal brothers but remain "committed" to military power. "Upon whom this might be turned and for what reasons remains a crucial question." Latham concludes: "To move beyond the positioning of liberalism as the master referent of post-Cold War change, at a minimum the myth of liberal heroism will need to be abandoned." pp. 111-12.

49. Gates Jr., *Loose Canons*, p. 176. A somewhat recent book by Alex Callinicos, *Theories and Narratives: Reflections on the Philosophy*

*of History*, deals with the changing relationship between social theories and historical narratives. Callinicos argues that social theory can effectively contribute to our better understanding of the past. To this end he analyses the ideas of Francis Fukuyama's Hegelian conceptualization of history, to Hayden White's postmodernist attempts to visualize past through human representation. In the book he attacks a Eurocentric theory of history wondering "how a critique of oppression can proceed except on a nonrelativist basis." He takes up Rorty's argument and bends it to suit his purpose. See Richard Rorty, *Contigency, Irony and Solidarity* (Cambridge: CUP, 1989), p. 191. Callinicos employs the Rortian rhetoric that moral and political action is not based on "some universalistic notion of moral autonomy or human rights but the narrower solidarities which emerge in specific historically contingent circumstances." Though Callinicos accepts Rorty's idea that our construction of "us" is more localized than universal, Callinicos finds it hard to believe that Rorty can question the humanistic basis of man's generosity to others. Nevertheless, Callinicos's objection to Rorty's argument is more fundamental. He wants to know: "Who are the *we* shared membership of which is to the basis of moral and political action? Solidarities 'smaller and more local than the human race' necessarily exclude as well as include. The politically effective 'we' in the antebellum American South excluded slave. Abolitionists challenging the 'peculiar institution' appealed, among other things, to the very fact that black slaves were as much human beings as free whites. Looking back, we condemn various historically constituted solidarites as too narrow, in an ethically relevant sense—classical Athens, for example, for excluding women, slaves and metics from the 'we' of free citizens. But how is this condemnation to be grounded?" (Callinicos, *ibid*., p. 197). The ongoing controversy about multiculturalism can best be exemplified by the publication of two books and their varied reception in America. The first is Todd Gitlin's *The Twilight of Common Dreams* (Henry Holt, 1995). And the second David Hollinger's *Postethnic America* (Basic Books 1995) Gitlin's book provides a rich historical and psychological analysis of American culture, leading to the clash of cultures in contemporary America. However his strongly leftist and highly confrontational position has met with strong reactions from multicultural critics furthering their brand of aggressive political identity. Hollinger's is a more balanced and well-argued work on multiculturalism that looks beyond the present controversy proposing ways to circumvent it. However, both agree that the inherent contradiction in multiculturalism is responsible for its dismal failure. Multiculturalism, they believe, lacks the ability to balance singular cultural difference with universal cultural unity. After all multiculturalism ultimately ought to exist within the framework of social solidarity and must contribute to social unity. And therefore, both authors critique the notion of multicultural alterity standing against the idea of cultural togetherness. Since a multicultural identity underscores cultural difference it puts on hold the notion of human solidarity, making it look somewhat suspect. Moreover its emphasis on legitimating and empowering identity makes it see the notion of human solidarity as a plea for ethnocentrism.

50. Amy Kaplan, "Violent Belongings and the Question of Empire Today: Presidential Address to the American Studies Association, October 17, 2003," *American Quarterly*, Vol. 56, No. 1 (March 2004). Kaplan writes: "A nation of immigrants, a melting pot, the western frontier, manifest destiny, a classless society—all involve metaphors of spatial mobility rather than the spatial fixedness and rootedness that homeland implies. . . . How many U.S. citizens see themselves as members of a diasporic community with a homeland in Ireland, Africa, Israel, or Palestine—a place to which they feel spiritual or political affiliation and belonging, whether literally a place of birth or not? Does the idea of America as the homeland make such dual identifications suspect and threatening, something akin to terrorism? Are you either a member of the homeland or with the terrorists, to paraphrase Bush? And what of the terrible irony of the United States as a homeland to Native Americans?" (pp. 8-9). The neo-conservative belief of democratizing the world has been attacked from within the western world by the discipline of anthropology. Clifford Geertz believes that man does not possess universal nature but universal potential that are realized in specific situations. Since he does not possess a composite universal nature it becomes difficult to appeal to a collective ethical core in moments of crisis. We constantly see scapegoats in others and, symbolically or literally, sacrifice them in the hope of eventually exorcising our own phobias, guilt-ridden fantasies and vices. Kenneth Burke, who sees a process of "vicarious atonement" at

work here, has analyzed this process of exteriorization and symbolic renewal at length. Burke believes that the scapegoat becomes a "chosen vessel" that is employed by others to "cleanse themselves" by heaping the "burden of their iniquities" on it. The violent intensity with which the ritual of displacement is conducted decides the "curative" power of the scapegoat. The victim and the residual violence become not only instrumental in restoring individual and social healing but fusing with each other in a symbiosis. In other words we first project our guilt, mortification and inadequacy on a person then we malign and ostracize him. In this manner we regain health and well-being. This complex process of identity formation works in the following manner: first to malign difference, then to elevate it to the level of a religious sacrifice, and then feel empowered. Can we escape this process of conceptualization? Is there a way out? Burke suggests that identity may be constructed not in terms of solidarity but in terms of a "fundamental kinship with the enemy," someone against whom we define ourselves. Self and other can stand facing each other like prismatic mirrors refracting unseen aspects of each other. Even while we are constructing a sense of difference we are inextricably intertwined, sharing somewhat similar histories, undergoing not altogether divergent fates. Burke goes further to suggest that aspects of the self may be seen as aspects of the other and vice versa. This implies in Derrida's logic to understand and appreciate the ways in which the "other" constructs itself as different aspects of the ego or "I."

51. Niall Ferguson, *Empire: The Rise and Demise of the British World Order and the Lessons for Global Power* (New York: Basic Books, 2002), p. 370. Ferguson's revisionist history of the British Empire rebukes America for its denial of empire and exhorts it to take the mantle of the white man's burden. Also see Amy Kaplan, p. 3.
52. See Kaplan, "Violent Beginnings," p. 4. J.M. Coetzee maintains that empires always fear their own demise—One thought alone preoccupies the submerged mind of Empire: how not to end, how not to die, how to prolong its era." *Waiting for the Barbarians* (New York: Penguin, 1982), p. 31.
53. Amy Kaplan, pp. 5 and 12-16.

# The Interplay of Doubles in Edwidge Danticat's Fiction[1]

**Alice Mills**
**Universtie' de Caen, France**

The first generation of Haitian writers of the diaspora were banished from the Haitian literary world for treason, treason in that they had betrayed the place of origin and hence the place of reception of their work. Writers like Anthony Phelps, Emile Ollivier, Paul Laraque, Jean Metellus, René Depestre and Dany Laferrière were the victims of this ethnic perception of literary reality, which qualifies as illegitimate the works of writers of the diaspora. With Danticat's work the betrayal seems complete. Neither place nor language is preserved, because Edwidge Danticat took up writing with an American literary memory, reminiscent of the tone of Maya Angelou, Toni Morrison and the hundreds of female voices that had been erased for centuries. This work was admitted and supported by the literary institutions of the United States, making Danticat's work the epitome of revolt, a literary production denied a passport of authenticity and legitimacy of origin. And . . . we can be thankful for that! (Saint Elois 61, Trans. from the French).

When the usual criteria are no longer of any use in identifying the origins of a body of work, it is no doubt best to let the writing itself suggest them. The importance of the concept of the double in *Breath, Eyes, Memory*, *The Farming of Bones* and *Krik? Krak!*, in the short story *Seven* and the introduction to *The Butterfly's Way* seems to me to reveal a culture which, before being Haitian or North American, was African. My interest in the presence of the double in Danticat's writing has been primarily inspired by the work of Dominique Diard, Andrée-Anne Kekeh Dika, Angelia Poon, Renée Shea, Nancy Gerber, April Shemak and Marie José N'Zengou-Tayo. My interest differs from theirs, however, in that the theme of the double is only implicitly or briefly addressed in their articles and does not constitute one of their fundamental aspects. Yet the subject seems to me to justify detailed examination because of its constant presence and complex nature, and the many forms it takes.

Among the more obvious expressions of the theme of the double, are its physical representations. Twins appear under their most common guise, that of two children born during a twin birth, but also in the form of characters who give the impression of twin-ness because of their behavior or physical resemblance.[2] Note that there is also in Danticat's work a particular form of twin-ness inspired by the marasa tradition, an African religious belief or cultural practice that is deeply entrenched in the Caribbean.[3]

The character of the pregnant woman, the union of two lives and two bodies in one, is also one of the physical representations of the double. Conversely, elements whose duality is due not to the union of two entities but to the division of the original entity can also be included among these representations: in Danticat's universe mattresses, ceilings, houses, paths, the sky and the world split apart frequently, while machetes cut bodies and faces in two. Hispaniola itself was arbitrarily divided into two nations, each possessing, to a greater or lesser degree, a population divided between rich and powerful elite and the masses maintained in a state of fear and poverty. Although they differ in essence, one might also cite the situations which, throughout Danticat's novels and short stories, possess a quality of duality because they are repeated in time and space: Haitians flee to the United States in order to escape the murderous police in Haiti, but in America are assassinated by the local police. Haitian mothers' practice of verifying their daughters' virginity also belongs to the sphere of repetition since the daughters will in turn, and despite the trauma of the experience, proceed to examine their own children in the same way.

Another dual situation is that of characters who in several works insist on the official inscription of their names, their eyewitness accounts or their stories, even though such registration is often absurd[4] or dangerous. The theme of inscription, a recurrent one with Danticat, offers interesting possibilities for study. Thus, the act of inscribing itself, irrespective of the fact that it is repeated throughout Danticat's work, is often an act intrinsically double in nature. Angelia Poon in "Rewriting the Male Text" has noted quite rightly that when Emilie (in "The Missing Peace") insists on writing down the names of the soldier-assassins, it is not only their patronymic that she is making official, but also the memory of their victims. In much the same way, I would add that when Célianne (in "Children of the Sea") slashes her face after having been raped, her gesture, instead of plunging her into oblivion, draws attention to her person and serves as a reminder of the assault of which she has been a victim.[5] Célianne's act also partakes of another type of duality, that of the encoding of atrocity: the mark of the wounds left by the knife on her flesh sends out a message identical to the message conveyed by a pen's marks on paper. Using different media, her character and the narrator perform the same act of inscribing the violence directed against them. Célianne writes her story on her body before throwing it into the sea; the narrator writes his in a notebook that he surrenders to the waves.

For Danticat, scars express the inexpressible, and the collective language of wounds to the flesh often parallels that of the individual word. One after the other throughout Danticat's works, older women remind their granddaughters that a name written on a piece of paper is meaningless and that only the physical presence of a person matters. Yet, the author shows the absurdity of a rivalry which consists in opposing the spoken and the written word, since any distinction between flesh and paper tends to be leveled in fires and massacres, revealing the fragility of both documents and bodies.[6]

Certain double figures exhibit a mingling of contradictory component parts.[7] Thus the heroine's mother in *Breath, Eyes, Memory* is described as a "living corpse" and the heroine views her as "two people. Someone who was trying to hold things together and someone who was falling apart" (218). The mother, speaking about herself, confirms this contradictory duality: "I am a fat woman trying to pass for thin. A dark woman trying to pass for light. And I have no breasts" (189). This mother, androgynous because of her lack of breasts, becomes a part of the imaginary aspect of sexual bi-polarity.[8] The heroine of *The Farming of Bones*, Amabelle Désir, is also marked by a contradictory duality. Her companion Sebastien, named after a saint who died twice, describes her as "A woman/child with . . . what we see and what we don't see, the good and the bad" (3). Amabelle who declares that she has "chosen a living death" (283), is perhaps also double in the sense that all orphans become their own mothers.[9] Torn between two countries, Haiti and the Dominican Republic, she experiences duality on several levels. She reports that during the 1937 massacre "a crossroad split our trail into two paths" (167) and at that moment the wounded face of a young woman "flapped open" (168). Finally, Amabelle's life is double because it is organized around the dynamics of the mirror,[10] the future that the heroine will never experience reflects a past of which she knows nothing: "All my heirs would be like my ancestors: revenants, shadows, ghosts" (278).

Generally speaking, the dynamics of reflection work as a structuring function within Danticat's work, since the structure of certain paragraphs and pages, chapters and short stories, is based entirely on a mirror-like composition.[11] The short story "Seeing Things Simply" makes use of a construction in which the end reflects the beginning. The first sentence: "Get it, kill it!" (*Krik? Krak!* 125) is reflected in the final words of the story: "Get him, kill him" (141). In both cases the pronoun refers to a cock, which has apparently become humanized and gained in virility between the beginning and the end of the story, since "it" has become "him." The fact that the sentence is repeated in a slightly modified form, however, in no way disqualifies it as a mirror. What we have here is simply an instance of the African tradition of "Signifying" described by Henry Louis Gates as "repetition and difference, repetition and revision in the Anglo African narrative tradition" (*Signifying* XXV). Many traces of this tradition can be found in Danticat's writings. The short story "New York Day Women" ends with the words "shame is heavier than a hundred bags of salt" (154), a playful repetition of "salt is heavier than a hundred bags of shame" (150). In the same way, the short story "Caroline's Wedding" which makes use of the African tradition of questions and answers closes with the answer to a riddle asked several times throughout the text.

The mirror structure also functions because different works refer to one another in the African American tradition of "Signifying," of the "Talking Book" and of "Speakerly Texts."[12] The last paragraphs in *Breath, Eyes, Memory* mention butterflies and the tears of statues, thereby echoing the short stories "Nineteen Thirty Seven" and "Children of the Sea." Sometimes, however, the dynamics of the mirror draw their force from an internal narrative development which is replete with repetition. The epilogue of *Krik? Krak!* repeats the following sentence four times: "You remember thinking while braiding your hair that you look a lot like your mother" (*Krik? Krak!* 219, 221, 222, 223). In *Breath, Eyes, Memory*, the words "his name is Sabastien Onius" (281) are also repeated four times on a single page and endow the text with an incantatory rhythm. Furthermore, since the novel opens with these words, one senses the complexity in this interplay of reflections, which both crystallizes the text and projects it beyond itself.

Danticat's writing also exhibits what Henry Louis Gates calls "a double voiced narrative mode" (*Signifying* 110-13) since the author interweaves several dual cultural traditions. The sentence used for expressing acknowledgments in *The Farming of Bones* is an example of this: "Mèsi anpil, Muchas gracias, Thank you very much" (311).[13]

Danticat not only makes use of the confrontation on American soil between two parallel discursive spheres—one originating in Africa, the other in Europe—but also uses American-English to write narratives inspired by events experienced in Creole, French and Spanish. Within this cultural universe, which is already extremely complex, the French of the Haitians who have remained on their island encounters the French of the Haitians who have emigrated to the United States, those who are called the "traveled" (*les voyagés*) and who are thought of as cowardly and arrogant.[14] Furthermore, the language of the Haitians who have stayed in the country takes two distinct forms: the silent body language of those who have been tortured and mutilated and the spoken languages of those who have not.[15] Thus several types of language are used, each with several linguistic registers.

A study of the two versions of the same short story, i.e. "From the Ocean Floor" and "Children of the Sea," points to an additional level of complexity in Danticat's use of language since the narrative, as it distances itself from Creole and French, the author's native tongues, becomes more pessimistic. The American English text, "From the Ocean Floor" includes a number of French expressions, for example, "Haiti est comme tu l'as laissée, same merde, same bullshit." Or again: "It was just his con de tête." In "Children of the Sea," a version of "From the Ocean Floor" expurgated of both its French and colloquial expressions and published a few years later in *Krik? Krak!*, the words "same merde, same bullshit" are transformed into "same hole, same everything," and "It was just his con de tête" becomes "It was just his head" (4, 7). This sterilization of the story's language, eliminating both the multiplicity of tongues and linguistic registers since even the colloquial English disappears, is accompanied by a loss of hope: the end of "Children of the Sea" describes the drowning narrator's last thoughts while the possibility of rescue has not been excluded in "From the Ocean Floor."

Looking at duality in Danticat's writing in the general sense, one notes that she alternates bold and normal typefaces in certain works. The two types of characters are used to distinguish between the words of two different narrators in "New York Day

Women" and "Children of the Sea," but in *The Farming of Bones* they appear to express the different registers of a single narrator, who is virtually split into two parts, one living in reality, the other in a dream world.[16] Here the word "shadow" recurs frequently.

To continue with the theme of the double voice, it is appropriate to note, as does Nancy Gerber, that Danticat is both a woman poet and a "woman-speaking-subject."[17] One can apply to all of Danticat's narratives what Gerber says about *Breath, Eyes, Memory*: "Sophie's text frames interpolated stories told by the other Caco women. . . . A polyphonic text . . . the stories themselves . . . mirror the themes . . . that resonate in the larger first person narrative" (189). Of the different forms taken by the double, I would like to stress one of its particularly interesting aspects, the unexpected dynamics of some of its forms.

Doubles resulting from combinations or associations traditionally perceived as natural (two arms, two eyes, two legs), and those resulting from the association of two components necessary to the creation of an archetypal image (for example, mother plus child = maternity, and man plus woman = couple), appear with Danticat to be the object of a deconstruction of traditional unions or associations. This deconstruction is necessarily related to the notion of struggle and rivalry, leading to the destruction or sacrifice of one of the components. Thus, arms, which are universally conceived in pairs formed of equal components, lose their equality with Tibon (*The Farming of Bones*): one of his arms is atrophied and the other hypertrophied. The couples formed of lovers, double because they are two but also because they resemble each other physically or psychologically, are inevitably destroyed through the disappearance of one of them. The fate of twins is hardly more enviable: they are suspected of trying to strangle each other in their mother's womb. Note that the possibility of survival is granted only to the feminine component. Lastly, the image of maternity is almost always tragic. Either the child dies in the womb or at birth, the mother herself dies while giving birth, or death takes both the mother and the child. Mothers who have adopted children must also face the death of the child they have welcomed before, in turn, losing their minds and dying themselves.

It is possible to view these unexpected struggles between elements of a similar or complementary nature as a metaphor for the particular situation of the black population in the Caribbean. The idea of fratricide is explicitly taken up in *The Farming of Bones,* in which the Dominicans kill their own people whom they mistake for Haitians. As a rule, blacks mistreat other blacks. Tibon the Haitian regularly beats up a Dominican friend because "He won't say what I want him to say, that we're the same, me and him, flesh like flesh, blood like blood" (182).

In "Children of the Sea," a woman says: "They treat Haitians like dogs in the Bahamas. . . . To them we are not human. Even though their music sounds like ours. Their people look like ours. Even though we had the same African fathers who probably crossed the same seas together" (14).

Another possible reading of the unjust fate reserved for the components of the double could be drawn from African tradition. Esu Elegbara, one of the main characters of African legend, moves on legs of unequal length in order to keep one foot on the ground and one in the sky at all times. Such an interpretation is interesting in that it provides a link with the themes of the real and the imaginary universes already mentioned in relation to the alternating use of bold and normal typefaces.

A second form of the unexpected coexistence of the components of a double is due to the exactly opposite scenario since in Danticat's writing elements usually opposed to one another coexist harmoniously in spite of their intrinsically or culturally incompatible natures. This is particularly true when considered from a western point of view, which is more likely to reason in terms of clear-cut separation than is the African custom. With Danticat, the principle of fluidity seems to determine the transfer of one aspect of the double into its opposite and define the coexistence of the trivial and the extraordinary, of the amiable peacefulness and the absolute horror of Haitian everyday life.[18] The different ways in which

Danticat's characters view parsley is one example. An everyday cooking ingredient and cleaning tool (parsley is used as a sponge in Haiti), the plant becomes an instrument of torture during periods of political upheaval, since Dominicans identify Haitians by asking them to pronounce the word in Spanish (*perejil*), which is difficult for Haitians, and then stuff it down their throats. Yet the references to parsley made by the characters reveal a surprising degree of calm given the extreme ambiguity of its symbolism. Their acceptance of the plant's diverse and varied uses is on the whole detached. Amabelle who is taken for dead after having been suffocated with parsley concludes simply: "We used parsley for our food, our teas, our baths, to cleanse our insides as well as our outsides. Perhaps the Generalissimo, in some larger order, was trying to do the same for his country" (203).

In much the same way, Haitian policemen in *The Farming of Bones* don the uniforms of the Dominican soldiers charged with exterminating them without any apparent scruples. The Haitian president himself sports a medal awarded to him by the Dominican general responsible for the massacre of the Haitian people. The coexistence of the best and the worst reigns supreme even at the bottom of the mass grave, where for one victim the strangeness of that situation revives the pleasant memory of his young bride's surprise at waking up in his bed for the first time.

No doubt the victims' relative detachment can be explained in part by their shock and confusion but the text does not say so explicitly. Perhaps also because of the frequency of abnormal occurrences, whether rape, torture or murder, they finish by becoming part of the norm. Here again nothing is explicitly stated. The acceptance of the monstrous as part of the everyday could, however, be strengthened by a culture and religious practices mixing the most contradictory of traditions. Do not Danticat's characters celebrate in Erzulie a divinity who rapes and kills men while preserving the gentleness and chastity of the Virgin Mary?[19] Perhaps the most remarkable aspect in all this is not so much Erzulie's bi-polar unity (after all Khali in India and many other divine figures are similar in nature[20]) but the union within the same figure of two elements one of which, Christianity, is traditionally perceived as excluding all other religious affiliations, in this case, voodoo.[21] It would appear that the coalescing and mingling of antagonistic values is one of everyday life's realities in Haiti.

Danticat's writing shows that the division of the original entity into two clearly separated elements (bodies, houses, paths cut in two) is only one of the possible forms that the splitting apart can take. Often, the original entity changes progressively, and we witness a reciprocal invasion of spheres considered as mutually exclusive, if not universally at least by traditional patriarchal communities. This explains the frequent occurrence of the theme of androgyny in Danticat's work, or rather, of a particular form of androgyny, since it originates exclusively in the acquisition of male characteristics by women. They are mutilated and their heads shaved in wartime, their breasts are removed for medical reasons in peacetime. Although the amputation is performed with sharp tools, this operation is not an instance of excision, since the intention is not to affirm through separation the masculine and feminine sexualities. The result tends to become, on the contrary, a symbol of the union of these gender principles by means of the sacrifice to which these women are subjected: they gain in virility without losing the essence of their femininity. Thus, in *Breath, Eyes, Memory* the heroine's mother whose breasts have been removed nonetheless becomes pregnant.

It is interesting to read Danticat in light of Griaule's work on Sudanese mythology or, more recent, the work of Gates on Yoruba culture. Marilyn Houlberg's and Vèvè Clark's research on Haitian vaudoo also shows to what extent bisexuality is an essential concept in certain regions of Africa. Perhaps the dynamics on which rests the tradition of the marasa, a derivative of African myths not rooted in the patriarchal tradition, throw light on what to a Western mind may seem a disconcerting acceptance of irreconcilable contradictions. According to Clark, the marasa is a Caribbean adaptation of the Mawu Lisa, a divine figure who is both male and female and is one of the creation myths of Benin. This natural coexistence of opposite elements, this bi-polarity, appears, therefore, to be an everyday reality in Caribbean culture.

Danticat's works frequently refer explicitly to the marasa tradition, which prevents Haitians from going completely mad because it explains the most monstrous acts as a result of the split personality of the people who commit them. Likewise, the human and the inhuman frequently coexist in the personality of politicians:

> There were many cases in our history where our ancestors had *doubled.* Following in the *vaudoo* tradition, most of our presidents were actually one body split into two: part flesh and part shadow. That was the only way they could murder and rape so many people and still go home to play with their children and make love to their wives. (*Breath, Eyes, Memory* 155)

It would, however, be difficult to interpret Danticat's references to the marasa in terms of her regarding the tradition as susceptible of providing a satisfactory solution to the contradictions of Caribbean society and the horror of the situation in Haiti.[22] Probably because of the particular nature of her themes, including the cruelty of human beings towards their fellows, Danticat would appear to be challenging the reader to find a positive meaning or logic in the events she describes. It is just as difficult for the reader to detect any semblance of a narrative resolution. The prospect of a solution is not excluded but nor is it hinted at.[23]

The study of the endings of Danticat's novels and short stories is particularly interesting, and I return here to the theme of the mirror-like construction, in which the beginning is reflected in the ending. The author refuses to close her narratives with an event providing the answer to the questions posed by the text as a whole or orienting it in a particular direction. Danticat suggests an ending that opens on to a space offering multiple paths of returns in keeping with African tradition. The idea that, in one way or another, both history and stories repeat themselves, that nothing really ever ends, resonates particularly strongly with an author whose fiction often merges with reality. Renée Larrier justifiably observes that even though *The Farming of Bones* takes the form of a novel it nonetheless contains documentary-like aspects including the reproduction of a letter from President Stenio Vincent to the Minister of Foreign Affairs George Léger. This impression of reality is further emphasized by the fact that the book is dedicated and signed by Amabelle Désir.[24] This constant shifting back and forth from fiction to reality is echoed quite naturally in the fact that a great number of Haitians are still harvesting sugarcane in the Dominican Republic under terrible conditions, as outlined in the report of the Inter-American Commission for Human Rights.[25]

Danticat's fiction is sometimes directly inspired by past and present reality: in Haiti those who oppose the incumbent powers continue to be assassinated and the entire population lives in terror of the "*Père Lebrun*," the flaming tire hung around the neck of troublemakers. But if Danticat's fiction is inspired by reality, it also anticipates certain real events which in turn become a source of inspiration. Thus, the destiny of the imaginary narrator of "Children of the Sea," a radio host in Haiti wanted by the "*Tonton Macoute*" death squads, anticipates the very real fate of Jean Dominique, a journalist for Radio Haiti Inter assassinated in 2000 only a few years after the publication of the short story. Jean Dominique's death, in turn, became the subject of Danticat's preface to *The Butterfly's Way*.[26] The violence of the country's political framework is matched by the violence of the prevalent diseases, aids and typhoid fever, and of cyclones that are all the more deadly because of deforestation. In the prevailing climate of fear and uncertainty, perhaps Haitian mothers, like Danticat's characters, take refuge in the strict observance of ancient customs whose rituals provide reassurance but condemn their daughters to ignorance and servitude to men.[27]

Where does the writer's imagination begin? How can we circumscribe the reality which nourishes her writing? The driving force behind a spiral[28] which mirrors its own curves, Danticat's double feeds on both terror and the feeling of well-being, both real and imaginary. To paraphrase the final words in

*Krik! Krak?*, she bears witness to the way the Haitian people have lived, died and lived again,[29] transforming the figure of duality that animates her novels into a metaphor for the problematic meeting of cultures that haunts Haitian society as much as do her imagination and the imagination of other writers.

## NOTES

1. I first presented the ideas expressed in this article on February 23, 2002 at a conference held at the University of Paris VII organized by the Cercle d'Etudes Afro-Américaines. Since I am not a specialist of the Caribbean, I did so with reservations. Several specialized studies, and in particular one by April Shemak, have since confirmed my analysis and encouraged me to publish my ideas.
2. In Renee Shea's "The Dangerous Job of Edwidge Danticat," Danticat is quoted as saying "the idea is that two people are one but not quite, they might look alike and talk alike but are, in essence, different people." (385)
3. See the work of Vèvè Clark and Marilyn Houlberg on Haitian voodoo.
4. The most striking case may be the insistence of the old man in "Children of the Sea" to have his name inscribed on a piece of paper which he knows will immediately be swallowed up by the sea, as he will be himself.
5. In the case of Emilie and Célianne, there may be an attempt to re-appropriate power through the act of inscription, a desire to "have the last word." The marks left by these characters on paper or on their own bodies tend to free them from the power others have over them. In *Breath, Eyes, Memory*, Sophie mutilates herself in order to escape the humiliation of the vaginal examination her mother subjects her to. Marie José N'Zengou-Tayo, in "Rewriting Folklore," has interpreted the act of writing down the names of the soldier-assassins as a form of magic by which Emilie holds them in her power. Note that these gestures are an act of volition on the part of the heroines while most characters suffer their mutilation passively.
6. The body as the seat of memory in *The Farming of Bones* is the subject of April Shemak's study "Re-Membering Hispaniola."

7. Maybe these figures echo the Haiti described by Haitian writers. In *The Butterfly's Way*, Edwidge Danticat, Joel Dreyfus and Marylène Philips take up the idea that Haiti, "the poorest nation of the Western hemisphere" is also a country rich in art, literature and glorious historical events. (XVI, 57,115)
8. Although her component parts are not contradictory here, she is also double because of her pregnancy, her allegiance to two countries, Haiti and the United States, and her conviction that she and her daughter are "two fingers on the same hand. Two eyes on the same head" (98).
9. "My parents had drowned, leaving us both to parent our childhood dreams out of ourselves" (*The Farming of Bones*, 27)
10. The double as reflection calls to mind water, the original mirror. In fact, Danticat's characters like to examine their reflection in water. The short story "Nineteen Thirty Seven" offers an illustration of a doubling split between the image of a little girl and her mother, who resemble each other and together look at their reflection in the river.
11. One could argue that the novel *The Farming of Bones* works on this principle. First, the narrative is divided into two parts of equal length: one in which the heroine shows deference to the values of mainstream society, and another in which she is liberated from them. Second, the first chapter opens with a sentence which is repeated four times in the next—to-last chapter, enhancing the mirror-effect.
12. "Intertextuality represents a process of repetition and revision, by definition. A number of shared structural elements are repeated, with differences that suggest familiarity with other texts." (Henry Louis Gates, *The Signifying Monkey*, 60)
13. The French version of this novel entitled *La Récolte douce des larmes* adds "merci" to the acknowledgements.
14. "Members of the diaspora would be classified—justifiably or not—as arrogant, insensitive, overbearing and pretentious people who were eager to reap the benefits of good jobs and political positions in times of stability in a country they had fled during difficult times. Shamefacedly, I would bow my head and accept these judgments when they were expressed, feeling guilty for my own physical distance from a country I had left at the age of twelve years during a dictatorship that had forced thousands to choose

between exile or death." Edwidge Danticat, (*The Butterfly's Way*, xvi).

15. See April Shemak's "Re-Membering Hispaniola: Danticat's *The Farming of Bones*.
16. This idea is in keeping with Danticat's introduction to *The Butterfly's Way*: "My country [. . .] is one of uncertainty. Haiti possesses nine departments on its geographical map and the tenth was the floating homeland, the ideological one which joined all Haitians living in the *Dyaspora*." (xiv) Further on she adds, "The *Dyaspora* are people with feet planted in both worlds." (xv)
17. "The doubled female voice of woman-poet-author and woman-speaking-subject" ("Binding the Narrative Thread" 189).
18. The general characteristics of water, which is universally perceived as having a dual value since it is a source both of life and of destruction, are reinforced through the intensity of storms in Haiti and the Dominican Republic. The weather plays a key role in *The Farming of Bones*, in which the heroine loses her parents because of the violence of the rainfall but finds a lover thanks to another storm. History itself helps to further overstate the ambivalence of water. The sea that once brought slaves now carries away desperate boat people, and the rivers mingle Dominican and Haitian blood. The essence of water would be pure cruelty if the tears and the lives they have swallowed were not transformed into holy water, and bodies of water a place of meditation, love and communion. The role of water in Danticat's writings recalls Gilbert Durand's observation that water, in losing its translucence, becomes thicker and colored, as if haunted by blood. Durand was referring to a geographical body of water which had become almost organic by dint of its thickness, midway between love and horror.

    Water as a universal symbolic object and because of its inherent duality can be submitted with relative ease to reversals of meaning and to a *doubling*, which together lead to the process of double negation (*Les Structures Anthropologiques de l'Imaginaire* 252, 253): We find an illustration of this in "Children of the Sea" where the sea is transformed from a place of refuge—it allows fugitives to escape the "*Tonton Macoute*" death squads—into a place of menace, the water invading their small craft, before finally returning to being a protective cradle when it embraces the shipwrecked. The narrator's last words before drowning: "I go to them (the children of the sea) now as though it was always meant to be, as though the very day my mother birthed me, she had chosen me to live life eternal, among the children of the deep blue sea, those who have escaped the chains of slavery to form a world beneath the heavens and the blood-drenched earth where you live. Perhaps I was chosen from the beginning of time to live there with Agwé at the bottom of the sea. Maybe this was my invitation to go." (28) We can see clearly here that being engulfed by the sea does not desecrate but, on the contrary, makes sacred. Water makes euphemizing possible. There is a semantic inversion here, a transfiguration of the meaning and of the objectives of the human beings themselves, although the characters' material and physical destiny remains inescapable. However, the defining principles of water, fluidity and ductility, determine the transfer of one aspect of the double into its opposite.

19. According to Henry Louis Gates, "Erzulie"also means "love of mirrors" (*The Signifying Monkey* 227).
20. See Eliade and Soustelle.
21. Rodney Saint Eloi, in a short article on Danticat published in 2001 ("L'Ecriture Bizango" 58) also mentions the "Bizango" as a mythical Haitian figure that recalls the *duality* of the subject. Bizango, according to Saint Eloi, "is also a secret society marked, among other things, by a dual attitude and unsuspected mutations of identity on the part of the members of the cult: man/beast, day/night. In fact, the Bizango is a master in the art of reconciling opposites." For Maximilien Laroche, whom Rodney Saint Eloi quotes, the Bizango "refers through anti-phrases, like shadow to the light, to this ever-changing figure of the mythology of the renaissance in Haiti."
22. The use of the principle of the marasa raises many questions and might be seen as legitimizing the expression of cruelty. Vèvè Clark vehemently objects to the idea that the marasa could be viewed as a cultural and religious tradition capable of solving its adepts' problems.
23. A traditional interpretation would see the dynamics of sacrifice in the disappearance of one of the elements of the double, the annihilation of one of the parts making the survival or self-realization of the other possible. Yet, such a view hardly seems relevant when referring to narratives in which the fate of the survivor often turns out to be worse than death. The same can be

said of the notion of borders. In "Re-Membering Hispaniola," April Shemak has noted concerning *The Farming of Bones* that "Danticat's text challenges prematurely facile celebrations of borderlands." (87) Shemak argues that Danticat's vision of the border does not totally correspond to Gloria Anzaldua's theory (*Borderlands: la Frontera, The New Mestiza*) in that according to Anzaldua borderlands are places of creativity, socialization and freedom, while in Danticat's writing the border, whether concrete or symbolic (i.e. the Massacre river or the hymen of young raped or self-mutilated girls) remains a place of horror and of unresolved tension, even if it can be read as a space for communion and love originating in a shared experience of horror.

24. See Renee Larrier's "Girl by the Shore: Gender and Testimony in Edwidge Danticat's *The Farming of Bones*."
25. According to the *Daily News* of October 23, 2000, "most cane-cutting, and much labor is performed by Haitians who are contracted en masse by employment brokers."
26. The short story "Seven," which mentions the murder of a Haitian in the United States, bears a resemblance to the story of Patrick Dorismond, who was shot down for no justifiable reason by the New York police in 2000. It is also reminiscent of the story of another Haitian-American, Abner Louima, who was brutalized and raped by a policeman at Brooklyn police headquarters in 1997.
27. In "Rewriting Folklore," Marie-José N'Zengou-Tayo writes: "Concerning the importance of virginity . . . Danticat dares to speak about a practice ("the test") that has always been silenced in Haitian culture and society. Bastien documented customs surrounding the "non virginity" of brides and indicated how mothers' honor is at stake . . . but he did not mention preventive practices to ensure the preservation of their daughters' virginity. I tried to obtain confirmation of this practice: though it was implicitly confirmed, I was told that any official answer would be an absolute denial of it. Ira Lowenthal, who documented gender and sex discourse in a small village in the South of Haiti, is also silent on the matter. . . . It would be tempting, therefore to dismiss the "test" as a device totally made up by Danticat as a means to denounce women's part in passing on patriarchal customs detrimental to them. Yet . . . some popular sayings . . . lead us to wonder if there is not some (symbolic) truth in Danticat's fiction" (127, 128).

28. For Vèvè Clark the tradition of the marasa is binary only at first glance, because it reveals opposites. In fact this tradition is an invitation to go beyond binary opposition towards a cyclical and spiral reading of the elements concerned. Clark's interpretation, which is reminiscent of the theories of Henry Louis Gates and Gilbert Durand, suggests an interesting approach to the analysis of Danticat's narratives.
29. The sentence itself reads "and this was your testament to the way that these women lived and died and lived again."

## Works Cited and Consulted

Anglesay, Zoe. "The Voice of the Storytellers: An Interview with Edwidge Danticat." *MultiCultural Review* (Sep. 1998): 36-39.

Anzaldua, Gloria. *Borderlands: la Frontera, The New Mestiza.* San Francisco: Aunt Lute, 1987.

Bastien, Rémi. *Le Paysan haitien et sa famille: Vallée de Marbial.* (*The Haitian Peasant and His Family in the Marbial Valley*). Trans. Linette and André-Marcel d'Ans. Paris: Karthala, 1985. (1951).

Braziel, Jana-Evans. "Daffodils, Rhizomes, Migrations: Narrative Coming of Age in the Diasporic Writings of Edwidge Danticat and Jamaica Kincaid." *Meridians: Feminism,-Race,-Transnationalism* 3.2 (2003): 110-31.

Brice-Finch, Jacqueline. "Edwidge Danticat: Memories of Maafa." *MaCommere: Journal of the Association of Caribbean Women Writers and Scholars* (2001): 146-54.

Clark, Vèvè. "Developing Diaspora Consciousness and *Marasa* Consciousness." *Comparative American Identities: Race, Sex and Nationality in the Modern Text*, ed Hortense Spiller. NewYork: Routledge, 1991. 40-61.

Danticat, Edwidge. *Breath, Eyes, Memory.* New York: Vintage, 1994.

_____. *Krik? Krak!.* New York: Vintage, 1995.

_____. *The Farming of Bones.* New York: Penguin, 1998.

_____. Introduction. *The Butterfly's Way*, ed. Edwidge Danticat. New York: Soho, 2001

Diard, Dominique. "Exil et migration." (équipe "Voi (es)x de l'exil et des migrations). Caen, *Cahiers de la Maison de la Recherche en Sciences Humaines* (octobre 2003). 183-96.

Durand, Gilbert. *Les Structures Anthropologiques de l'imaginaire.* Paris: Dunod, 1992. (Paris Bordas, 1969 pour la première édition)

Gates Jr., Henry Louis. *Figures in Black, Words, Signs and the "Racial" Self.* New York: Oxford University Press, 1987.

_____. *The Signifying Monkey: A Theory of African-American Literary Criticism.* New York: Oxford University Press, 1988.

Gerber, Nancy F. "Binding the Narrative Thread: Storytelling and the Mother-Daughter Relationship in Edwidge Danticat's *Breath, Eyes, Memory.*" *Journal of the Association for Research on Mothering* (Fall-Winter 2000): 188-99.

Goldblatt, Patricia. "The Implausibility of Marriage." *Multicultural Review* (Sept. 2001): 42-48, 73.

Griaule, *Une Mythologie Soudanaise.* Ann. Univ. Paris, XVIIe année, n° 2, 1947

Hewett, Heather-Ann. *Diaspora's Daughters: Buchi Emechta, Julie Dash, Edwidge Danticat and the Remapping of Mother Africa. Dissertation Abstracts, International Section-A: The Humanities and Social Sciences* 62.7 (2002). University of Wisconsin.

Houlberg, Marilyn. "Magic Marassa: The Ritual Cosmos of Twins and Other Sacred Children." *The Sacred Arts of Haitian Vodou*, ed. Donald Cosentino. Los Angeles: UCLA Fowler Museum of Cultural History, 1995. 267-83.

Horn, Jessica. "Edwidge Danticat: An Intimate Reader." *Meridians: Feminism,-Race,-Transnationalism* (Spring 2001). 19-25.

Kekeh-Dika, Andrée-Anne. "Entre ville et village: Quelles destinées pour le féminin chez Edwidge Danticat?" in Duboin, Corinne (ed. et introd.). *La ville plurielle dans la fiction antillaise anglophone: images de l'interculturel*, Toulouse, France: PU du Mirail, 2000.

Lahens, Yanick. "L'Apport de quatre romancières au roman moderne haitien."

Laroche, Maximilien, *Bizango, Essai de mythologie haitienne.* Quebec, Université GRELCA, n° 14, 1997.

Larrier, Renee, "'Girl by the Shore': Gender and Testimony in Edwidge Danticat's *The Farming of Bones.*" *Journal of Haitian Studies* (Fall 2001): 50-60.

N'Zengou-Tayo, Marie-Jose. "Rewriting Folklore: Traditional Beliefs and Popular Culture in Edwidge Danticat's *Breath, Eyes, Memory* and *Krik?Krak!.*" *MaCommere: Journal of the Association of Caribbean Women Writers and Scholars* (2000): 123-40.

Ortiz, Lisa—Marie. "Modes of Auto Ethnography: Genealogical, Autobiographical and Historical Recovery in the Novels of Alvarez, Cliff and Danticat." *Dissertation Abstracts, International*

*Section-A: The Humanities and Social Sciences* 61.3 (Sep. 2000) 989, Wayne State University.

Poon, Angelia. "Re-Writing the Male Text: Mapping Cultural Spaces in Edwidge Danticat's *Krik?Krak*! and Jamaica Kincaid's *A Small Place.*" Jouvert: *A Journal of Postcolonial Studies* (Winter 2000). 30 paragraphs.

Saint Eloi, Rodney. "L'Ecriture Bizango: Edwidge Danticat, le go between." Notre Librairie: *Revue des Littératures du Sud* (Janvier-Mars 2001): 58-61.

Shea, Renee, H. "Edwidge Danticat." *Belles Lettres* (Summer 1995): 12-15.

_____. "The Hunger to Tell: Edwidge Danticat and *The Farming of Bones.*" *MaCommere: Journal of the Association of Caribbean Women Writers and Scholars* (1999): 12-22.

Shemak, April. "Re-Membering Hispaniola: Edwidge Danticat's *The Farming of Bones.*" *Modern Fiction Studies* (Spring 2002): 83-112

Tabuteau, Eric. "American Dream, Urban Nightmare: Edwidge Danticat's *Breath, Eyes, Memory* and George Lamming's *In the Castle of My Skin.*" Alizes: Revue Angliciste de la Réunion, 2002. 95-110.

Watchel, Eleanor. "A Conversation with Edwidge Danticat" *Brick* (Fall 2000): 65-66, 106-19.

Wucker, Michele. "Edwidge Danticat: A Voice for the Voiceless." *Americas* (May-June 2000): 40-45.

# Reconfigurations of Nation Space: From Jacobs to Morrison

**Jasbir Jain**
**University of Rajasthan, Jaipur**

Black writers have had always to contend with the adjective 'black'—a term of identification with a group, a kind of representation thrust on them and yet, at the same time, a term of exclusion from the dominant mainstream. This exclusion has been ironically framed both by history and the politics of power—their visibility of color has been the base of this invisibility. Pushed into non-citizenship, confined into subordinate roles and segregated spaces both literally and figuratively, the African Americans have also had to contend with doubleness of belonging and their writing has signified this struggle. Each step forward towards extracting another inch of space, each step forward towards the dismantling of the binaries between black and white, between ethnos and nation has been in itself a landmark.

What makes a text a 'landmark' and bestow on it the status of a 'classic'? The two terms cohere at some point or do they ask for a distinction on the basis of genre—like creative writing and critical writing? The difference may work at the level of statement and art, in the aesthetics of the work leading one into a larger debate about the production of meaning and of knowledge, into the ways one 'knows' requiring one to work a series of frameworks—ontological, phenomenological, psychological, political, and epistemological.[1]

To begin with there is the matter of recognition and impact: a landmark need not always be recognized at the time of its origin. It often acquires this recognition in retrospect: and its value is similarly subject to re-evaluation. In fact, it is this possibility of re-evaluation, that goes on to make it a classic as it marks a shift in time and space: the first requisite thus would be its capacity to be re-read, to reveal hidden depths, to respond to the exigencies of the reader's present, in short to go beyond the confines of the page, to render the relationship between the written word and its meaning one of constant expansion.

The four texts I wish to focus on span a period of nearly a century and a half—Harriet Jacobs's *Incidents in the Life of a Slave Girl* (1861), bell hooks's *Ain't I a Woman* (1981) and *Feminist Theory: From Margin to Centre* (1984) and Toni Morrison's *Playing in the Dark* (1992)—are texts which work across genres and contend with political situations as well as a language, which in Morrison's terms, is laced with 'hidden signs of racial superiority, cultural hegemony, and dismissive 'othering' of people and language which are by no means marginal' (xii). The very medium of articulation, which is neither neutral nor objective, is loaded against them. Thus as they write, they create new categories, replace the rhetoric, invent new images, and refer to other histories.

Harriet Jacobs's fictionalized autobiography has a subtitle 'written by herself.' Resistance is expressed and redefinition sought through this act of writing which is an act of appropriation. Harriet was self-educated, and had to hide this fact from her white masters, though later on she began to write for the newspapers and also wrote her book during the years 1852-58. She went on to seek publication for it. Finally it was only in 1861, through the services of L. Maria Child that the book could be published. The title is worth our attention for two things—'Incidents' (it is not 'Life', not 'Adventure', not 'heroism' but 'incidents'), and 'Herself'—a reflexive pronoun acting as a substitute for a name and reflecting on this act of writing which is instrumental in this self-assertion. It also brings about a change in her slave status: it provides her with an agency.

bell hooks in *Ain't I a Woman* (1981) takes up the title of her work from Sojourner Truth's well-known speech at the 2nd

Annual Convention of the Women's Right Movement at Ohio (1852) when Truth flung this phrase repeatedly at her audience to prove that in no way are women inferior to men where physical strength or emotional endurance is concerned. She was attacking not one but two binaries—'white and black' and 'men' and women'—and thus make a claim for equality. hooks built on it to intervene in the assumption that white feminism was representative of all women. Following it up, three years later, with *Feminist Theory: From Margin to Centre* (1984), she sought to go beyond feminism, while Toni Morrison in *Playing in the Dark* (1992) constructs the concept of 'writerly reading' (as different from Barthes's 'writerly writing'), which requires an enormous capacity to imagine the other, and thus enter into the spaces of the creative process. Morrison takes the reader along through her reading of canonical writers like Mark Twain, Edgar Allan Poe, Willa Cather and Ernest Hemingway and several others to explore their hidden absences, the dark shadows lurking in their work. As the foundation of the American dream is laid, the black slave population is the 'other' they create as a substitute for their past which they have rejected or escaped from, in substitute for the absent aristocratic 'other'. This black 'other' is easier to contend with. Morrison, rather than place herself in opposition as the 'other' enters the self of the white 'other'. She writes: 'The ability of writers to imagine what is not the self, to familiarize the strange and mystify the familiar, is the test of their power' (15) and she began to look for the signs and codes, the literary strategies the white writers had employed to accommodate this racial encounter.

All four texts are written by women, yet none of them is purely or solely a woman's text. They go beyond gender to contest the space for freedom, for value, for a cultural presence and to address the category of power. It is not whiteness alone that has to be negotiated but what is at stake is something more crucial than it, it is the freedom to be—in all its fullness—personally, socially and culturally. Morrison's work is subtitled 'whiteness and literary imagination' as she proceeds to reveal the hidden black presence integrated into this white literary imagination. These lectures were part of the William Massey lectures in the history of *civilization* (emphasis mine): the work is thus an announcement of having arrived right in the midst of it, to have surfaced up to visibility.

The earliest of these writers Harriet Jacobs, writing in the mid-nineteenth century, had none of the advantages that bell hooks and Toni Morrison were to have later on—access to education, choice, or to freedom of movement and citizenship. And because of these factors her narrative is the boldest even if less sophisticated than the work of hooks and Morrison. It works across genres—an autobiography, it seeks help from fictional names and forms. Critics like Jean Fagan Yellin have commented upon its affiliation with the novel of romance as it is occasionally interrupted by direct address to the reader. Yet, even in this it goes on to reverse the formula of the seduction novel by refusing to rehabilitate the narrator within marriage. Richardson's shadow can be traced as both *Pamela* and *Clarissa* constantly haunt the reading of this autobiography but its concerns are markedly different as its chapter divisions indicate. As they go on to comment on the nature of the family, the partial and prejudicial application of law, the biased concept of justice, the mockery of the ideals of democracy, it moves beyond the fictional limits to dialogue with racial prejudices. It records history and redefines the notion of black motherhood. It is at one level, a fugitive slave narrative and at the same time an anti-slavery document, a persistent knocking at the 'conscience' of the nation.

It would do well to remember, that this is approximately the period when Harriet Martineau and Frances Trollope had traveled to America and written about its great democratic values and institutions as well as slavery.[2] Jacobs's account represents the underside of the story, the experience of a female slave in Edentown, North Carolina, who fights for a right to her body and her motherhood and in order to achieve them, has to use her intelligence and often resort to deception and subterfuge, especially when we learn that during her seven-year period of hiding in the low, narrow attic of her grandmother's house, in order to mislead her pursuers, she conspires with friends to have letters posted from the North. Her early attempts at self-education, her carefully planned movements, the physical discomfort ranging from the time in the swamps, the burial underground in a white woman's kitchen and the long self-imprisonment without any physical exercise or social company in a three-foot high attic for seven long years astound one's imagination and are all acts of courage which require emotional restraint. One is amazed at the maturity of her young son, who once he hears a cough from the attic discourages his sister from playing nearabouts for fear of attracting attention. The pleasures of childhood, the joys of motherhood and man-woman relationships—all are destroyed in this racially-divided world between the master and the slave. As Jacobs portrays parallel family structures, Dr. Flint and his wife, his son and daughter-in-law, her own parents' brief relations and her own grandmother's relationship with her children and grandchildren, all kinds of kinship patterns come in for examination. Yet the contrast does not run along color divisions. There are several relationships among the whites which project continuity and compatibility. Relationships are also formed across lines of color—Linda Brent is aided and abetted by several white people, neighbors, slave traders and slaveholders. This absence of a color division simultaneously dismantles the opposition between white and black as well as between civilized and savage. It questions the norm of white superiority and projects an individual-based notion of morality. The well-kept black homes, their linen, their housekeeping skills, go on to offer a contrast to the 'poor' white, who like them are victims of the same economic system but unlike them are unconscious of this victimhood.

Jacobs works across these boundaries in order to attack the larger institutions of law and religion. A nation which had gone to seek freedom for itself also proceeded to build its strength on norms of subjugation and slavery. There are several references to the Fugitive Slave Law passed in 1850, a law that required citizens to assist in the capture of slaves. The recurrent references to Dr. Flint's sexual advances towards her, the use of the word 'property' and the speculation of the monetary worth of a slave, the exclusion of slaves from appeal to law—all these comment on the white concepts of justice and power. Similarly, slaves attended separate churches meant for them within the same faith thus carrying on the discrimination in matters of religious observance. Religion was also considered a strong antidote to aspirations for freedom. Jacobs points out that after the alarm caused by Nat Turner's insurrection, the slaveholders considered it appropriate "to give the slaves enough of religious instruction to keep them from murdering their master' (197) but there was a great difference between the tenets of Christianity and the practice of religion in the South (204). This practice, later on in the narrative, is contrasted with her experience of religion in England where she lived in the house of a clergyman who was a true disciple of religion (330). In fact, her short chapter on her stay in England offers a counter discourse to English travelogues on America and its institution of slavery.[3]

As she moves across a wide canvas ranging from descriptions of other slaveholders, the division of the blacks into domestic workers and plantation workers, the implementation of law and the practice of religion, and narrates her emotional experiences—her early love which came to an untimely end, the counter-lover she later took and who fathered her two children, her unfulfilled maternal feelings—Jacobs contrasts the space she occupies narrow and confined with the space she relates to across memory and history. By framing her narrative through the novel of seduction before transferring it into one of consent, she by displacing the white lover makes a statement about the construction of the self as well as the nature of a sexual relationship. Despite physical and legal limitations she strives to acquire an agency. Her notion of motherhood also moves away from the black 'foster' mother or the slave breeder to one of a mother who protects and nurtures her children. Her struggle for the rights of education and freedom is a struggle for citizenship and equality—yet in itself, it is an incomplete narrative, "The dream of my life is not yet realized—I do not sit with my children in a home of my own." (350).

The authenticity of Harriet's narrative has been testified to both my her contemporaries like Amy Post and George Lawther[4] and researchers like Yellin who have worked in the archives to locate people places and incidents.[5] Maria Child, the white woman, whose help she had to seek in order to be published, also provides another testimony.[6] Yet it needed a subtitle 'Written by Herself' to authenticate not merely the happenings but also their telling—the voice of the narrator, the first person tracing of the journey of the self in an environment of hostility—to acquire an agency.

This arrival at a subjectivity, when framed in the context of political realities, reveals other forces that it needs to confront. Linda Brent's struggle is against slavery, against Dr. Flint and misappropriation of the female body. It is resistance to appropriation. The hidden factor of the 'white' woman as opponent is only marginally revealed in the behavior of the two Mrs. Flints—mother-in-law and daughter-in-law. For them the black woman is the 'other', who threatens the security of their marital relationships. Such an oppositional relationships could not in any way bring black and white women together on the question of political or human rights. Racism, for black women, was the primary struggle which relegated sexism to a secondary category. In fact racism incorporated within it, a reversal of sexist roles. hooks writes about the masculine roles that black women had to assume, laboring in the fields and plantations. They were seen as 'surrogate' men by white male slavers (hooks 1981: 22-23).

The course of social role-creations also differed widely in the two cases. While white women were gradually freed from the puritan fundamentalist view of being embodiments of sin and evil and temptresses, black women were inversely loaded with this discarded baggage and seen as prostitutes, whores (hooks 1981: 26-31,39) and as 'breeders' of a work force. The myth of the matriärch also came in handy to portray them as inherently more strong and domineering than white women, and pushed them into the role of female castrators responsible for the castration of men. In all this it was the body that was the site.

Harriet Jacobs's struggle was for a right to the body and the concept of freedom which for her, even when directed towards citizenship, is best understood as control over the body, over relationships and mobility, and the right to education and family. In some ways, her continued stress on purity of body and the legality of marriage are in consonance with the approved standards of white morality.[7]

bell hooks places the relationships between the black men and women in the political context where white interventions were constantly at work playing them against each other.[8] In all these shifts the black woman was the victim. The mistaken belief that a strong black patriarchy was the only way to end racism further brainwashed black women against feminism.

It was the issue of suffrage, the right to vote, that further widened the schism between white and black, and between men and women. White racial imperialism held on to the consolidation of power on the ground of race, while black patriarchy rendered it useless for black women and forced them back to fight on the same ground. hooks by tracing the history of black women's struggles in *Ain't I a Woman* (1981) goes on to continue the narrative by directly intervening in the elitist, white middle-class feminist movement in *Feminist Theory: From Margin to Centre* (1984). The history and the issues of the black feminist movement have been so multi-layered and different that they cannot be swept into any homogeneous category. hooks goes on to locate the black movement right in the political context and emphasizes the role of economic contexts in a capitalistic society. Her effort is to build a more encompassing concept of the human. In *Feminist Theory* she stresses the need for black women to recognize the special vantage point their marginality has given them. They can, she observes, "criticize the dominant racist, classicist, sexist hegemony as well as (to) envision and create a counter-hegemony" (15). But in the succeeding chapters of the book, she proceeds to dismantle such a binary opposition. Man-woman relationships are not necessarily oppressive; they can be liberatory as well. She dismisses the idea of opposition and puts forth one of growing up in a relationship of compatibilities and forging solidarities. hooks proceeds to discuss multi-ethnicity and focuses on the need to understand one another's cultural codes (56), the need to respect differences, and to evolve a sense of community (57). Individual experience can in no way be gathered under any one homogeneity, thus the need to work through 'difference' and go on to evolve an area of understanding. The emphasis has shifted from self to self-effort, from a 'given' to a 'constant evolution', expanding the notion of human will to move beyond choice to conscious, concerted effort. Hence the shift from mere 'support', which may be unqualified approval often requiring suspension of critical judgment (Jane Rule qtd. hooks, *Feminist Theory* 62) but solidarity can work across differences. And finally she also wishes to break the idea of women alone working for feminism, an approach which excludes the other half relocating them in the role of oppressor. Women, hooks firmly believes, can no longer allow feminism to be another arena where antagonism between the sexes is the rule; strategies for including men in the struggle need to be involved.

Jacobs and hooks, even as they locate themselves within women's position and that too as black women, move outside those positions to recognize positive relationships across racial and gender divisions. They are concerned with social and political structures which oppress and use one human being against the other as a medium of oppression. Moving outside these histories and experiences, each in consonance with the demands of her times, defines freedom and nationhood.

Jacobs's Linda Brent is conscious of the 'land where I was born' as is hooks of the diverse cultures which constitute the nation. Toni Morrison goes even further than them to work through the notion of culture and literary imagination. She works backwards through the nineteenth century to raise questions regarding the absence, the marginal presence, and the subordinated role assigned to the black by the white canonical writers. And as she travels backwards, she builds up a cyclical frame of history which relates the past to the present. The hostility often experienced by the blacks even in their contact with those who were believed to be anti-slavery or sympathetic to their cause can be perceived in the writing of men like Twain, Poe, Hemingway and others. Willa Cather's *Sapphira and the Slave Girl* projects, in one way, the story of Linda Brent written from a white woman's perspective. The novel, Morrison observes, "turns in the end into a kind of memoir, the author's recollection of herself as a child witnessing the return, the reconciliation, and an imposed 'all rightness' in untenable, outrageous circumstances" (27). Writer after writer, as they constructed and fed the American dream which they pursued as newcomers to the land, turned to romance, rather than to history and in this liberatory form, their imagination was free to play on the power of blackness, "The slave population, it could be and was assumed, offered itself up as surrogate selves for meditation on problems of human freedom, its lure and its elusiveness" (37). Later she adds, "The concept of freedom did not emerge in a vacuum. Nothing highlighted freedom—if it did not in fact create it—like slavery." The slaves symbolized not only 'not-free' but also 'not-me,' thus through polarities and through exclusion, the category of power through whiteness was constructed to build an image of America as "new, white and male" (43). Americans falling outside this range need to be classified with adjectives of color and hyphenated identities.

Morrison asserts that the black presence has always been a constituent in the construction of the American political and literary culture—it has been there in the framing of the constitution; in the enfranchisement struggles and laws, in jurisprudence and theological discourse, in fact, everywhere. Toni Morrison by compelling her reader/listener to read along with her these major canonical texts forces upon them the recognition of the black presence—"one of the most furtively radical impinging forces on the country's literature." She goes on to add that the contemplation of this black presence is central to any understanding of American literature and should not be permitted "to hover at the margins of literary imagination" (5). It is not only the subjugated populations that have been receivers of knowledge or have absorbed the white man's value structures and role models, but this subjugated population has been instrumental in constructing the major and championed characteristics of American culture (individualism, masculinity, freedom, etc.).

None of these three writers stays confined to any exclusive category, none of them visualizes separatist spaces: family, freedom and solidarity matter to them as does a shared culture. Jacobs's persistent concern with law, justice and morality, and the norms of citizenship, hooks's questioning of white feminism's stereotypes and sexist categories, Morrison's' view of how polarities can work together, are approaches that enlarge the human discourse and go on to define the 'human' anew. They are all questionings of the master narrative and work through definitions of self breaking through the imposed mould of the 'loathed' other, a cast projected on them through cultural constructs. Morrison also engages with the work of writers to understand the process of intellectual domination—how it is created and perpetuated (8). Yet this questioning of power is not a route to power—it is not to end as an 'exchange of dominations'. She goes on to argue that the concept of freedom did not emerge in a vacuum. It defined itself in opposition to non-freedom (38), that "autonomy, authority, newness and difference, absolute power—each one is made possible by, shaped by, activated by a complex awareness and employment of a constituted Africanism" (44). Among the various strategies that these writers have employed is one which she classifies as metaphysical condensation (the others are economy of stereotype, metonymic displacement, fetishization, dehistoricizing allegory and patterns of explosive disjointed allegory), which allows the writer to transform social and historical differences into universal differences, "collapsing persons into animals prevents human contact and exchange" and closes off the "possibility of communication" (68). Freedom thus does not mean freedom from chains but also a freedom from namelessness and nationlessness (73); it implies the coming into being of a self working against self-loathing, a freedom from the category of the inferior 'other', acquisition of an agency, a humanness with the possibility of an independent will. What then is a landmark—a classic? A text which contests boundaries, evokes human memory, provokes intellectual thought and negotiates power, is distinct from hegemony, and brings about a change not only in history but also in the reader. Toni Morrison falls back on Antonia Byatt's description of certain kinds of readings—"when the knowledge that we *shall know* the writing differently . . . runs ahead of any capacity to say what we know. In these readings, a sense that the text has appeared to be wholly new, never seen before, is followed, almost immediately, by the sense that it was *always there*" (qtd. Morrison xiii). It is this simultaneity of knowledge and ignorance, this timelessness, a certain dehistoricization, that creates a shareable world across barriers, and helps define the human. From this point of view these three writers go on to create a counter-discourse not only to white perspectives but also the hegemonic discourse of black patriarchy as their notion of self goes on to encompass other realities of human existence—political rights, aesthetic norms and knowledge constructs.

## NOTES

1. As I have chosen one fictionalized autobiography and three theoretical texts, this query may be a natural fallout—do we classify a classic differently from a landmark? Would it be possible to argue that creative writing can constitute a classic and a theoretical text a landmark? Such a distinction would be hard to maintain for great works of art are never closed texts even when they present specific realities. They extend their meaning and relevance to our times.
2. Frances Trollope wrote her travelogue *Domestic Manners of the Americans* in 1832 and Harriet Martineau wrote *Society in America* in 1837.
3. There is a reference to Amelia Matilda Murray's 1856 work, *Letters from the United States, Cuba and Canada* where Murray had projected a positive picture of slavery (*Incidents* 330).
4. Refer to the Appendix to *Incidents* in the Modern Library edition, the text which I have used for reference, 351-53. There are several references by Harriet Jacobs herself during the course of the

narrative which repeatedly stress the authenticity. In fact the opening line is "Reader, be assured this narrative is no fiction" (119).

5. See Yellin's Introduction to *Incidents,* Cambridge, 1987. It is also included in the Modern Library Edition, 2000.
6. L. Maria Child helped her in finding a publisher (the narrative was, in the first instance, published anonymously), and she wrote in the Introduction that "the author of the following autobiography is personally known to me." (Child, Modern Library Edition, 2000, 121-22).
7. For more details see hooks's *Feminist Theory* 47-48, where she refers to Anne Scott's summing up of the 19th century idealized woman. Also see pp. 91 and 182.
8. bell hooks refers to historian Eugene Genovese and quotes: "Sensible masters actually encouraged a limited sexual division of labor among their slaves and saw some advantages in strengthening the power of male in the household" (qtd. hooks, *Ain't I a Woman*, 45).

## List of Works Cited and Consulted

Gates, Henry Louis, Jr. "Foreword: In Her Own Write." *Incidents in the Life of a Slave Girl*. Ed. Valerie Smith.

hooks, bell. *Ain't I a Woman: Black Women and Feminism.* Boston: South End Press, 1981.

_____. *Feminist Theory: From Centre to Margin.* Boston: South End Press, 1984.

Jacobs, Harriet. *Incidents in the Life of a Slave Girl: Written by Herself.* Ed. L. Maria Child. Introduction by the Editor, originally to the first edition 1861. Also included in the Modern Library edition, 2000. Edited with an introduction by Jean Fagan Yellin. Cambridge, Massachusetts: Harvard University Press, 1987. Valerie Smith, ed., Introduction by Harriet Jacobs. New York: Oxford University Press, 1988.

_____. *Incidents in the Life of a Slave Girl* in *Narrative of the Life of Frederick Douglas, An American Slave & Incidents in the Life of a Slave Girl.* Introduction by Kwame Anthony Appiah, Notes and Biographical Note by Joy Viveros. New York: Modern Library, 2000.

Morrison, Toni. *Playing in the Dark: Whiteness and Literary Imagination* (1992). London: Picador 1993.

# Writing to Right: Harriet Jacobs's *Incidents* as Re-definition of Womanhood

**Punam Gupta**
**Dev Samaj College for Women, Chandigarh**

From the 'Demonic Sinner' of the puritan era to the 'Domestic Saint' of the mid-nineteenth century, the image of the woman had not undergone any real change. Her entire identity was trapped in her image as a sexual being, who unless lorded over by the male as master, was prone to lust and sinfulness. Men remained self-appointed arbiters and overseers of female virtue and chastity. In the nineteenth century ideology of femininity and the cult of domesticity that came to be constructed on both sides of the Atlantic, the ideal woman was cast in the image of an angel in the house or a serene queen on a domestic pedestal. This Goddess was to have the cardinal virtues of beauty, piety, purity, submissiveness and domesticity. She was to be lazy, helpless, decorous, dependent, not sexual and not worldly at all. The message was that a frail and ethereal woman without sexual feelings was worthy of male love, respect and consideration. The duty of this 'nobler half of humanity' was to elevate men's sentiments and inspire higher virtues in them.

In both the American north and south, this patriarchy-fostered "feminine mystique" (Robert Staples's term) had far-reaching cultural ramifications. The behavior of upper and middle class women became governed to a large extent by these esoteric norms, for women feared that it was within these parameters that they would be defined as woman or not woman. What social custom ordained, popular and literary conventions further enforced. Nineteenth century women's magazines *The Ladies' Repository, Godey's Lady's Book, The Ladies'*

*Companion*—all carried instructions, at times bizarre, as to how young girls and even older women were to manage weirdly slim waists by fitting themselves into tightly-laced corsets, or to create an interesting paleness by drinking vinegar or to practise the art of fainting to appear delicate to men. At its most extreme, the ideal of the frail and sickly female glorified the dead or the dying woman. A true woman who had lost her purity, definitely preferred death to disgrace. Barbara Welter suggests: "in the women's magazines at least, her intellect was geared to her hymen" (100). The whole idea was to subjugate woman into passivity.

Women's education was meant to include a minimal training in modern languages, a study of drawing, water coloring, embroidery and music. Louisa May Alcott's 1869 novel *Little Women* peopled with four young girls growing up in a middle class household is perhaps most representative of this trend. Alcott clearly suggests that a woman's happiest kingdom is home. The book is replete with instances of 'lady like' behavior. Meg, one of the sisters puts it, "it really seems like being a fine young lady, to come home from my party in my carriage, and sit in my dressing gown, with a maid to wait on me" (45). At another place she mourns, "I wonder if I shall be happy enough to have real lace on my clothes and bows on my caps" (106).

There was always the anxiety of the 'falling' of those insubordinate upper middle class women, who asserted not only their sexual liberty but also their emotional and intellectual needs. Thus, counterpoised to the glowing portrait of angelic ladies was always the image of the whore, and that of the fearful and demonic madwomen, murderesses or scheming sorceresses, as these social and intellectual climbers came to be called. In Nathaniel Hawthorne's novel *Blithedale Romance,* written in 1852, Zenobia, the passionate and self-willed dark heroine of the novel tries to live intellectually, but her 'diversified capacities' fail to sustain her. It is her heart that finally rules her. Rejected in love, she chooses to drown herself. Her punishment, Hawthorne seems to suggest, is justified because she has refused to accept her sometime lover's dictum that "woman is a monster . . .

without man as her acknowledged principal" (511). Zenobia is also unfavorably compared to her timid, insubstantial and lovable half-sister Priscilla, who is sought after by both the men in the novel—Coverdale and Hollingsworth.

Whereas the reality of the upper middle class woman did not always match up to the above-mentioned norms, this cult of true womanhood and domesticity had no meaning with respect to the life of the working woman. Whether married or single, the women of the lower classes were obliged to labor in both the private and the public spheres. Worst were the living and working conditions of black slave women in America. Bred like cattle to produce crops of new workers, subject to sexual exploitation by their white masters, frequently separated from their husbands and children, forced to perform endless hours of unpaid labor in cotton fields and plantation houses, these women were the most oppressed of all nineteenth century female workers. The misogyny of white/male America found its manifestation in creating certain degrading myths with respect to black women, which were diametrically opposed to the norms of true womanhood.

The black woman was cast in the images of concubine, breeder, mule and mammy. Overt sexuality emerged in the image of the black woman. It is no coincidence that glorifying the de-sexualized identity of the white lady was almost co-terminus with the rape of the black woman. This rape was, however, projected by the whites, both in life and in literature, as voluntary prostitution on the part of black women. It was assumed that black women were eager to give sexual favors even in return for petty gifts like a new pair of shoes or a scarf. Victor Séjour in his story *The Mulatto* (1837) says that "virtue . . . is so rare among women, above all among . . . slaves . . . who, every day, see their shameless companions prostitute themselves to the colonists, thereby only feeding more licentiousness" (qtd. Gates and McKay 292-93).

The second myth of black (non-)womanhood was that black women are breeders—female animals, who have an extraordinary ease of breeding, but being heathens they have no love or maternal instinct for their offspring. In *Uncle Tom's Cabin* (1852), an anti-slavery text by the white writer Harriet Beacher Stowe, the trader who wants to buy Eliza's child, tells the worried master, "these critters ain't like white folks" and suggests that if Eliza is given a new gown or earrings, she will forget her child's separation (9). To the white man, black children were property, to be used and traded at will. Yet another myth that prevailed with respect to slave women was that they are strong, unfeminine and masculinized to do arduous field jobs and domestic chores. They can stand whipping and lashing. They were called castrators who worked while their men did not, and that they were domineering, loud and outspoken.

The selfless mammy/nanny image was another mythification of the black slave woman. As Aunt Jemima—unclean, fat, asexual, she accepted her inferiority and found her life's fulfillment in serving the whites. Aunt Chloe, the devoted cook of the Shelby household in *Uncle Tom's Cabin*, thinks 'Missis's' beautiful hands are not meant for work. She is only supposed to sit in her parlor. She says her own "great black stumping hands" are suited to chores. Even after she learns of her husband's sale by the Shelbys, she calmly serves dinner to the whole master's family. Though the Shelbys back out on their promise of buying back Tom, Chloe continues to call her mistress "too good."

Much worse, however than the mythification of black women's lives and character was the internalization of the cult of true womanhood and domesticity by the black women. They were not proud of their ability to work with and like men in the fields. They wanted to adhere to the sex role patterns of the white patriarchal system. The norm of beauty and fragility they aspired to was Anglo-Saxon. In her book, *Ain't I a Woman*, bell hooks quotes Henry Watson, an Alabama plantation owner of the 1860s, as saying that black female laborers "desired to play the lady and be supported by their husbands 'like the white folks do'" (48). In literature the analogue to the white lady was created in the figure of the tragic mullata—fair, pious and pure. In his 1853 novel, *Clotel,* the black abolitionist, William Wells Brown says, "Indeed most of the slave women have no higher aspiration than that of becoming the finely dressed mistress of some white man" (48). Currer, the black mother of Clotel and Althesa in Brown's novel *Clotel*, brings up her beautiful mulatto daughters like 'ladies' who can attract attention at balls and parties. When Clotel succeeds in attracting the attention of Horatio, the son of a rich gentleman, Currer is very pleased at "her daughter's conquest" (41). When the life of this mulatta takes a tragic turn, she chooses to die by drowning. Mag and her daughter Frado in Harriet Wilson's 1859 novel, *Our Nig* look upon marriage as a means to subserve their own comfort. It would be pertinent to quote bell hooks, "By completely accepting the female role as defined by patriarchy, enslaved black women embraced and upheld an oppressive sexist order and became along with their white sisters both accomplices in the crimes perpetrated against women and the victims of those crimes" (49). Through most of the 19th century thus, woman remained in part a 'cultural creation' on the basis of mythical aspects of the requisites of womanhood. The self-concept of the woman became almost completely bound up with her 'biological destiny'.

Written at the peak of the period of the prevalence of the cults of true white womanhood and of the myth of the black whore, Harriet Jacobs's *Incidents in the Life of a Slave Girl, Written by Herself*, published in 1861, is a landmark text. It exposes both the myths as ideological constructs of the dominant white and male order. It further defines Jacobs's own black womanhood on self-created parameters of the specificity of her unique political-economic context and historical experience and, above all, from the need to shape her own subjectivity and spirituality.

Linda Brent, the narrator of Jacobs, opens the book with what she calls the "unusually fortunate circumstances" of her childhood: loving parents, a family home, an extended family and a kind and caring mistress. All this comes to an end when Brent is twelve and her "kind mistress sickened and died." Although promised that this mistress's will would free her, Brent is instead "bequeathed" to the mistress's niece, who is a child of five years. At this point she becomes subject to the child's father,

her new master Dr. Flint. The rest of Jacobs's account details her attempts to evade Flint's sexual harassment, which begins when she approaches adolescence: "a sad epoch in the life of a slave girl. My master began to whisper foul words in my ear. . . . He tried his utmost to corrupt the pure principles my grandmother had instilled. My soul revolted against the mean tyranny" (44-45).

Dr. Flint relentlessly pursues Linda for sexual favors. When she refuses him, he tells her "foolish girl! You don't know what is for your own good. I would cherish you. I would make a lady of you" (56). At another time he promises to make her "happy" by "redeeming her character." When Flint still finds Linda unrelenting, he offers to build her a secluded house to give "me a home of my own, and to make a lady of me" (82). Linda says, "The war of my life had begun and one of God's most powerless creatures, I resolved never to be conquered" (31). To avoid Flint's advances, she ultimately takes three actions.

First, Linda enters into a sexual liaison and has two children with a white man in the town, Mr. Sands, a decision she describes as a "desperate" "plunge into the abyss" (83).[1] Insisting on her own responsibility for her 'immoral' act, she asserts that "I knew what I did and I did it with deliberate calculation" (83):

> It seems less degrading to give one's self, than to submit to compulsion. There is something akin to freedom in having a lover who has no control over you except that which he gains by kindness and attachment. . . . He was a man of more generosity and feeling than my master, and I thought my freedom could be easily obtained from him. . . . I also felt quite sure that they [her two children] would be made free. (85)

Second, Brent takes refuge in the garret of her grandmother's house, a "dismal hole . . . only nine feet long and seven wide" (175). She stays in this hole for seven years. Insisting again upon her own responsibility, Brent chooses freedom from sexual harassment over the freedom from material comfort she could have obtained by becoming Flint's mistress: "It seemed horrible to sit or lie in a cramped position day after day, without one gleam of light. Yet I would have chosen this, rather than my lot as a slave, though white people considered it an easy one" (237).

Third, Brent manages to have her children bought by Sands and have them sent north. Then in a sailor's disguise and with the help of a few faithful friends, she herself escapes north. Here after much effort she meets her children. She works hard as a nursemaid in white households to earn enough to give a good education to her children. Though Flint tries to pursue her even here, she manages to escape him through her cunning. In the end her kind white mistress Mrs. Bruce purchases her freedom. Flint is dead. Linda ends her story by saying: "Reader, my story ends with freedom; not in the usual way, with marriage. . . . The dream of my life is not yet realized. I do not sit with my children in a home of my own" (302).

My reading of *Incidents* is based on the idea that Jacobs confronts problematic stereotypes of the 'true woman' and of the black 'non-woman' as objectifying constructs of the dominant patriarchal order, thereby subverting their value. She understands that to allow stereotypes to prevail or to let pass is as much an oppressive force as to create them. *Incidents,* thus is Jacobs's re-visionist and corrective engagement with the then prevailing imperialist/patriarchal order and aims at a re-definition of womanhood.

Linda's story compels us to think how slavery converts into liabilities the very qualities of beauty and dainty femininity that 'true' women were taught to cultivate, or that which many black women aspired to. She says: "That which commands admiration in the white woman only hastens the degradation of the female slave." (46). Thus beauty which is an asset to the self-concept of the white woman is only to be dreaded in the slave woman. The covert dynamics of economic exploitation, racism and sexism burdened the slave girl with heavy responsibilities and at times she had to be the breadwinner at an early age. Linda says that a slave girl in her position will become "prematurely knowing concerning the evil ways of the world," (83) thereby pushing her into early womanhood. In this confusion of blurred role identities, daintiness and fragility were nothing but a farce with respect to the female black slaves.

As to notions of purity and morality, Linda suggests that these are complex issues, not simple ones: "The condition of the slave confuses all principles of morality and, in fact, renders the practice of them impossible" (86). Jacobs says that though "Slavery is terrible for men; but it is far more terrible for women. . . . Superadded to the burden common to all, *they* have wrongs, and sufferings, and mortifications peculiarly their own" (119). The 'demon Slavery,' Linda suggests, precludes easy pronouncements of right and wrong and therefore, "the slave woman ought not to be judged by the same standard as others" (86).

Brent provokes the reader to put into perspective her action of taking on a lover and becoming an unwed mother as a unique human reaction of hers to the condition of utter degradation in which she was cast. It is her self-defined handling of the dynamics of rape that she was faced with as a slave woman. Through her conduct, Jacobs wants the reader to understand that some behavior patterns and alternative attitudes are only functional adaptations to negative external conditions. Yvonne Johnson says that Jacobs "presents herself as a moral person in the midst of an immoral system" (22). Jacobs challenges her readers to defy her. Also, through her assertion of self-willed sexual autonomy, Jacobs displays the strength of mind that was an essential requisite for slave women to save themselves from total inner brutalization and to enable them to retain a measure of self esteem.[2] Houston Baker suggests that "this new code of ethics emphasizes a woman's prerogative to control her own sexuality—to govern the integrity of her own body" (52). By rejecting all offers of 'ladyhood' made by Flint, Jacobs also sets at rest the 'always wanting to be white men's mistresses' and 'women of easy morals' theory with respect to black slave women.

Not only is Brent not driven insane or to suicide by her 'fall', as the "death vs. virtue" paradigm of women's writing of her time suggested, she refuses to fulfill another feminine characteristic of the true woman, that is submissiveness. Barbara Welter suggests: "Women were the passive, submissive, respondents. The order of dialogue, was, of course, fixed in heaven" (102). For Linda in her situation, submissiveness amounts to unwomanly vulnerability, and is therefore meaningless. She effectively uses dialogue in her narrative to subvert this tradition of submissiveness. After repeated insults and threats from Flint, Brent tells him, "You have struck me for answering you honestly. How I despise you!" (61). At another point she says: "you have no right to do as you like with me" (62). When Flint calls Linda's lover a "puppy," she thunders, "If he is a puppy, I am a puppy. . . . The man you call puppy, never insulted me" (61). Given her master's coercive methods, Linda suggests that entering into verbal warfare with him was a measure of self-defence for her, as for many slave girls like her. It is no self-aggrandizing, amazonic assertion but a self-defensive one, given her peculiar positioning and otherwise degrading and oppressive situation.

Another trait that a 'true' woman was expected to exhibit was domesticity. An 1840 article in a ladies' magazine admonished ladies to retire from "the busy highways of ambition" and to "wander in the shady green lanes of domestic life" (qtd. Johnson 21). The domestic novels of Cummins and Warner of the 1850s typically ended happily, the heroine finding bliss and fulfillment in marriage, family and her home. Jacobs had to confront this situation, too, in her narrative by laying bare the need for self-dependency and by insisting on the right to support her children within her own domestic and woman-centered economy. Beth Maclay Doriaini calls it a "new domesticity" (219). There is no lament in her at not being provided for by a husband. Doriani suggests that Jacobs chooses "economic independence, not marital dependence" (211). Jacobs has broadened the definition of woman as homemaker and mother to include economic and political dimensions. To her, workplace is not corruptive. Mothering figures as the most important and articulated aspect of her life. While her narrative has some touching incidents of love, care and concern with her children, she willingly makes the sacrifice of being separated from her two children, only to ensure their freedom and safety.

The narrative structure of *Incidents* is structured around an alternative discourse of womanhood and motherhood as against the prevailing discourses of the nineteenth century. Linda asserts the need for a vigorous self-concept for the slave woman. She was not a no-woman but a woman whose womanly qualities were inherent in her strength of mind, her intelligence, her resourcefulness, her economic independence, her talking ability (even if it meant talking back), and an external shield of strength, tenacity and invincibility blended with an inner core of tenderness, compassion and a capacity to love.

While to most slave women and men—writers of slave narratives in her time, freedom meant emancipation from slavery, and to the newly simmering feminist voices (mostly white), freedom meant coming out of their cloistered houses, Linda dates her freedom from the day of her self-imprisonment in her granny's garret. It is her negotiation of the meaning of true freedom. Freedom to Linda meant freedom from possible sexual assault. The struggle for sexual autonomy, therefore, becomes a crucial organizing device for the whole narrative structure of *Incidents in the Life of the Slave Girl*.

## NOTES

1. In calling her action 'a desperate plunge', Linda seems to co-opt with the principles of white morality, but one needs to put such statements in perspective. Her readers were going to be mostly white women, and Jacobs wanted her book to be sold and to be read by these women, who were used to the sentimental fiction of her time.
2. Linda's 'unconventional' behavior, Jacobs seems to suggest, might be a 'façade' that many slave women had to maintain in order to save themselves from appearing vulnerable. bell hooks has elaborated this viewpoint in her book, *Ain't I a Woman.*

## Works Cited and Consulted

Alcott, Louisa May. *Little Women*. London: Children's Press, 1958.

Baker, Houston A., Jr. *Blues, Ideology, and Afro-American Literature: A Vernacular Theory*. Chicago: U of Chicago P, 1984.

Brown, William Wells. *Clotel, or The President's Daughter*. Introduction. Arthur Davis. New York: Macmillan, 1970.

Carby, Hazel V. *Reconstructing Womanhood: The Emergence of the Afro-American Woman Novelist*. New York: OUP, 1987.

Doriani, Beth Maclay. "Black Womanhood in Nineteenth-Century America: Subversion and Self-Construction in Two Women's Autobiographies." *American Quarterly* 43.2 (June 1991): 199-222.

Foreman, P. Gabrielle. "The Spoken and the Silenced in *Incidents in the Life of a Slave Girl* and *Our Nig*." *Callaloo: An Afro American and African Journal of Arts and Letters*. 13 (1990): 313-24.

Gates, Henry Louis, Jr., and Nellie Y. MacKay, ed. *The Norton Anthology of African American Literature*. New York: W.W. Norton, 1997.

Gilbert, Sandra M. and Susan Gubar, ed. *The Norton Anthology of Literature by Women: The Traditions in English*. New York: Norton, 1996.

Hawthorne, Nathaniel. "*Blithedale Romance*." *Complete Novels and Selected Tales of Hawthorne*. Introduction. Norman Holmes Pearson. New York: Modern Library, 1937. 439-585.

hooks, bell. *Ain't I a Woman: Black Women and Feminism*. Boston MA: South End Press, 1981.

Jacobs, Harriet. *Incidents in the Life of a Slave Girl*. Intro. Valerie Smith. New York: OUP, 1988.

Johnson, Yvonne. *The Voices of African American Women*. New York: Peter Lang, 1999.

Staples, Robert. *The Black Woman in America: Sex, Marriage and the Family*. Chicago: Nelson Hall, 1974.

Stowe, Harriet Beecher. *Uncle Tom's Cabin or Life among the Lowly*, ed. Kenneth S Lynn. Cambridge: The Belknap Press of Harvard UP, 1962.

Welter, Barbara. "The Cult of True Womanhood: 1820-1860." *Our American Sisters: Women in American Life and Thought*, ed. Jean E. Friedman and William G Shade. Boston: Allyn and Bacon, 1973.

# Walt Whitman's "Song of the Open Road"—A Sufic Perspective

**Roshan Lal Sharma**
**Government PG College, Solan (HP)**

Walt Whitman's "Song of the Open Road" (Whitman 149-59) is characterized by "elation," "buoyant invitation to adventure" and a "confident promise" of a rich and varied experience of life along with the meaningful exploration of universal consciousness. W.S. Kennedy rightly conjectured that Whitman must have felt inspired by the description of the road given by George Sand in his novel *Consuelo*: "What is there more meaningful than a road? It is the symbol and the image of an active and varied life. . . . And then that road is the passage of Humanity, the route of the Universe" (qtd. Bradley and Blodgett 149). No wonder that the poem was titled "Poem of the Road" in 1856 and was given its present title in 1867.

Thus it will not suffice to go by the literal import of Whitman's carefully chosen metaphor of the "open road" as it has multiple socio-political, philosophical and mystical implications. In a sense the poem offers tremendous scope to be studied from various perspectives. The present paper, however, seeks to examine the Sufic implication of the poem in terms of the concepts of *Tawhid*, *Wahdat al-wujud* and *Sama* as enunciated in Sufism. Whitman's "open road" metaphorically suggests the path taken up by a Sufi quester who, steeped as he is, in '*Sama*-consciousness,' seeks to experience *Tawhid*—a state of oneness with God perceived as the Beloved in Sufism.

It would be pertinent to make clear at the outset that even though Whitman had no formal grounding in Sufism, there is evidence of his knowledge as well as assimilation of its essence in the poem "A Persian Lesson" (*LG* 553), written thirty five years after "Song of the Open Road" was composed, and first published in the section *Good-Bye My Fancy* (1891). In this poem, which is "an accurate reflection of Sufi mysticism" (Bradley and Blodgett 552) a "greybeard sufi" addresses a group of "young priests and students" in "the fresh scent of the morning air" on the "slope of a teeming Persian rose-garden":

> Finally my children, to envelop each word, each part of the rest,
> Allah is all, all, all—is immanent in every life and object,
> May-be at many and many-a-more removes—yet Allah, Allah,
> Allah is there. (*LG* 553)

Thus, it becomes evident that Whitman had the understanding of the "complex symbolism" and quintessential aspects of Sufism that are the core concern of this paper. The above lines explicitly state that "Allah is all . . . immanent in every life and object." This is precisely what *Tawhid* implies. Moreover, like an enlightened *Murshid* (Master/teacher of Sufism epitomized by the "greybeard sufi" in the poem delivering his "o'erarching and last lesson"), Whitman unambiguously understood about "the urge and spur of every life" along with "the invisible need of every seed." He says:

> It is the central urge in every atom,
> (Often unconscious, often evil, downfallen,)
> To return to its divine source and origin, howsoever distant,
> Latent the same in subject and in object, without one exception.
> (*LG* 553)

As such, the influence of Sufi mysticism on Walt Whitman may not be denied outright. It is relatively an unexplored domain that calls for a concerted effort to unravel the sufic implication of the thematic thrust of Whitman's poetic universe along with the complex symbolism and imagery that he had to resort to in order to achieve what Max I. Baym terms as "universal unanimism (a poetic ideal of a collective life), marked by grandeur and beauty" (Baym 71).

Viewed overtly, "Song of the Open Road" emerges as Whitman's powerful statement on liberty and the central metaphor of the "open road" used therein signifies, as Emory Halloway in his Introduction to Whitman's *Leaves of Grass* observes, "an open democratic road leading to better things" (Whitman xx). Moreover, as Matthiessen observes, the poem "announces a dynamic philosophy of forward movement, struggle and triumph" with the characteristic Whitmanesque "severely energetic" calls to arise and stride on (Matthiessen 568). Nevertheless, the poem also offers ample scope to be viewed in the light of Sufic concepts of *Tawhid*, *Wahdat al-wujud* and *Sama* as enunciated in Sufism. In fact, Whitman's poetic consciousness seems to include all three of them. *Tawhid* is the pivot around which all other concepts are woven in Sufism. It signifies a state in which none other than the One exists. Literally too, *Tawhid* means 'one.' Technically it refers to the doctrine of God as One Reality (also called Divine Unity/ God's Unity/ Absolute Reality), which is "unitive" in character manifesting through a "variety of forms" (Khosla 222). In fact, the Sufis believe in the oneness of being, and by being, they mean God's Being. They maintain that every aspect of creation is included in God's Being (*Wujud*). The Sufi master in Whitman's "A Persian Lesson" reveals the same as he speaks: "Allah is all, all, all—is immanent in every life and object." In fact, *Tawhid* is realized when the quester develops the capacity to see *One* behind *many*. Highlighting the importance of *Tawhid* in Sufism, I.H. Azad Faruqi observes:

> Sufism aims at the personal experience of the central mystery of Islam, i.e. *Tauhid* (Unity of God). In the Islamic experience of religion, it is through the realization of *Tauhid,* or the fact that there is nothing to be worshipped, nothing to be adored except God, that contact with the Holy is achieved. The whole religious complex of Islam pivots *Tauhid,* and all its intricate parts and details are determined by the central concept. Throughout the ages Sufis have tried to realize this basic *élan* of Islam. (Faruqi 1)

Thus, through *Tawhid* Sufic doctrine of unity is postulated. It means that "God is One, Alone, Single, Eternal . . . Merciful,

Compassionate . . . Creating, Sustaining" (Arberry 10). *Wahdat al-wujud* is yet another technical term in Sufism, which is associated with the school of Ibn al-Arabi (560-638 A.H.), the great Andalusian Sufi theosophist. It has the same root as that of *Tawhid*. For instance, the terms *wahid, ahad, wahda* mean 'one,' and *ahadiya, wahdaniyya* signify 'oneness'/ 'unity.' Literally *wujud* refers to 'being' but in Sufism the concept of *Wahdat al-wujud* signifies "Oneness of Being or Unity of Existence." (Golkhosravi 2001). It "means that the real existence cannot be attributed to anything except God" (Faruqi 4). Arabi's concept of *Wahdat al-wajud* signifying the pantheistic conception of *Tawhid* was opposed by Shaikh Ahmad Sirhindi (the Mujaddid, b.971 A.H.). Shaikh Ahmad put forth his argument against "direct religious experience," technically known as *Kashf*, which means "unveiling" in the sense of the "apprehension of facts and events as well as truths, mundane and celestial, by inner sight or light" (Faruqi 4-6). His conception of *Tawhid* is based on his stance against Arabi's perception of *Wahdat al-wujud* (the unity of being that is synonymous with "Unityism," "Identyism" and pantheism). Shaikh Ahmad firmly believed that "We cannot know God through kashf-o-shuhud or intuition and mystic experience. Hence, we should revert to Revelation and to 'Ulama-i-zahir or divines [theologians], because their conception is derived direct from Revelation" (Faruqi 117-18). He treats mystical experience of *Wahdat al-wujud* as subjective lacking "objective validity." Furthermore, he maintains:

> God is Khaliq or Creator of earth and heavens, mountains and oceans . . . minerals as well as of human beings with all their potentialities. In short He is the Creator of all things. . . . He is the only Divine Being; there is no one else who possesses the same sifat or qualities, and He alone deserves 'ibadat' or worship. He encompasses or comprehends everything, is everywhere with us. (Faruqi 121-22)

As such, what Shaikh Ahmad asserts is signified by the term technically called *Wahdat-i-Shuhud* meaning "apparentism" which means that "by creation of the world no change is wrought in the being of God,—He remains intact" (Faruqi 161). In

*Wahdat al-wujud* ("unityism"), however, "change enters in the being of God itself, for it is He who modifies Himself and becomes the contingent world" (Faruqi 160). In this way we may say that the realization of *Tawhid* is the goal of Sufi seeker. It is the absolute belief in Allah/God/Beloved as One, "Alone" and Eternal. *Wahdat al-wujud* (perception of Divinity in an infinite range of forms in the physical universe), logically and naturally corroborates *Tawhid.* Both the concepts may be technically different but in the later tradition of Sufism, they are treated as synonymous with each other. For instance, Farid Al Din Attar differentiates the two concepts as "identity-in-difference" and "difference-in-identity" (Khosla 166).

Literally *Sama* in Arabic means 'hearing' or 'audition.' In Sufism, it aims at inducing of a state of ecstasy during the performance of *Dhikr* (meaning 'mentioning,' 'remembering,' and 'thinking' in Arabic) with the help of music, singing and dancing. *Dhikr* implies a meditative remembrance of Allah's/ God's Name and *Sama* adds musical dimension to it. Through continual singing, musical chanting of the Holy Name, and dancing, the seeker tries to establish an uninterrupted communion with God through ecstasy.

Thus, *Sama* in Sufism implies listening to music, singing, dancing and also ecstasy. Rumi perceived divinity in music. He emphasized the importance of *Sama* in religious service. Characterized by "vitality," *Sama* is extremely important in Sufism "as a means of partaking in the experiential dimension of spiritual achievement" (Sharma 317) as observed by Regula B. Qureshi in his article "Localising Islam: Sama in the Royal Court of Chisti Saints." Rumi's followers were known as the "Whirling Dervishes." He knew that *Sama* in the form of singing and dancing had the capacity to intensify "the flame of love." Attaching a mystical dimension to *Sama*, K. Khosla pertinently observes: "The dance symbolizes the ecstasy both of dying to self and of attaining to life everlasting, *Fana* (total transmutation) and *Baqa* (everlastingness)—a doubly rapturous experience" (Khosla 195). In a state of ecstasy and deep spiritual rapture, the Sufic quester is intently focused at the Beloved/ God.

He continuously remembers God who is perceived as the Beloved with special, rhythmic music and peculiar gyrating movements. Like a drunken lover, the Sufic seeker is absolutely oblivious of himself as well as everything else except the Beloved/ God during the performance of *Sama*. Analyzing the impact of *Sama* on the listener/the quester, Regula B. Qureshi aptly observes, "In the performance of *sama,* music and poetry fuse together, and have a special effect on the listener. They reach a spiritual state which expresses itself in gestures—weeping, vocalizing and ultimately a dance of ecstasy" (Sharma 319). Some of the great Sufi Masters believed that the seekers (*Murid*) on the initial stages of the Sufic path should not be allowed to participate in the *Sama.* It was because without the guidance of an enlightened master (*Murshid*), there was the possibility of the seeker's getting strayed on the path to realize God. Abu Hafs Omar as-Suhrawardi remarks:

> Music does not give rise, in the heart, to anything which is not already there. So he, whose inner self is attached to anything else than God is stirred by music to sensual desire, but the one who is inwardly attached to the love of God is moved, by hearing music, to do His will. . . . The common folk listen to music according to nature, and the novice listen with desire and awe, while the listening of the saints brings them a vision of the Divine gifts and graces, and these are the gnostics to whom listening means contemplation. But finally, there is the listening of the spiritually perfect to whom, through music, God reveals Himself unveiled. (Qtd. Hammarlund 12).

Even though the Islamic orthodoxy denounces the practice of *Sama*, most of the Sufi orders find it useful as it helps in focusing the mind. Secondly, it helps in attaining *wajd* (ecstasy). Those who intently hear *Sama* at times are seen shedding tears of joy (Sharda 46). Keeping in mind the multiple implications of the concept of *Sama* as postulated and practised in Sufism, it can be said that Whitman's protagonist in "Song of the Open Road" seems to be steeped in '*Sama-consciousness*' given his exuberance and flamboyance that have the charge of "original energy" that gushes with equal intensity and force in "Song of Myself" too.

Viewed in Sufic terms, the I-protagonist of "Song of the Open Road" exhibits a highly evolved spiritual state of being characterized by ecstasy, bliss, celebration and the joy of having attained a "unitive" vision in which the difference between the Creator (God) and the creation (phenomenal world with its diverse attributes) does not exist. The poet-protagonist has already experienced *Tawhid* ("unitive" state of being) after having gone through the stages of *Wusla* (union with the Beloved/ Divine), *Hal* (state of rapture) and *Muqam* (state of ecstasy). It becomes evident from the mystical vision of the I-protagonist in Whitman's poem "Song of Myself" which was written a year before in 1855. He seems to have realized the Sufic states of *Tawhid* and *Wahdat al-wujud*, which implies a perception of the essential Oneness of Being expressed as "Onc Identity" by him. A year later, the poet-protagonist's "tone of celebration" that gives the very "substance" to "Song of the Open Road" (Zweig 285), takes an ecstatic turn thereby expressing "the sheer joy of movement and diversity of experience" (Miller 102).

Spurning the cozy, comfortable and static state of being, the poet is "afoot" to venture out on the "open road" with a "healthy" and a "free" state of mind. Instead of getting glued to the spot, the poet prefers movement on the "open road" so that he can get directly involved "with nature in the innocence and validity of its *naturalness*, its original and uncorrupted form" (Miller 102). Now "good-fortune" hardly holds any charm for the poet as, "I [the poet] myself am good-fortune" (Section 1). After realizing the futility of "indoor complaints, libraries, querulous criticisms," the poet like an *Arif* (gnostic)[1] sets out to explore "earth" (nature) which is in the closest proximity. He does not show any interest in the "constellations." In fact, he knows about the origin, source and mystery of the universe, which is man since he partakes of the Divine Essence. Hence, it is the "earth" along with the "men and women" who fill his being thereby giving it a meaning. He cannot get rid of his "old delicious burdens," which signify his fellow beings who have been with him in the past and who will always be with him in all times to come. He himself acknowledges this in his *Preface* to the 1855 edition of *Leaves of Grass*:

> Past and present and future are not disjoined but joined. The greatest poet forms the consistence of what is to be from what has been and is. He drags the dead out of their coffins and stands them again on their feet . . . he says to the past, Rise and walk before me that I may realize you. He learns the lesson . . . he places himself where the future becomes present. (20)

As such, the "old delicious burdens," in fact, are eternal presences in him comprising his "Self" which has cosmic proportions. In Section 6 of "Song of Myself," the poet grows curious about the lot of the dead young and old men, women and children. As he observes the "smallest sprout of grass," he gets convinced about the fact that actually there is no death. He realizes that death in no way arrests life. It rather paves the way to resurrection, rejuvenation and renewal of life. Thus, we may view the poet's "delicious burdens" in terms of the sense of continuity that the poet has imbibed and assimilated to be used at a later point in time.

The metaphor of the "open road" assumes symbolic overtones at the beginning of Section 2 when Whitman chants:

> You road I enter upon and look around, I believe you are not all
> That is here,
> I believe that much unseen is also here. (Section 2)

For the poet, the existing phenomenon is composed of different particles of earth. Similarly every particle of earth contains within itself the essence of all existing things. Since the essence remains inherently invisible, its existence cannot be denied. Therefore things may/may not be visible to the physical organ called eye. Sufis view the phenomena in terms of visible and invisible worlds. They postulate that the existence of the universe lies in between the physical existence (*wujud*) and the physical non-existence (*adum*) i.e. between the phenomenal realms of *it is* and *it is not*. Sometimes the revealing glance of

*Arif* (Gnostic) leads him to acquire knowledge of his origin and the beginning of his manifestation, in what realm of existence (world) was he hidden before his birth (in the phenomenal world) and where will he go after his death. *Fikr* (concentrated mental effort to look into the wonders of Nature) guides him to the truth of man's existence, and finally, to the Ultimate Truth.

After looking around, the poet is able to suggest that something which is not visible ("unseen"). It indicates that the poet, like the Sufi *Arif,* has the knowledge, nay, the realization of the invisible phenomena, which may not be perceptible with the physical organ of seeing. Here the road symbolizes life with all its diverse facets. The road, the poet says, openly receives everyone without discrimination whether that be the black, the drunkard, the poor or the rich. It is beyond petty choices, preferences and denials. Interestingly, the poet's consciousness enlarges along with the expanse of the road. Viewed in Sufic terms, Whitman is firmly established in *Sama-consciousness*, in which the aspirant (*Murid*) not only listens to the music, or dances, but he is also [under the able guidance of the master (*Shaikh/Murshid/Wali*)] made to watch how the consciousness expands gradually with music taking an ecstatic turn. However, the *Sama-consciousness* is in the service of *Tawhid* ("unitive state of being"), which is the propelling force behind Whitman's poetic consciousness as evident in "Song of the Open Road."

In Section 3, the poet enlivens various objects that he greets on the open road through meticulous and exhaustive cataloguing. It signifies Whitman's "efforts at describing an endless journey of the poet's imagination across infinity" (Baym 72). He welcomes them all—visible as well as invisible. Whitman refers to the "paths" that are "latent with unseen existences" and "the spirits" of "the living and the dead." In fact, his experience of "infinitude" is vast and all-encompassing. The rich cadence of the music that runs parallel to the expanding earth, expanding consciousness of the I-protagonist, and the "cheerful voice of the public road" charge the whole atmosphere mystically:

> The earth expanding right hand and left hand,

> The picture alive, every part in its best light,
> The music falling in where it is wanted, and stopping where it is not wanted,
> The cheerful voice of the public road, the gay fresh sentiment of the road. (Section 4)

The poet is fearless to venture out as he has an inner assurance of the fact that the "open road" can "express" him better than he can. He ordains himself to pursue the open road boldly. No one can limit him, nor can anyone restrain/hold him as "divesting" himself "of the holds," he moves out "loos'd of limits and imaginary lines." His actualization of the state of *Tawhid* comes to the fore when he chants ecstatically, as if in a trance:

> I inhale great draughts of space,
> The east and the west are mine, and the north and the south are mine.
> I am larger, better than I thought,
> I did not know I held so much goodness. (Section 5)

In Section 51 of "Song of Myself" also, Whitman talks about his 'largeness: "I am large, I contain multitudes." D.H. Lawrence contests this "vast extension, or concentrated intensification into Allness" along with "cryptic *One Identity*" of Whitman. For Lawrence, the "last and final truth" is "the quick"/ "the quick of quicks," which is "the single individual soul." What he means is that in "extending himself, Whitman still remains himself; he does not become the other man, or the other woman, or the tree, or the universe" (*LG* 845). Lawrence perceives Whitman's "One Identity" as "a prison of horror" (*LG* 846). At the same time, he acknowledges Whitman's experience of cosmic consciousness by saying that "It is man's maximum state of consciousness, his highest state of spiritual being. Supreme spiritual consciousness, and the divine drunkenness of supreme conscious. It is reached through embracing love" (*LG* 845). Whitman's cosmic consciousness perfectly approximates Sufic state of *Tawhid* as well as *Wahdat al-wujud*, which mean being one/ 'at-one-ment' with One and Abiding Reality after having gone through the temporal and the material.[2] Whitman, the mystic's poetic stance becomes problematic to Lawrence due to the latter's emphasis on "the single and overweening self," "the quick of quicks," "the single individual soul" and "each vivid soul" (Bradley and Blodget 842-50). However, it is worth-mentioning that Whitman's poetic chants have inherent potential to be micro-reduced as well as macro-expanded. Lawrence's "quick" as well as "quicks" are intrinsically embedded in Whitman's poetic universe which is why the "I" and the "Kosmos" are "One Identity." If we see the whole issue in Blakean light, we will realize that it is the perception of the simultaneous co-existence of the "contraries" which is more important than the uni-polar, lopsided perception of reality. The vision, no doubt, is "unitive." Moreover, the central thrust of Sufism as well as Transcendentalism is that the Divine Essence permeates the animate as well as the inanimate objects in this universe, and that the goal of human life is the union with the Divine.

In Section 6, Whitman blissfully reveals about the "secret" known to a mystic only. He sings, "Now I see the secret of the making of the best persons, / It is to grow in the open air and to eat and sleep with the earth." It is suggestive of the mystical perception of the poet. As Hazrat Inayat Khan observes, "The mystic sees the law in all things and this gives him an insight into life. . . . The law of the mystic is not the law of the people. It is the law of nature; it is the real law" (Vol. X 18). In this way, the poet has the fundamental understanding of the existing phenomenon. He knows that the "Wisdom is of the soul" and that it cannot be gotten from pursuing the academic curriculum. Wisdom, according to the poet,

> Is the certainty of the reality and immortality of things, and the excellence of things:
> Something there is in the float of the sight of things that provokes it out of the soul. (Section 6)

Thus, the poet has the capacity to see the invisible "in the float of the sight of things," and to stay focused at/getting nourishment from only "the kernel of every object" (Section 6). The term "float" also suggests the "flood" or "flowing" of the appearances that provoke wisdom out of the soul (Bradley and Blodgett 152). It is akin to the perception of a mystic: "Things which seem real to an average person are unreal in the eyes of the mystic; and the things that seem unreal in the eyes of the average person are real in the eyes of the mystic" (Khan Vol. X 14). Through his mystical chants, Whitman enjoys *Wajad,* which is a "state of sacred ecstasy which the Sufis experience at Suma [*Sama*], may be said to be union with the Desired One," (Khan Vol. II 60) that is God/Beloved. He can hear everything, which is audible to the subtler ear, e.g. the *silent* "talk of those turning eye-balls" (Section 6) and *what* he interchanges "so suddenly with strangers" (Section 7). The poet sings joyously about the "efflux of the soul" and the deep impact it has on his expanding consciousness. In the following Section, the "efflux of the soul" and "the open air" are charged with delight that Whitman feels within:

> The efflux of the soul is happiness, here is happiness,
> I think it pervades the open air, waiting at all times,
> Now it flows unto us, we are rightly charged. (Section 8)

The delight that the poet experiences, is the "joy of transience" and it is gotten at the cost of "the rejection of the static and the materialistic" (Miller 103).

Whitman gives a call to those who are comfortably curled up in their "sweet," "laid-up stores" and "convenient" dwellings to come and travel with him. He is fed up with the superficial anchorages and regressive moorings of petty material considerations. He assures them that Nature will unfold her wonders and mysteries once they are out on the open road:

> The earth is rude, silent, incomprehensible at first, Nature is rude
> And incomprehensible at first,
> Be not discouraged, keep on, there are divine things well envelop'd,
> I swear to you there are divine things more beautiful than words can tell. (Section 9)

Thus, only those who are earnest having a genuine urge to explore the mysteries of Nature may join the poet who is the mystic traveler. However, the suggestion is quite clear that it is not the path of complacence. It requires conviction as well as commitment to take up this path renouncing the temptations and allurements of the material world. The open road signifies momentum; stasis is for the complacent ones. The poet is adventurous and can hence leave the sheltered port without any qualms. He wants to "sail the pathless and wild seas" (Section 10) for which the "best blood," "health, gayety, self-esteem, curiosity" are required. He invites the "materialistic priests" to explore Nature and her elements provided they have the "courage," "endurance" and the "determin'd bodies." He neither wants a "diseas'd person" nor a "rum-drinker" to pursue the open road which may even be shard-strewn at many junctures. Cajoling and goading his fellow beings, Whitman tells them never to accumulate wealth. Nor does he want them to fall into the mire of stasis.

If we analyze it from a Sufic perspective, Whitman has an apparent preference and an irresistible urge for mobility along with a sense of insecurity in the worldly sense. It basically signifies freedom with least sense of attachment in it. For a Sufi quester, a false sense of security is the biggest trap. Viewed thus, the open "road becomes a figure of change, growth, and learning" (Zweig 242). The poet's appeal does not stop here. In fact, it becomes more intense as he catalogues the journeyers from diverse walks of life who dared to sing the song of this path that leads to ultimate freedom given its cosmic dimensions. In Section 14, the poet reiterates the importance of movement by saying that "active rebellion" against the conventional grooves of habit, is a must. He chants thus:

> My call is the call of battle, I nourish active rebellion,
> He going with me go well arm'd
> He going with me goes often with spare diet, poverty, angry enemies, desertions. (Section 14)

The choice of the open road, therefore, is not an easy one. It implies a tremendous amount of courage to be on one's own. The "hardships of individualized life" (Miller 103), the displeasure of one's near and dear, the strength of mind, and an endless urge to realize "the essence of things" are some of the important tips that Whitman's "vagabond poet" gives to any earnest seeker of the open road which symbolizes every conceivable aspect of this universe. In the concluding Section, the poet asks the reader to give up everything that has material connotation, and become an active participant in his journey to know the quintessence of being on the open road. He extends his hand as well as his love to help the reader tread the path successfully. To speak metaphorically, the open road signifies the path of mysticism as well as the Sufic path to realize the quintessence of being, which cannot be trodden by everyone.

Finally, it will be worthwhile to note that even the Sufic states of *Tawhid* and *Wahdat al-wujud* are not static in any sense. The experience of the realization of both these states of being, is dynamic as it is embedded in *Sama-consciousness*. It is eternally mobile. From the above analysis of the poem, one may emphatically sum up that the so-called "success" on the spiritual path in no way implies any kind of formal closure of active seeking/striving. In Sufic terms, even after attaining the "unitive" vision (*Tawhid*) or the pantheistic vision (*Wahdat al-wujud*) through the varied manifestations of phenomenal world, the seeking on the part of the seeker does not come to an end. In fact, it is led to some onward movement. To quote Whitman:

> Have the past struggles succeeded?
> What has succeeded? yourself? . . . Nature?
> Now understand me well—it is provided in the essence of things
> that from any fruition of success, no matter what, shall
> come forth something to make a greater struggle necessary.
>
> (Section 14)

Thus, we can see that "Song of the Open Road" remarkably presents how Whitman is 'at-one-ment' with the Sufic concepts of *Tawhid* and *Wahdat al-wujud.* He uses the central metaphor of the "open road" to express his poetic vision which is "unitive," "uniting" and cosmic in form. Moreover, it is *Sama-consciousness* of the poet, which is at work as the intrinsic principle, permeating diverse aspects of creation and varied facets of experience, as delineated in the poem.

# NOTES

1. In Sufism, an *Arif* means a 'gnostic' who grapples with the complex and intriguing questions concerning the source of intelligence, intellect, discernment, understanding and perception in human structure. He also tries to know about the enigma of human life, its origin and its spiritual source, which enables him to perform such bodily functions as walking, seeing, and hearing. He is mainly curious to know about the real Omnipresent source of all human actions and of man's power called the Soul of all souls (*ruhul Arwah*).
2. Richard Maurice Bucke places Walt Whitman in the category of enlightened people like Buddha, Christ, Blake, etc. on the basis of the level of cosmic consciousness that he attained. He categorises consciousness into simple consciousness (belonging to animal kingdom), self-consciousness (concerning man) and cosmic consciousness (belonging to mystics and sages). According to Bucke, "The prime characteristic of *cosmic consciousness* is . . . a consciousness of the cosmos, that is, of the life and the order of the universe. . . . Along with the consciousness of the cosmos there occurs an intellectual enlightenment or illumination which alone would place the individual on a new plane of existence—would make him almost a member of a new species." (Bucke 3)

## Works Cited and Consulted

Arberry, Arthur John. *The Doctrine of the Sufis.* New Delhi: Kitab Bhawan, 1994.

Baym, Max I. *A History of Literary Aesthetics in America.* New York: Frederick Unger, 1973.

Bucke, Richard Maurice. *Cosmic Consciousness.* New York: Penguin, 1991.

Faruqi, Burhan Ahmad. *The Mujaddid's Conception of Tawhid.* Delhi: Idarah-i Adabiyat-i, 1977.

Faruqi, I.H. Azad. *Sufism and Bhakti.* New Delhi: Abhinav, 1984.

Golkhosravi, Mehrad. "'Panentheistic' View of Divine Love in Man and Nature: A Comparative Study in Whitman's *Leaves of Grass* and Maulana Jalal al-Din Rumi's *Mathnavi.*" University of Barcelona. 2001. See the website: <www.publicacions.ub.es/revistes/bells13/PDF/articles>

Hammarlund, Anders et al., ed. *Sufism, Music and Society in Turkey and the Middle East*. Istanbul: Swedish Research Institute, 2001.

Khan, Hazrat Inayat. *The Sufi Message,* Vol. II. Delhi: Motilal Banarasidass, 1988.

_____. *The Sufi Message,* Vol. X. Delhi: Motilal Banarasidass, 1990.

Khosla, K. *The Sufism of Rumi*. Dorset: Element Books, 1987.

Matthiessen, F.O. *American Renaissance: Art and Expression in the Age of Emerson and Whitman*. Delhi: OUP, 1973.

Miller Jr., James E. *Walt Whitman*. Allahabad: A.H. Wheeler, 1962.

Sharda, S.R. *Sufi Thought*. New Delhi: Munshiram Manoharlal, 1974.

Sharma, Shankar Dayal, et al., ed. *Contemporary Relevance of Sufism*. New Delhi: Indian Council for Cultural Relations, 1993.

Whitman, Walt. *Leaves of Grass*. London: Dent, 1971.

_____. *Leaves of Grass*. New Delhi: Prentice-Hall of India, 1986. Ed. Sculley Bradley and Harold W. Blodgett.

Zweig, Paul. *Walt Whitman: The Making of a Poet.* Harmondsworth: Viking, 1985.

# Intertextuality and the Canon: Reinterpreting Fitzgerald's *The Great Gatsby*

**Somdatta Mandal**
**Visva-Bharati University, Santiniketan**

Derived from the Latin *intertexto,* meaning to intermingle while weaving, the semiotic notion of intertextuality, first introduced by Julia Kristeva in the late Sixties, is used to designate the various relationships that a given text may have with other texts. These intertextual relationships include anagram, allusion, adaptation, translation, parody, pastiche, imitation, and other kinds of transformation. Breaking the traditional notions of the author's 'influences' and the text's 'sources,' she argued that all signifying systems are constituted by the manner in which they transform earlier signifying systems. In the literary theories of structuralism and post-structuralism, texts are seen to refer to other texts (or to themselves as texts) rather than to an external reality. The term 'intertext' has been used variously for a text drawing on other texts, for a text thus drawn upon, and for the relationship between both. Kristeva further refers to texts in terms of two axes: a *horizontal axis* connecting the author and reader of a text, and a *vertical axis,* which connects the text with other texts (69). Uniting these two axes are shared codes: every text and every reading depends on prior codes. "Any text," she argues, "is constructed of a mosaic of quotations; any text is the absorption and transformation of another" (66).

Since intertextuality refers to far more than the 'influences' of writers on each other, the objective of my paper is to explore how the 1925 canonical American text, *The Great Gatsby,* a novel that T.S. Eliot announced to be "a remarkable book . . . the first step that American fiction has taken since Henry James," is read and interpreted many decades later through two multiethnic publications, both memoirs, namely Wu Ningkun's *A Single Tear: A Family's Persecution, Love, and Endurance in Communist China* (1993) and Azar Nafisi's *Reading Lolita in Tehran: A Memoir in Books* (2003). We are well aware that the term 'Gatsby' has become a generic term used in the American context to allude to a lot of things—the jazz age, the fabulous parties, the idea and pursuit of the American Dream, the democratic idealism when Gatsby is said to have "risen from a platonic idea of himself" waiting eternally for the 'green light' to emanate from the end of Daisy's dock. Trying to teach the Fitzgerald text in environments hostile to Western ideas and according to 'prior codes' bring forth unprecedented problems both in communist China and in the Khomeini regime in Tehran during the height of religious fundamentalism, and therefore becomes a new means of assessing the canonical text intertextually and interculturally.

Wu Ningkun's *A Single Tear* is a gripping narrative that tells the story of a young, conscientious and sensitive Chinese professor of English, who was educated in America, whose decision to return to China from America after the 1949 Mao Zedong revolution has lasting and potentially tragic implications for both him and his family. Like many Chinese who emigrated to other parts of the world after the World War II, Wu answered to the call of his homeland as he believed that China will be able to enter a better, prosperous and independent phase with the new Mao regime. Leaving his doctoral dissertation at the University of Chicago incomplete, he was pressed to join the department of Western languages and literature at Yenching University in Peking. Though not particularly political, and ignorant of Marxism, he agreed, abandoning his prospects in literary America. Although quickly disillusioned, Wu and his family remain subject to persecution, imprisonment, deprivation, poverty, betrayal and humiliation. By the time of Mao's death in the 1970s, the Wu family has been moved—separately and together—from city to country and back again, persecuted for their religious beliefs as Christians, and distrustful of neighbors and friends with the constant denunciations that have become standard. After enduring this pogrom for forty years, the family ultimately survived and when Wu wrote this memoir he believed that the truthful account of his experiences over three tragic decades, though intensely personal, would "contribute to a compassionate understanding of history and men" (viii).

One may ask, how does Gatsby come in here? Well, in the very first chapter of the memoir, aptly entitled "The Return of a Native, 1951-52" Wu Ningkun narrates how he left America without "any doubt in [his] mind that he would eventually go home and put [his] expertise to some good use for a new China." Full of optimism, he thought that he "would be welcomed as a patriotic intellectual who had given up an attractive profession in the most affluent capitalist society to come home and serve the socialist motherland" (4). Soon after joining the university, all the professors were ordered to examine their past for pro-American bourgeois ideology and subjected to criticism by students at public meetings. It was in this "self-criticism" session that Ningkun was first denounced politically for exposing his students to capitalistic propaganda like *The Great Gatsby.*

> When it was my turn, I spoke of my tardy recognition of the great things the party had done for China. I admitted I had perhaps wasted too many years steeping myself in the study of bourgeois Western literature when the Chinese people were fighting for a new China under the leadership of the Communist party, and I expressed readiness to remold my ideology, which had been formed in Nationalist China and the United States. I thought I had gone pretty far in getting to the bottom of things. No sooner had I finished, however, than a bespectacled second-year English major jumped to his feet and called my self-criticism "superficial" and "evasive." He brandished a paperback American novel one of the seniors in my class had borrowed from me. My righteous accuser pointed to the cover, which pictured a hand with painted fingernails holding a glass of wine, and demanded with indignant eloquence, "Is this the kind of crap you've brought back from the U.S. imperialists to corrupt the young minds of New China with?" The novel was *The Great Gatsby.* I was much more "backward"

> than I had realized, but I was not prepared to dump Fitzgerald's classic. Nonetheless, I had to make a more humble self-criticism a few days later before I was "passed." (20)

The tragedy of course did not end there but actually began. Summing up at the end of the session, the chairman pointed out that his "thinking had been polluted by [his] American education and by his reluctance to cast off 'bourgeois individualism' and accept ideological remolding" (30). As Marxists who believed in facing the facts and relieving the load on one's own mind by telling the party all, Ningkun was looked upon as some sort of a suspect and the next stage was to make him take a pledge to step up his "thought reform." Also, this was only his first taste of the arbitrary treatment of the individual by the all-powerful state, which would become the inflexible law of life in the decades to follow. That he was a bourgeois rightist seemed a foregone conclusion. In an interview given to the CNN in 1997, Wu states how this examination and confession was most frustrating. He felt he was so conscientious in coming home, so he got more and more frustrated and he got more and more angry, so he kept talking and talking and talking. He got himself into more and more trouble, because he did not know at the time, everything he said was actually monitored and whatever he said among his colleagues or to other people was actually recorded in detail. By 1956, once again he found himself "the number-one political villain" (57) and finally, at a general faculty-staff meeting the day before the festive National Day, he was "formally denounced as a 'poisonous weed' of the worst kind—an 'ultrarightist, a backbone element of the reactionary right wing of the bourgeoisie" (59). In Wu's own words this was how things went:

> My heinous crimes were characterized as anti-party, anti-people, and antisocialism, which made me a "Three-Anti" counter-revolutionary and an enemy of the people. The charges were numerous: I was born in a reactionary landlord family; I had served in the reactionary Nationalist Air Force; I had absorbed U.S. imperialist education; the motive of my return to China was unclarified; I was involved with the counterrevolutionary clique

> the ABC; I had taken part in their latest counterrevolutionary gathering; I maliciously attacked the Great Campaign to Uproot Hidden Counterrevolutionaries at a lynching; I openly clamored for freedom of speech for rightists to overthrow the socialist China; I shouted the counterrevolutionary U.S. imperialist slogan "Give me liberty or give me death!"; I attacked the Soviet Union and Chairman Mao's policy of "leaning to one side"; I blasphemed Chairman Mao's great Marxist theory of art and literature; I was dying to deep-fry Communists in cauldrons of boiling oil; I had harbored the active counterrevolutionary Jiang the Younger in my home during the great anti-rightist campaign; and so on and so forth. Indignant revolutionary comrades shouted for me to "hang my head and admit my guilt." Placed in a chair by myself facing my tribunal, I burst into tears and pleaded guilty. My compulsory confession, in which I thought I had gone far in besmirching myself, was denounced as insincere and treacherous. (59-60)

For those interested in knowing the end of this harrowing tale, Wu then found himself being torn from his young family and packed off for thought reform in a forced-labor camp in the Great Northern Wilderness, on the Soviet border facing Siberia, when the starving prisoners and their frightened visitors were beyond shedding a single tear. With nothing much but a copy of *Hamlet* in an old laundry bag, one is profoundly touched by Wu's habit of quoting Shakespeare to himself at particularly bad moments. Nearly starved and nearly frozen, he survived some of the Maoist experiments and was released, only to be denounced again, as a 'cow demon' in the infamous Cultural Revolution of the 1960s. Wu was finally rehabilitated in 1979-80. Jay Gatsby, who is said to have risen "from a Platonic idea of himself" thus became the catalyst of this sincere professor's downfall.

Fitzgerald's text plays a greater role in the next memoir, Azar Nafisi's *Reading Lolita in Tehran* published in 2003. Like Wu Ningkun, literature professor Azar Nafisi returned to her native Islamic Republic of Iran in 1987 after a long education abroad. Winning a fellowship from Oxford, she taught English literature at the University of Tehran, the Free Islamic University and the University of Allameh Tabatabai, that had been "singled out as the most liberal university in Tehran" (9). In the fall of

1995, she was expelled from the University of Tehran for refusing to wear the veil and left Iran for America in 1997. Every Thursday morning for those last two years, Nafisi indulged herself and decided to fulfill a dream. She secretly gathered seven of her most committed female students to read forbidden Western classics in the privacy of her own home. "The theme of the class was the relation between fiction and reality" (6). As Islamic morality squads staged arbitrary raids in Tehran, fundamentalists seized hold of the universities, and a blind censor stifled artistic expression, the girls in Nafisi's living room risked removing their veils and immersed themselves in the worlds of Jane Austen, F. Scott Fitzgerald, Henry James and Vladimir Nabokov. She recollects how each student took off more than their scarves and robes in her room, gained outline and shape gradually becoming her own inimitable self. "Living in a culture that denied any merit to literary works" Nafisi records in details the bleak reality of the times:

> Our world under the mullah's rule was shaped by the colorless lenses of the blind censor. Not just our reality but also our fiction had taken on this curious coloration in a world where the censor was the poet's rival in rearranging and reshaping reality, where we simultaneously invented ourselves and were figments of someone else's imagination. (25)

In this extraordinary memoir, the students' stories thus become intertwined with the ones they were reading. As Michiko Kakutani states in *The New York Times,* "the refuge from ideology that art can offer to those living under tyranny, and art's affirmative and subversive faith in the voice of the individual" become the hallmark of this memoir.

But first we have to understand how Fitzgerald travels back to the 1979 revolution. At the very beginning of the second part of her memoir entitled "Gatsby," Nafisi narrates, how like Wu Ningkun, she had returned to her homeland with a lot of optimism and promise. From the airplane she saw suddenly a blanket of lights that signaled that she had arrived at Tehran and she felt that always on arrival there was a particular moment of epiphany. Like Jay Gatsby waiting for the green light at the end of Daisy's dock, "For seventeen years," she says, "I dreamed of those lights, so beckoning and seductive. I dreamed of being submerged in them and of never having to leave again." (81) Along with her other personal items, the customs officer picked up *Ada, Jews without Money, The Great Gatsby* "as if handling someone else's dirty laundry. But he did not confiscate them—not then. That came sometime later." (82) On joining the English Department at the University of Tehran, she offered to teach a course where she would do a comparative study of the literature of the Twenties and Thirties, the proletarians and the non-proletarians. The best person for the Twenties for her was of course Fitzgerald, though she was curious to know why in the Thirties, people like him were pushed out by a new breed of writers. In trying to be "somewhat fair politically," (89) side by side with *The Great Gatsby* and *A Farewell to Arms,* she planned to teach works by Maxim Gorky and Mike Gold.

Before the new term began in September 1979, Nafisi had to spend most of her time hunting for the books on her syllabus. In one bookstore, as she was rummaging through a few copies of *The Great Gatsby* and *A Farewell to Arms,* the owner approached her.

> "If you're interested in those, you'd better buy them now," he said, shaking his head sadly. I looked at him sympathetically and said smugly, "There's too much demand for them. They can't do anything about that—can they?"
>
> He was right. In a few months' time, Fitzgerald and Hemingway were very difficult to find. The government could not remove all of the books from the stores, but gradually it closed down some of the most important foreign-language bookstores and blocked the distribution of foreign books in Iran. (91)

The first day she went to the university armed with the trusty *Gatsby*. "It was showing signs of wear: the dearer a book was to my heart, the more battered and bruised it became." (92) Anxious about how her class would receive her as she was anxious about the political upheavals in the country, she found the students unusually quiet. Her hands were full of all the books and xeroxes she had brought for the class, "an eclectic mix of revolutionary writers whose works had been translated into Persian and 'elitists' such as Fitzgerald, Faulkner and Woolf" (93). She asked her students what they thought fiction would accomplish, why one should bother to read fiction at all. One thing the authors she would be teaching had in common was their subversiveness and she told the students how the best fiction always forced one to question what one took for granted. One day, when her leftist students had cancelled classes protesting the fresh murder of three revolutionaries, Nafisi was caught up by a few students. They had already read *Gatsby* and wanted to know whether Fitzgerald's other books were similar to it. Nafisi remembered this incident for a long time and wrote:

> We went on talking Fitzgerald as we walked down the wide staircase, past the various tables with their political goods for sale and the rather large crowd assembled in front of a wall plastered with newspapers. We walked onto the hot asphalt and sat on one of the benches by the stream running through the campus, and talked like children sharing coveted stolen cherries. I felt very young, and we laughed and we talked. Then we went our separate ways. We never became more intimate than that. (96)

We are then told about one of her colleagues, who always worried about losing his job. Having just divorced his wife, he had to maintain her, plus his home and swimming pool and somehow inappropriately kept comparing himself to Gatsby, calling himself Little Great Gatsby. But Nafisi's first culture shock came when one day she had a stimulating discussion on the implications of the words *literature, radical, bourgeois* and *revolutionary* with one of the best students of her class, Mr. Bahri. At the end of the talk she was so excited that she reached out to him in a gesture of goodwill and friendship. He silently, deliberately, withdrew both his hands behind his back, as if to remove them from even the possibility of a handshake. Bewildered and "too much of a stranger to the newness of revolutionary ways," (98) she was later informed by a colleague that the gesture meant that no Muslim man would or should touch a *namaharam* woman—a woman other than his wife, mother or sister. Still that aborted handshake did not prepare her fully to dislike Mr. Bahri, though she developed a habit of blaming him and holding him responsible for everything that went wrong.

Initially Nafisi felt the impending problems of teaching *Gatsby.* Amid shouts of "Death to America" and every now and then the burning of the American flag, the text seemed a strange choice for students burning with revolutionary zeal. Later, in retrospect, Nafisi felt that it was the right choice as the values shaping the novel were the exact opposite of those of the revolution. "Ironically, as time went by, it was the values inherent in *Gatsby* that would triumph, but at that time we had not yet realized just how far we had betrayed our dreams" (108). Because of the constant interruptions, the *Gatsby* text was begun in November 1979 but could not be finished until January 1980. Nafisi's choice of the text was not based on the political climate of the time but on the fact that it was a great novel. Though she read and reread *Gatsby* "with greedy wonder," she was held back by a strange feeling that she did not want to share it with anyone. Her students were "slightly baffled" with the text. The story of an idealistic guy, so much in love with this beautiful rich girl who betrays him, could not be satisfying to those for whom sacrifice was defined by words such as *masses, revolution,* and *Islam.* Passion and betrayal were for them political emotions, and love far removed from the stirrings of Jay Gatsby for Mrs. Tom Buchanan. Adultery in Tehran was one of so many other crimes, and the law dealt with it accordingly: public stoning.

As the teacher tried to explain to her students that *Gatsby* was an American classic, in many ways the quintessential American novel it was also different from the ideologies of her own country. "We in ancient countries have our past—we obsess over the past. They, the Americans, have a dream: they feel nostalgia about the promise of the future." (109) She then tried to explain the concept of the American Dream. When they come to the point in the text when Gatsby is visiting Daisy and Tom Buchanan's house for the first time and Tom has a sudden insight into their relationship, a student cut in to add that that is because Tom "is in love with the money and not with Daisy. She is only a symbol." Another voice from the back of the room asks, "But what use is love in this world we live in?" (110) When the teacher asks what kind of a world would be suitable for love, Mr. Nyazi's hand darts up. "We don't have time for love right now," he said. "We are committed to a higher, more sacred love." When a female student Zarrin turned around and said sardonically, "Why else do you fight a revolution?" Mr. Nyazi turned very red, bowed his head and after a short pause took up his pen and started to write furiously. The teacher diffused the tension by adding that a novel was not an allegory and to read a novel was to "inhale the experience" (111).

The next day Mr. Nyazi met Professor Nafisi in earnest and all goodwill, and his complaint was about Gatsby. He said he was telling her for her own good and he was serious. He was not against Mr. Gatsby himself but against the novel. The novel was immoral. It taught the youth the wrong stuff; it poisoned their minds—surely she could see? She reminded him that Gatsby was a work of fiction and not a how-to manual. But the gentleman was adamant, "Maybe Mr. Gatsby was all right for the Americans, but not for our revolutionary youth." There was, for Mr. Nyazi, no difference between the fiction of Fitzgerald and the facts of his own life: "*The Great Gatsby* was representative of things American, and America was poison for us; it certainly was. We should teach Iranian students to fight against American immorality," he said.

In those days of public prosecutions, Nafisi suddenly had a mischievous notion and suggested that they put *Gatsby* on mock trial in class. Mr. Nyazi would be the prosecutor, and he should also write a paper offering his evidence. There would also be a lawyer for the defence and a defendant; the rest of the class would be the jury. They would also need a judge, a defendant and a defense attorney. Since no one volunteered to be the defence, the teacher had to defend it. Zarrin volunteered to be Nafisi's lawyer and wanted to know if the teacher was Fitzgerald or the book itself. They decided that the teacher would be the book; Fitzgerald may have had or lacked qualities that they could detect in the book. It was agreed that in this trial the rest of the class could at any point interrupt the defence or the prosecution with their own comments and questions. But no one wanted to speak for *Gatsby*.

*The Great Gatsby* thus became the set-piece in the courtroom drama in the classroom. "And so began the case of the Islamic Republic of Iran versus *The Great Gatsby,"* (124) writes Nafisi. After a long invocation "In the Name of God," Mr. Nyazi, the Islamist prosecutor ranted against the novel for its ambiguity about the characters' decadence:

> Imam Khomeini has relegated a great task to our poets and writers. . . . He has given them a sacred mission, *much* more exalted than that of the materialistic writers in the West. . . . Our task as our Imam has stated, is to purge the country of the decadent Western culture. . . . This is an Islamic court, not *Perry Mason.* I can present my case the way I want to, and I am setting the context. I want to say that as a Muslim I cannot accept *Gatsby*. . . .
>
> I have enough evidence—every page, *every* single page of this book is its own condemnation. . . . And if you want to see cultural rape, you need go no further than this very book. . . This book preaches illicit relations between a man and a woman.
>
> The one thing good about this book is that it exposes the immorality and decadence of American society, but we have fought to rid ourselves of this trash and it is high time that such books be banned. . . . This book is supposed to be about the American dream, but what sort of a dream is this? Does the author mean to suggest that we should all be adulterers and bandits? Americans are decadent and in decline because this is their dream. They are going down! This is the last hiccup of a dead culture! (124-27)

When Zarrin was summoned to defend her case she accused the prosecutor of committing "the fallacy of getting too close to the amusement park. He can no longer distinguish fiction from reality." (128) "*Gatsby* is being put on trial because it disturbs us," she stated. "This is not the first time a novel—a non-political novel—has been put on trial by a state." She cited the famous trials of *Madame Bovary, Ulysses, Lady Chatterley's Lover* and *Lolita* and explained how in each case the novel won.

The point that seemed to trouble the judge as well as the prosecutor was the lure of money and its role in the novel. It is about wealth but not about the vulgar materialism that had been hinted upon. While both the sides elaborated on their own points of view, Nafisi became rather excited. She wanted to tell them that the book "is not about adultery but about the loss of dreams." (133) and kept going back to Fitzgerald's own explanation of his novel: "That's the whole burden of this novel," he had said, "the loss of those illusions that give such color to the world so that you don't care whether things are true or false as long as they partake of the magical glory." So she advised her students in more concrete and practical terms:

> You don't read Gatsby to learn whether adultery is good or bad but to learn about how complicated issues such as adultery and fidelity and marriage are. A great novel heightens your senses and sensitivity to the complexities of life and of individuals, and prevents you from the self-righteousness that sees morality in fixed formulas about good and evil. (133)

Mr. Nyazi was of course unable to understand the logic. "But ma'am, there is nothing complicated about having an affair with another man's wife. Why doesn't Mr. Gatsby get his own wife?" he added sulkily. When it was time to hear from the jury, a few of the leftist activists defended the novel. Nafisi felt that they did so partly because the Muslim activists were so dead set against it. In essence, their defense was not so different from Nyazi's condemnation. They said that they needed to read a fiction like *The Great Gatsby* because they needed to know about the immorality of American culture. They felt they should read more revolutionary material, but that they should read books like this as well to understand the enemy. It was much later that Nafisi discovered that "most students had supported Zarrin but very few were prepared to risk voicing their views, mainly because they lacked enough self-confidence to articulate their points as 'eloquently' as the defense and the prosecutor. Some claimed in private that they personally liked the book" (135). Nafisi's colleagues who were surprised that the debate in class was

Fitzgerald versus Islam instead of Lenin versus the Imam, praised Mr. Bahri for quieting down the voices of outrage and somehow convinced the Islamic association that she had "put America on trial" (137). Personally, the *Gatsby* "trial" had opened a window into Nafisi's own feelings and desires. A totalitarian regime would have to dislike uncertainty or doubt, for its existence would rely heavily on absolutes: good, evil, God, etc. Nafisi shows us that the absence of doubt contributes to the disappearance of empathy, the very heart of any novel. The "blind censor" does not empathise; he only wants to wipe out imagination. The text thus becomes an allegory of the struggle between Iran's Islamists and Leftists to control the legacy of the revolution. At the end of the trial, while trying to explain to Mr. Nyazi that dreams are perfect ideals, complete in themselves and cannot be imposed on a constantly changing imperfect, incomplete reality, Nafisi undergoes a kind of self-discovery:

> When I left the class that day, I did not tell them that I myself was just beginning to discover: how similar our own fate was becoming to Gatsby's. He wanted to fulfill his dream by repeating the past, and in the end he discovered that the past was dead, the present a sham, and there was no future. Was this not similar to our revolution, which had come in the name of our collective past and had wrecked our lives in the name of a dream? (144)

Years later, as she read faxes and emails from some of her former students in Iran in her office in Washington D.C. Nafisi tried to decipher something beyond the hysteria of their words:

> I would like to know where Mr. Bahri is right now, at this moment, and to ask him: how did it all turn out, Mr. Bahri—was this your dream, your dream of the revolution? Who will pay for all the ghosts in my memory? Who will pay for the snapshots of the murdered and the executed that we hid in our shoes and closets as we moved on to other things? Tell me, Mr. Bahri—or, to use that odd expression of Gatsby's, Tell me, old sport—what shall we do with all these corpses on our hands? (153)

To conclude I reiterate the idea of intertextuality with which I began this article. According to some critics the term is not a mere cross-referencing or interdependence of texts, it also includes the attitude that one text exhibits towards another. Taking the term in its widest sense, these two memoirs also exhibit the boundary-crossings between texts. With multiculturalism changing the face of the American literary scenario, the Barthesian idea—that writing is always an iteration which is also a re-iteration, a re-writing which foregrounds the trace of the various texts it both knowingly and unknowingly places and displaces—takes on an added meaning in this analysis. In the meantime, we just keep waiting for more of Jay Gatsby's cross-cultural travels around the globe.

### List of Works Cited and Consulted

Chandler, Daniel. *Semiotics for Beginners.* Online version. http://www.aber.ac.uk/media/documents

Culler, Jonathan. *The Pursuit of Signs: Semiotics, Literature, Deconstruction.* London: Routledge & Kegan Paul, 1981.

Fitzgerald, F. Scott. *The Great Gatsby.* New York: Scribner's, 1925.

Kristeva, Julia. *Desire in Language: A Semiotic Approach to Literature and Art.* New York: Columbia University Press, 1980.

Nafisi, Azar. *Reading Lolita in Tehran: A Memoir in Books.* New York: Random House, 2003.

Ningkun, Wu. *A Single Tear: A Family's Persecution, Love, and Endurance in Communist China.* London: Hodder & Stoughton, 1993.

_____. Interview given in New York City on 8th February, 1997 to the CNN series on COLD WAR. Tape no. 10492. <http://www.CNN Cold War—Interviews Wu Ninglun.htm>

Sturrock, John. *Structuralism.* London: Paladin, 1986.

# Through the Lens Darkly: Accented Filmmaking in Mira Nair's *The Perez Family*

**Pin-Chia Feng**
**National Chiao Tung University**
**Hsin-chu, Taiwan**

Among the South Asian women filmmakers, Mira Nair is undoubtedly the most prominent and productive one. Starting as a student of sociology who recorded the social changes of Indian society through her documentaries, Nair has moved into feature films with her widely acclaimed *Salaam Bombay!* (1988) and into Hollywood with her later productions. Through the camera lens Nair looks closely at India, diasporic experiences, and North America. Nair first provides insight into Indian society with her documentaries *Jama Masjid Street Journal* (1979), *So Far from India* (1982), *Indian Cabaret* (1985), *Children of a Desired Sex* (1987), and a portrayal of the subalterns in *Salaam Bombay!* (1988). In the historical drama *Kamasutra* (1997) and the contemporary melodrama *Monsoon Wedding* (2002), Nair further reviews women's position in India. She also chooses to represent diasporic experiences through the melodramatic form in *Mississippi Masala* (1992), *The Perez Family* (1995), and *My Own Country* (1998). As her film career matures, she takes on even more diversified subject matters. In her recent feature film *Hysterical Blindness* (2002) Nair looks into the lives of lower-middle class white women, records the aftermath of 9/11 in a short documentary "India" (2002), and adapts William Thackeray's *Vanity Fair* into a period drama. Except for the nineteenth-century setting of *Vanity Fair* (2003), there appear to be two main foci of Nair's filmic oeuvre: lives of the South Asian diaspora; and those of the minorities in American society—immigrants, peoples of color and the lower classes, victims of diseases, etc. This paper focuses on Nair's "accented" representation of diasporic experiences in *The Perez Family*, in which Nair documents lives of Cuban boat people making their way into Miami. The first part of the paper is a brief introduction to the controversies over Nair's career in order to contextualize Nair's filmic works in general and *The Perez Family* in particular. It is followed by a close reading of the heterogeneous "accents" in *The Perez Family* to expound on the ways in which Nair represents the formation of a new Cuban American family and probes beneath the surface of the containment of a romance comedy, thereby leaving a cinematic landmark on the American optic consciousness.

In his chapter "Bombay Cinema and Diasporic Desire," Vijay Mishra historicizes the origin of the Indian diaspora as coming out of "two quite distinct moments in the history of capital. The first moment (of classic capitalism) produced the movement of indentured labor to the colonies (South Africa, Fiji, Trinidad, Guyana, etc.) for the production of sugar, rubber, and tin for the growing British and European markets" and results in what he terms "the old Indian diaspora of plantation labor"; the second Indian diaspora, or the post-1960s "diaspora of late capital" (236), Mishra points out, is "distinguished by the movement of economic migrants (but also refugees) into the metropolitan centers of the former empire as well as the New World and Australia" (235). Born in India and educated both in India and the United States, Mira Nair belongs to this second diaspora, out of which grows "an important market of popular cinema as well as site for its production" (Mishra 236) and a special diasporic film culture of "the 'Brown Atlantic'" (Desai ix).[1] The multiple routes of Indian migrations in the Brown Atlantic provide Nair with the background of those "emigrants twice displaced" characters in *Mississippi Masala* and *My Own Country*,[2] who are forced to leave their African birthplaces and are finally relocated in the United States.

As a filmmaker Nair is always a controversial figure, not only because of her frequent choice of transgressive subject matter but also because she is relatively successful in the mainstream film industry. She is cited by Hamid Naficy as one of those minority filmmakers who benefit from "a social and professional mobility in the new land by means of cinema" and who "move out of minoritarian cinema into the mainstream by making popular films" ("Between Rocks and Hard Places" 133). Professional and social advancements are often regarded as signs of deviation from one's roots. Her gender and class identity—a middle-class woman with an elitist education—further renders her a suspect of intellectual compradorism. This upper mobility thus leads to polarized assessments of her film career. On the one hand, she has been criticized as "part of a tokenized minority of 'post-colonial' scholars and artists who function as both collaborators and resisters" (Ballal 95). Her films about India, such as *Salaam Bombay!*, have been criticized as providing insider's information to international audiences from the perspective of a native informer. On the other, she is praised as "a cineaste of uncompromising feminist postcolonial subjectivity in-the-making" (Foster 111) and as someone who deploys a "politics of provocation" in her films to shock her audiences into new awareness.[3] According to Alpana Sharma, the purpose of this kind of provocative filmmaking is to sharpen our senses through transgression: "Her camera opens out both ways: It asks us to look at its subject just as frankly as we look at ourselves looking, in the process breaking down the dialectic of inside and outside, subject and object, viewer and viewee" (92). In this respect Nair's explorations of polemic subjects are not seen as trading on shock value but offering a chance for reflective inspection that will lead to renewed insights. The sexually explicit scenes in *Mississippi Masala* and *Kama Sutra*, for instance, are not just meant to offer spectatorial excitement but to inspire a rethinking of the meaning of bodily pleasure, especially from a feminist perspective.

The controversies regarding Nair's film career, therefore, to a large extent are a result of her liminal status as a diasporic filmmaker from the Third World. Her own liminality in turn leads to a strong interest in marginal characters. Nair once stated: "I would have to admit that I have always been drawn to stories of people who live on the margins of society, on the edge, or outside, learning the language of being in-between, always dealing with the question: 'What, and where, is home?'" ("The Language of being in between"). This question of the definition and location of home for marginal people becomes a central problematic that Nair is working with in her filmic texts; almost all her main characters struggle to find a place called home: Ashok the immigrant worker in New York who is struggling with his duty to bring his family to the Big Apple in *So Far from India*; Krishna the abandoned child who has landed in the red light district of Bombay in *Salaam Bombay!*; Mina the Indian girl who was born in Uganda, works and lives in a Mississippian motel and falls in love with an African American carpet cleaner: Abraham Verghese the Indian doctor with an Ethiopian birthplace who is helping people in a small town of Tennessee to fight against the AIDS epidemic, just to mention a few examples. The pursuit of an elusive sense of "at-homeness" for the migrant/migrating characters is therefore almost always a structuring principle of Nair's films.

Nair's own diasporic background and this quest for "at-homeness" make her one of Naficy's "accented filmmakers"—"exilic and diasporic filmmakers . . . who work in the interstices of social formations and cinematic practices" (*Accented Cinema* 10). "By dint of their education, class affiliation, multilingualism, cosmopolitanism, and distance from the homeland," Naficy further points out, using Mina Nair as an example, "accented filmmakers are structurally outsiders, however much they desire to be considered insiders, either within their own native culture or in the host society" (*Accented Cinema* 70). This difficult position as outsiders finally results in a special double-voiced "accented style," which is a hybrid construct of "the cinematic traditions" of the dominant cinema and "the exilic and diasporic traditions" of the deterritorialized filmmakers (*Accented Cinema* 22). A question that is especially pertinent to Mina Nair is whether accented filmmakers can keep this special double voice and double consciousness throughout their careers without being consumed by the mainstream film industries.

Although, as mentioned, Naficy has also cited Nair as an example of minority filmmakers who have moved "up" to the mainstream, I would argue that Nair always strives to keep her "accent" and to incorporate different variations of the "accented style" that she has started with into her film productions, be they independently made or supported by the studios. Here *The Perez Family* becomes a case in point in that it is a film funded by a big studio and in which Nair has to practise a different "accent" than her own in her representation of marginal characters seeking to claim the United States as home. This film, which has received mixed reviews though being seldom discussed, is special among Nair's films about diasporic experiences in that it is at once a subject matter that Nair is unfamiliar with—about Cuban refugees in America—and one that is closest to her heart—about the lives of immigrants and exiles. How to make a film about a different ethnic community from her own and still remain a "faithful translator" of Hispanic culture is in every way a challenge for the Indian filmmaker. To put it another way: If Nair wants to maintain an accented style in this film, the second tradition in the film besides the Hollywood mode of melodramatic comedy becomes problematic; for by attempting to adopt the "accent" of the Cuban immigrant, Nair can very well be accused of appropriating the Cuban accent and performing a ventriloquial act. What makes her task even more difficult is how to balance the different traditions that seem to compete with each other since Nair reportedly has to struggle with the studio over the control of the film.

*The Perez Family*, adapted from a novel by Christine Bell, is made in the Hollywood tradition of romance comedy in its visualization of the interactions between immigrants and their naturalized habitats. Juan Raul Perez (played by Alfred Molina) is a Cuban plantation owner who has been imprisoned by Castro for twenty years. His wife Carmela (Anjelica Huston) and daughter Teresa have escaped to Miami in the meantime. Upon his release Juan takes advantage of the boatlift and sails to the U.S. to search for his lost family. On his route he came across Dottie (Dorita) Perez (Marisa Tomei), a cane cutter and part-time prostitute. The plot follows that of a comedy of mistaken identity in that Juan and Dottie are mistaken by the American immigrant officer as man and wife. Carmela's brother Angel fails to locate Juan because of this mistake and leaves Carmela heartbroken and Juan stranded in the refugee tent city inside the Orange Bowl. Dottie exploits the mistake by collecting three Perezes among the refugees to make up a family of four in order to get a sponsor for her entry into the U.S. and away from the football stadium. The Perez family ends up selling flowers on the street to people who are driving by. In the meantime, Carmela gives up on the hope of reunion with Juan and decides to start dating a police officer who has been called to her house by the alarm system installed by the neurotic Angel. Juan and Carmela are finally reunited, only to decide to follow their hearts instead of the marriage vow.

This comedy of romantic love in the diaspora is relatively less known among Nair's works and receives little critical attention. *The New York Times* reviewer Caryn James writes that the film "exists too much on the surface" although "that surface offers its own visual and aural glitter." In her analysis of *Mississippi Masala* Gwendolyn Audrey Foster cursorily states, "Like *Mississippi Masala*, *The Perez Family* uses the standard Hollywood romance formula as a tableau to stage political critique and to embody the visual pleasure of people of color" (Foster 126-27). The comments on the film's superficial and formulaic quality in fact reflect on Nair's accented style of filmmaking, in which the surface is actually the source of depth with the coexistence of conservative normality and radical potentiality in its deployment of Hollywood conventions. Nair uses Hollywood conventional elements in order to mobilize a critical inspection of the media imperialism. The voice of the visually colonized, in turn, will speak back to the American media empire.

The conventional plot of fantasy versus reality prevails in the film and is best exemplified in Dottie's obsession with John Wayne, which tropes on the frontier myth by alluding to the cowboy figure as the imagined embodiment of the American spirit of freedom. The Duke's cinematic presence as *the* American hero is produced and disseminated by the American mass media. It is Hollywood's commodified version of the American dream in which individualist heroism is celebrated in its capacity of fighting against social and natural adversaries. The celluloid cowboy who freely roams the "uncivilized" land of the West embodies the quintessential American cultural myth of freedom and mobility, which is then exported to the global market via a neo-imperialist conquering force of the mass media. Jinga Desai analyzes Nair's succumb to the "frontier myth or U.S.-domesticated nomadism" in *Mississippi Masala* in the film's emphasis on replacing the diaspora with the open space of the American West (73). Apparently the same myth is deliberately recycled in *The Perez Family*. Dottie becomes the ideal female spectator of the Hollywood westerns who is completely seduced by the visual pleasure of American macho heroism and the cinematic construction of America. Her repeated wishes of wanting to "fuck John Wayne" bespeak a heterosexual desire induced and produced by this visual pleasure. Nair underscores Dottie's obsession with Hollywood and Wayne by playing on geography. On their way to the Orange Bowl, Dottie spots the name Hollywood on a road sign and gets excited about how close John Wayne is. In a sense, the character Dottie is defined by this heterosexual fantasy peddled by the studios, which for Dottie safeguards her entrance into the American dream. It is also presented in the film that her sole motivation of going to the U.S. is to consummate her sexual fantasy with her hero. Her naivety is therefore both a comment on the seductive mode of interaction between Hollywood and its audience and that on the monovision of immigrants who embark on the journey away from home single-mindedly.

At a meta-filmic level, Dottie's naivety opens a space for Nair the filmmaker to reflect on the illusionary nature of

Hollywood productions and her own career as one of the providers of illusions. Nair deliberately reveals her self-reflexive intention through the Indian immigration officer (played by Ranjit Choudhry) who mercilessly disillusions Dottie with the news of the Duke's death and who also jokes about the cowboy/ Indian melodrama. The immigration officer's joke that the Indians on the silver screen in the Western are "[n]ot my kind of Indians" pokes fun at the historical misnaming. It alludes to Christopher Columbus's Orientalist geographic mistake that has created "Indians" out of Native Americans. The scene of Dottie's disillusionment also signifies a time lag that exists between the immigrant woman's media-produced America and the American reality. (Juan also does not know that Elvis is dead, which reinforces the sense of a time lag). The news of John Wayne's death supposedly should have shocked her into awareness of reality. Nair nevertheless seizes the opportunity to further critique the seductive power of Hollywood cinema as well as the Anglo-centrism involved in frontier heroism. During the showing of a John Wayne movie Dottie gets all excited and almost goes into a state of orgasm. Then the aged film stock gets burnt and interrupts her self-indulged erotic reaction, only to replace the image of the Duke with a "real" Anglo macho figure that seems to be a wish-fulfillment for Dottie—out of the burnt hole in the middle of the black and white film on the silver screen walks the Caucasian security guard Steve. Dottie ecstatically gazes at and reacts to this coincidence. By calling Steve "My United States freedom hero," Dottie is seen again as a visually colonized female spectator interpellated by the cinematic image into her "appropriate" position as a believer of American dream. Her celluloid cowboy lover is miraculously resurrected in the flesh-and-blood blond guard. The scene then cuts to Dottie and Steve violently make out at a corner of the stadium. However, once more Nair denies Dottie a fulfillment of her American dream. When she finally is about to consummate her sexual relationship with Steve who is suggestively in a cowboy outfit, Dottie discovers that Steve treats her as a prostitute, just like the overseer on the Cuban plantation that she has left behind. A distraught Dottie then walks out of Steve's apartment into the Miami night and back to the deserted stadium, where earlier Juan has struggled with the guards to protect his "son" Felipe from being forcefully removed and now only the grandfather is left. This second disappointment and the fear of losing her new family again finally guide her back to the fold of "her people" and the "proper" relationship with her assumed family. The sex that Dottie has saved for John Wayne is finally consummated with Juan, the Cuban John. Significantly, the next morning after they become a real couple Dottie decides to change her name back to Dorita. By giving up on the name that she gives herself upon landing on Miami and going back to her proper Cuban name, Dottie/Dorita is shown as "decolonized" and liberated from her fantasy. The romance of the two refugees of course again brings back the normative heterosexual discourse of Hollywood's melodramatic romance, but only after this visually produced romance plot has been thoroughly interrogated.

Once Dottie is completely disillusioned about the American cowboy, the rest of the drama concentrates on how the Cuban immigrants survive in the land of freedom. The film's Cuban "accent' is where Nair can mostly easily be criticized as superficial since it is about an ethnic community out of the Indian filmmaker's league. In this case what is at stake is Nair's role as a successful "cultural translator." Nair has accomplished this task by filming the Cuban community through "emphatic knowledge" (Foster 115) that can lead to border crossings.[4] On the one hand, she relies on her own lived experience as a diasporan to bridge the cultural differences of the two ethnic communities. The film also explores the reconfiguration of family and kinship system in the process of transnational migrations. The Perez family of the title is in fact a microcosmic representation of the Cuban immigrant community. Besides Juan and Dottie, the make-shift family also includes Grandfather Amarda the traumatized and disabled solider who prefers to run naked or climb up a high post to "look for Cuba," the homeland that he is forced to leave behind, and Felipe the street smart orphan who ingratiates into the family and exploits Dottie's maternal instinct. In a sense this Perez family is an exaggerated enactment of the freedom of choice in American democratic rhetoric. It also suggests the formation of a new Cuban American family that is built upon an alternative kinship system. Interestingly, there is another Perez family of blood relations consisting of Juan, Carmela and Teresa. The coexistence of the double versions of the Perez family signifies on the doubleness of the diasporic identity and thereby resists against any singularly "authentic" conceptualization and representation of an ethnic group. It also calls for a rethinking of the definition and location of home and family in a diasporic condition, a topic that Nair is most familiar with.

On the other hand, Nair reaches beyond the common denominator of diasporic experiences and strives to build appropriate socio-historical and cultural-religious contexts for the Cuban exiles in the film. The film is set in 1980 when the Mariel boat people left Cuba for Miami. As in *Mississippi Masala*, Nair does not dwell too much on the historical background of the exodus. Only a few clues such as the TV news broadcasting in Carmela's living room showing Castro in a newsreel serve as an indicator of the event; the film nevertheless demands extra-filmic literacy of the history behind the boatlift, from its audience. Through Angel's neurotic obsession with Carmela's security, the film also records the fear and distrust of the established Cuban American community against the newcomers, or "Marelitos" as Angel labels them. This excessive fear hints at intra-community divisions and disturbances, although they are significantly downplayed with the overall comic treatment. Cuban cultures also surface in the grandmother/spiritual healer figure who interprets Juan's obsessive concern with his bad teeth as really an anxiety for his manhood and virility and kind-heartedly tries to save Juan's "marriage" by sending Felipe to buy Juan some false teeth. The folk song that she keeps on singing becomes one of the theme melodies that are repeatedly played on the soundtrack. Interestingly, it is through this act of generosity that Felipe is incorporated into the Perez family since right after he runs into the gangster to whom he owes money, he in his hurry to escape is knocked unconscious and then claimed by the resourceful Dottie as her long lost son.

Cinematically, the filmic narrative framed by scenes of the island homeland creates a distinct sense of Cuban presence. After the credit lines the film opens with a band playing traditional music on a beach where a crowd of well-dressed bourgeoisie is enjoying a leisure outing on the sandy beach. Servants are seen preparing traditional food. The camera captures an overall sense of class well-being and family togetherness as it captures adults engaged in amiable conversations and children playing or napping. A young man in particular is seen dancing with a young woman. With the presence of nuns, schoolgirls and old women embroidering, the scene appears to picture lives of the Cuban middle class before the revolution. Then on the soundtrack the music fades away and is replaced by the sound of splashing ocean water and distant sound of a horn. The scene then cuts to an extra-long shot that views the beach from the angle of the ocean and then the young man is seen standing alone on the deserted beach, calling out the name Carmela and watching five people wading into the sea in their party dresses, including the young woman holding a child. A crab is seen crawling on his expensive shoes. When the scene abruptly changes into the darkness of a prison cell, we realize that the opening scene is actually Juan dreaming about his former life and the departure of his family to the other shore. The bright sunshine on the beach and the dimly lighted prison cell create a sharp contrast to highlight the change of social status of Juan. The contrast establishes the basic tone of the film in which dreams are pitted against stock reality both in Mariel and Miami. The beach scene is repeated in Juan's dream when he is sleeping in the same bed with Dottie. While he is still calling out the name Carmela, the girl in the dream has changed into Dottie, which subtly suggests a change of heart, though unrecognized, in Juan. The theme music is played again when Juan makes love to Dottie the first time, after he witnesses Carmela flirting with the federal officer and decides to "stop waiting." This message of the necessity to let go of the past is reiterated by Carmela when she is finally united with Juan. Here we are invited to see beneath the surface of the romantic comedy to detect a metaphor for the exilic condition. Carmela is virtually saying that the fear of letting go of the familiar past prevents the couple from getting new lives and they are therefore spending twenty years suspended between Cuba and the U.S. The act of dissolving the old marriage vow and going to their respective new loves allows them to embark on new lives. Thus at the end of the film the camera symbolically says good bye to the immigrants to the island by presenting a brief scene in which the camera is skirting the beach and the island from a bird's-eye view, which projects a last look at Cuba. Like the frames with roses presenting the credit lines at the beginning of the film which suggests romantic love, the three views of the beach present the progress of the Cuban immigrants in the new land.

The film also uses music and dance as an authenticating device to strengthen the overall Hispanic "accent." It opens with a stylized performance of traditional Cuban music in Juan's dream and towards the end another performance of Cuban music and dance at the community festival by Angel's mistress Flavia is staged. Dottie's dance on the boat on her way to Miami and the little girl who dances to the Cuban music in Little Havana as seen by Juan when he is searching for his way to Carmela's house are examples of the Hispanic dance culture. Nair's film is always very keen on the music and dance elements, which to a certain extent can be regarded as variations and ethnicized forms of the Bollywood song and dance tradition that Nair has grown up with. *The Perez Family* therefore also has a close affinity to Bollywood films in its deployment of music and dance performances, although in a rather reserved way than that of the Bollywood model.

Besides the double traditions of the Hollywood convention and Cuban cultural voices, therefore, there is also an "Indian accent" that is a predominant presence in Nair's films in which she navigates between different film genres and traditions of

Bollywood and Hollywood to represent characters of different classes and races. India is a constitutive element in her films with the constant use of Indian characters, especially with her cameo appearances in several films. For instance, in *The Perez Family* she plays a woman who drives by and buys flowers from Dottie because she is "tempted" by the flamboyant Cuban immigrant selling flowers at the beach front.[5] The Indian immigration officer who guides Dottie through the process of getting sponsorship and orchestrates the transportation of the Cuban immigrants in and out of the Orange Bowl stadium is another ostensive Indian presence in the film. The insertion of this Indian character in the film accentuates the comic aura with his wisecracking comments on Dottie and her American dream. With his official status as one who regulates the process of immigrants' naturalization, he apparently stands out as a signpost of successful assimilation into American institutions. However, his Indian accent at once adds on to the heteroglossic soundtrack of the film and signifies a part of the immigrant culture that is inassimilable. This inassimilable element, I believe, presents the very spirit of accented cinema and embodies an irreducible trace of the diasporic migration.

Mira Nair once commented, "Distance from a community is something which used to confuse me but now I use it as a tool for my films" (Anbarasan and Otchet). In his introductory essay to a collection of essays on exilic films and media studies, Homi Bhabha activates "an archaic root of the 'exilic'":

> it is worth remembering that the term also carries within it, invisibly, unconsciously, its Latin root, *Salire*, 'to leap.' It is the ethical 'leap' that requires us, in a kind of bounding, boundary-breaking movement to move, as Benjamin suggests, beyond 'our metropolitan streets and furnished rooms'; to revise our knowledge of some of the 'savage' discourses of power, possession, knowledge and belonging, that rise from the uncanny far-flung ruins and debris of metropolitan discourse. (xii)

The exilic movement of transnational migrations is therefore a way to refresh our jaded senses and to achieve new insights. Through representing the Cubans who sail across the ocean to search for a dream of freedom and rebuild their family in *The Perez Family*, we see how Mira Nair uses her filmmaker's lens to make these "leaps" possible for immigrants. Most important, this film with multiple "accents" also makes it possible for Nair herself to go beyond the boundary of the familiar Indian subject matter to document lives of different races, classes and ethnicities. The making of *The Perez Family*, therefore, signals a landmark for the diasporic filmmaker and the American viewing experience.

## NOTES

1. In Jigna Desai's *Beyond Bollywood*, a comparative study of "films in English from and about the 'Brown Atlantic' (South Asian diasporas in the United States, Canada, and Britain)" and Indian films, South Asian diasporic cinema is defined as "a developing cinema that negotiates the dominant discourses, politics, and economies of multiple locations. This political and cultural economy affects the form, production, and circulation of the films. South Asian diasporic cinema negotiates and traffics among the two largest global cinemas—those of Hollywood and Bollywood—as well as individual national cinemas including British, Canadian alternative U.S. and alternative Indian" (35).
2. See Binita Mehta's essay on *Mississippi Masala*.
3. Alpana Sharma argues, "Her entire filmography to date, while certainly not produced expressly with the intent to shock, characterizes Nair as a non-traditional filmmaker unafraid of controversy" (91).
4. Foster argues for the importance of the use of emphatic knowledge when we attempt to "speak for" the subalterns: "Certainly cultural and historical determiners must be kept in mind when making or talking about films on the 'culturally invisible,' the culturally silenced and politically oppressed subalterns of the world; but cultural/historical knowledge must not be repositioned as a new frontier/border or silencing mechanism itself" (115).
5. Nair is also the Indian gossip who reiterates the law of color and racial lines and resists any impingement against the traditional way of life both in *Mississippi Masala* and *My Own Country*.

## List of Works Cited and Consulted

Anbarasan, Ethirajan and Amy Otchet. "Mira Nair: An Eye for Paradox." <http://www.unesco.org/courier/1998_11/uk/dires/tet1.htm>

Ballal, Prateeti, Punja. "Illiberal Masala: The Diasporic Distortions of Mira Nair and Dinesh D'Souza." *Weber Studies* 15.1 (Winter 1998): 95-104.

Beth, Pinsker. "Filmer of the Bride; Mira Nair Talks About the Coming Monsoon." *The Independent Film and Video Monthly* 25.1 (2002): 30-32.

Bhabha, Homi. "Preface: Arrivals and Departures." Naficy vii-xii.

Desai, Jinga. *Beyond Bollywood: The Cultural Politics of South Asian Diasporic Film*. New York: Routledge, 2004.

Foster, Gwendolyn Audrey. "Mira Nair." *Women Filmmakers of the African & Asian Diaspora: Decolonizing the Gaze, Locating Subjectivity*. Carbondale, Il: Southern Illinois UP, 1997. 111-27.

James, Caryn. "Uno, Dos, Tres: A Miami Love Story." *The New York Times* May 12, 1995. <http://movie2.nytimes.com/mem/movies/review.html?title=&title2= PEREZ%20FAMILY. . .>

"The Language of being in between: The Biography of Mira Nair." <http://www.mirabaifilms.com/articles_6.html>

Mehta, Binita. "Emigrants Twice Displaced: Race, Color, and Identity in Mira Nair's *Mississippi Masala*." *Between the Lines: South Asians and Postcoloniality*. Ed. Deepika Bahri and Mary Vasudeva. Philadelphia: Temple UP, 1996. 185-203.

Mishra, Vijay. *Bollywood Cinema: Temples of Desire*. New York: Routledge, 2002.

_____. *An Accented Cinema: Exilic and Diasporic Filmmaking*. Princeton, NJ: Princeton UP, 2001.

Naficy, Hamid, ed. *Home, Exile, Homeland: Film, Media, and the Politics of Place*. New York: Routledge, 1999.

_____. "Between Rocks and Hard Places: The Interstitial Mode of Production in Exilic Cinema." Naficy 125-47.

Sharma, Alpana. "Body Matters: the Politics of Provocation in Mira Nair's Films." *Quarter Review of Film and Video* 18.1 (2001): 91-103.

## Filmography

Nair, Mira. *Children of a Desired Sex*. 1987.

______. *Hysterical Blindness*. HBO, 2002.

______. "India." *11'09'11—September 11*. Bac Films, 2002.

______. *Indian Cabaret*. 1985.

______. *Jama Masjid Street Journal*, 1979.

______. *Kama Sutra: A Tale of Love*. Trimark, 1997.

______. *Mississippi Masala*. SCS Films, 1992.

______. *Monsoon Wedding*. USA Films, 2002.

______. *My Own Country*. Showtime Networks, 1998.

______. *The Perez Family*. Samuel Goldwyn, 1995.

______. *Salaam Bombay!*. Cinecom, 1988.

______. *So Far from India*. 1982.

______. *Vanity Fair*. Gramercy, 2003.

# Landmarks in American Studies: The Example from Gertrude Stein, Picasso and the Armory Show

**Varghese John**
**Union Christian College, Alwaye**

This paper is partly on Gertrude Stein (1874-1946), the American experimental writer who emerged from the status of a literary outlaw to the distinction of a classic. It is also, briefly, about Pablo Picasso the Spanish painter with whom she shared much in artistic preoccupations and methods; about his cubist painting which ushered in a new understanding of artistic representation; about the Armory Show of 1913, an event that turned out to be a major landmark in American art and culture; and about the critical discovery of Stein as a modernist, postmodernist, and feminist. The paper also speculates on how the gradual popular, literary, and critical endorsement of twentieth century innovations in painting since the Armory Show must have been instrumental in the critical recognition of Stein.

Gertrude Stein has already been the subject of nearly twenty biographies, and this is certainly an indication of her increasing popularity. The scores of books and doctoral dissertations produced on her writings, besides the numerous articles that come out every year, are proof of her critical acclaim. The variety of Stein sites and hypertexts that occupy the 'web' suggest the diversity of interests she continues to evoke. At the Annual Conference of the Modern Language Association in Chicago in December 1999, one panel was named "Gertrude Stein: 125 Years of Continued Presence." The panel acknowledged: "because of Stein's continued presence, we finish the twentieth century with revised notions of what it means to be (post)modern, theatrical, ethnic, or lesbian."

The popularity of Gertrude Stein has been attributed to a variety of factors: the success of her cleverly titled and entertaining autobiography, *The Autobiography of Alice B. Toklas* (1933), in which she recreated the early twentieth century cultural ferment in Paris, with herself at its center (the book eliciting more than a hundred reviews in the first year itself); her successful tour of American lecture halls and college campuses as a celebrity in 1934 after three decades of expatriate life; and the recognition gained by Stein's artistic and literary friends like Picasso, Hemingway, Fitzgerald, Sherwood Anderson, Virgil Thomson, and many more. The academic world would appear to have caught up with the public interest, the first Gertrude Stein bibliography (by Julian Sawyer) appearing in 1941, followed by periodically updated checklists of writings by Stein; one of the first works of doctoral research on Stein (by Harry P. Garvin at the University of Michigan) being completed in 1950; the Yale edition of her unpublished writings appearing in eight volumes during 1951-58; the significance of Stein's views on subjects like time, genre, artistic representation and periodization (expressed without conventional theorizing) being recognized; the relation between her practice and precepts being explored; and several journals bringing out special issues for the Stein centenary in 1974. Stein's position was consolidated by the Eighties, with the perception that the avant-garde in a way represented the early beginnings of postmodernism and post-structuralism as well as much in feminist theory; and that Stein's writing, while effectively undermining hierarchical, patriarchal modes of signification, also problematizes marginalizations of several kinds.

An examination of Stein's reception as a modernist, postmodernist, and feminist will involve a study of the manner in which Stein responded to the artistic programs and polemics that surrounded her since her entry in 1903 into the Parisian milieu (of what Stephen Kern in the title of his 1983 book calls the "culture of time and space"). It will also involve a study of the tendency towards greater inclusiveness and crossing of disciplines that particularly characterizes recent Stein studies, the essential dynamics of American Studies.

The modernist movement, which began in the late nineteenth century, was a result of the scientific, philosophical, and political upheavals that began in Europe and formed part of the Enlightenment. The advances in Science, and Darwin's theory of evolution in particular, subverted the old perception of a religious and ethical order. Einstein's theory of relativity necessitated a new multiple perspective on the universe. Werner Heisenberg's formulation of the principle of uncertainty emphasized the importance of the viewpoint of the observer in determining reality, and the knowledge of reality came to be recognized as contingent on the perspective assumed by the perceiver. Sigmund Freud's theories about the unconscious and subconscious layers of the mind undermined the notion of the free and unitary personality. The different arts felt the need for new ways of representing space, time, and reality. It is generally understood how writers like Joyce and Eliot abandoned continuity of text in literature; artists like Picasso, Kandinsky and Paul Klee gave up perspective in painting; and musicians like Stravinsky and Schoenberg abolished harmony in music.

Realism has always been a fundamental mode in artistic creation from the earliest of times. The new understanding of the universe and of man brought in a new conception of the reality to be represented in literature and the arts. What was seen thus far as the natural way of seeing was now seen as nothing but a cultivated manner of perception. And it was realized that the reality that is perceived is essentially made up of fissures and discontinuities. The linearity implied in the ordering of material in conventional art and literature was found to be misleading. And each artist became preoccupied with the limitations of his/her medium.

Cubism, one of the major trends in modernist painting, was essentially a formalist art, concerned with the re-examination of pictorial conventions and norms. One of the paintings that ushered in the cubist movement was Picasso's *Les Demoiselles d' Avignon* (1907), and one of the major influences on this work was African sculpture. John Golding in his essay on cubism points out that "the Negro sculptor approaches his subject in a much more conceptual way; ideas about his subject are more important for him than a naturalistic depiction of it, with the result that he is led to forms that are at once more abstract and stylized, and in a sense more symbolic" (in Nicos Stangos 52-53). It was the interest in the formal aspects of painting that led to the evolution of cubist art.

Writers realized that it was the use of language that shaped the world around for human perception. And the conventional use of language with its linear ordering of reality was found to be inadequate in representing reality. It was the false linear ordering of conventional art that created the impression of coherent reality. In the perception of the modernists, reality was indeterminate and relational. It also included dreams, drives, and the consciousness of the perceiver. Reality was no more a coherent entity that lent itself to be rendered in linear fashion by the artist.

Gertrude Stein explains how travel in an automobile serves as a paradigm for the perception of reality as temporal, the different points of journey being experienced sequentially, in time. In contrast, travel in an airplane offers a view from above, the entire landscape existing as a piece in view at any moment. For the traveler in an automobile, the journey involves a sense of movement from one point to another. The view from the aircraft, on the other hand, remains nearly static, the changes perceived in the landscape from moment to moment being negligibly little. What little change is perceived may as well be the outcome of the shifts in the attention of the perceiver. The immensity of the view from the aircraft, with the numerous alternative possibilities of attention it offers, becomes for Stein a paradigm for the complex of the reality of twentieth century man's perception.

Gertrude Stein and Pablo Picasso first met in Paris in 1905 through the art dealer Clovis Sagot. Their acquaintance grew beyond the purchase of some of the earliest paintings of Picasso by Gertrude Stein and her art-collector brother Leo Stein. It developed into a mutually stimulating intimacy, though their talents belonged to two different media. They shared some of the burning concerns of early twentieth century art in the midst of what Roger Shattuck in the title of an impressive book on the epoch calls the "banquet years" of the *avant-garde*. There are interesting parallels between the ways in which both Picasso's innovations in painting and Stein's in writing derived from Cézanne's approach to his medium.

Stein's novel *The Making of Americans* and Picasso's painting *Les Demoiselles d'Avignon* are products of roughly the same historical moment and of comparable stages in the evolution of the two artists. They also share certain specific influences. The two works exhibit similarities of method, which also suggest similarities of basic concerns and convictions. Apart from the method of fragmentation common to both, they had each been planned to be a masterpiece. Both were begun primarily out of interest in the subject, but the formal interest soon took over. Both violate conventions of illusionism and employ a variety of styles.

Written sporadically during 1903-11 and first published in 1925, *The Making of Americans* in its original form ran into nearly a thousand pages, and is "a novel only in the loosest sense of the genre" (Kellner 45). As the title of the novel suggests, Stein's intention in *The Making of Americans* was to write a fictional account of the making of the American people. But the method she chose for this was to follow the fortunes of a family (the Hersland family which was modeled on her own) from its immigration to the United States, reaching up to the fourth generation, and moving across from Baltimore to Oakland in America. A keen awareness of the diversity among human beings made Stein give up the story of the family to devise a system to accommodate this diversity. Stein's primary interest turned to the analyzing and classifying of people. The narrative in effect becomes a record of the process of Stein's own understanding of human nature.

Besides her training in psychology and philosophy at Harvard, other factors too influenced Stein's understanding of human nature and reality, and her depiction of these in her writing. Her narrative method suggests the conviction that the process of knowing does not take place in the linear, chronological order presupposed by conventional narrative, or in the logical order of conventional expository prose. In the "*Translantic* Interview" of 1946, Stein told Robert Bartlet Haas that Paul Cézanne the French painter was one of the two major influences on her, the other being Gustave Flaubert (Haas 15). Leon Katz gives the evidence of Stein's "voluminous notes" for the impact of painting on her writing. And Jayne L. Walker concludes from the study of Stein's working notebooks that "she regarded Cézanne as the greatest master of the realization of the object itself, and Picasso as the only contemporary artist who was successfully following Cézanne's program." (3).

Stein pointed out that "Cézanne conceived the idea that in composition one thing was as important as another thing" (Haas 15). She went on to add that to her "[t]he realism of the composition . . . was the important thing, the realism of the composition of her *thoughts*" (6, emphasis mine). Once she became aware of this, she could no more be content with a narration of what she had already formulated in her mind. She would rather present the composition of the thought. She would also conceive of her fictional writing as a composition designed to produce a certain effect on the reader, not a slice of life meant for the reader's enjoyment of verisimilitude. Her writing thus becomes a composition meant to take the reader through a process in which numerous perceptions and impressions about people and events organize themselves in the mind through repeated occurrences and the associations they evoke.

The abstractionism and anti-illusionism in *The Making of Americans* consists of repeated descriptions of characters using variations of a limited vocabulary, as with the four women "strong to bear many children" (Stein 4), "the steady good one," "the little gentle weeping hopeless one" (50) and the "dreary little trickling woman" (59); returning time and again to the same characters and situations, frequently going back in time; occasional digressions on subjects with no apparent bearing on the rest of the narration (15,87); and detailed accounts of people associated with the Hersland family (172-73).

Without assuming the knowledge of everything, Stein uses language in such a way as to evoke impressions in the mind of the reader. Statements about characters often seem to convey knowledge about them. But the adjectives and the phraseology employed are such that the exact meaning remains vague and the knowledge conveyed is at best partial. The impressions, associations and bits of partial knowledge, some repeated, some supplemented incrementally, together organize themselves into a gradually accumulating sense of people and their relations, the diversity in human nature, and the apparent sameness and repetitiveness of everyday experience. While the book does not tell a story, it does present a world to the reader. Stein thus replaces conventional story telling by a more creative and original use of her medium, to which a parallel can be found in Picasso's use of his.

*Les Demoiselles* depicts five angular figures of nude or partially draped women, with some fruits in the foreground. One of the most striking features of the painting is the unusual fragmentation of the picture surface and distortion of the figures. The illusion of depth and volume expected in conventional painting is totally absent. Pierre Daix sums up and says: "Challengingly and irreversibly, Picasso at one bold stroke swept away the artifices of illusionism and set painting on an independent footing, as an autonomous art released from nature imitation and even from its own tradition" (31). This liberation from "the artifices of illusionism" is a common legacy from Cézanne, which Picasso shares with Stein.

Daix, among others, points out the unmistakable influence of Cézanne on Picasso's *Les Demoiselles d'Avignon* in its overall composition. Daix argues that Picasso must have seen a reproduction of Cézanne's *Five Bathers*, which hung on the wall of Derain's studio (which he used to visit). According to him, "on this same canvas by Cézanne he patterned the overall composition of his *Demoiselles d'Avignon*," though he broke the pattern on the right side of the picture "with the contrasting figure of seated girl taken over from another Cézanne picture of Bathers, the one with three women [then] owned by Matisse" (29).

More than this influence in overall design, Picasso learned from Cézanne's method, as Charles Altieri puts it, "how one could imagine space in painterly rather than sculptural forms" (22). From this Picasso realized the creative potential of his medium, which he was to substitute for its ability to produce conventional verisimilitude. This realization produced in him a yearning for formal freedom, which was one of the factors that goaded him into greater formal innovations in the successive preparatory studies he made for *Les Demoiselles*.

Both Gertrude Stein and Picasso, at crucial stages in their career, came under the profound influence of Cézanne whose fundamental thrust was on the creative potential of his medium, side by side with an acceptance of its limitations. The effect of this on either was an enhanced urge to explore anew the possibilities in their respective media. And the final outcome was the creation of two master works, *The Making of Americans* by Stein and *Les Demoiselles d'Avignon* by Picasso, each so radical and so significant as to constitute a new definition of the respective genre itself.

It was the Armory Show of 1913, which brought the innovations of European cubist painting to America. The event, organized by the Association of American Painters and Sculptors (AAPS) at the Sixty-ninth Regiment Armory in New York City, was described by Harold Rosenberg as the "Great Event in the history of American art." It exhibited nearly 1300 works, all of which had been produced after 1860, and nearly one-third of them were by Europeans. It also exhibited most of the leading new American artists. Alfred Stieglitz was the most widely acknowledged promoter of modernist painters in the United States at the time, as he gave exhibition space to all promising American modernist painters between 1910 and 1917. However, Douglas Tallack notes that the Armory Show laid "an artistic foundation by bringing European modernist paintings to the United States in much larger numbers than Stieglitz or any individual dealers could afford" (79). Among the major European movements represented at the Show were Impressionism, which was already fairly well known (Manet, Monet, and Renoir); Post-Impressionism (Van Gogh, Cezanne, and Gaugin); Neo-Impressionism (Seurat and Signac), and Fauvism (Dufy, Matisse, and Vlaminck). Cubism was represented by the works of Picabia, Picasso, Braque, Gleizes, Leger, and Duchamp. The "most important formal consequence of so much concentrated exposure to European modernism," according to Tallack, "was a challenge to realism or representational painting" (80). He quotes Peter Wollen:

> The history of art since the Renaissance until the modern period, had been one of homogenization: the exclusion of words from the picture-space, the restriction of point of view spatially and temporally (homogeneous space and single moment in time), the banishing of discontinuity [Qtd. Tallack 80).

The recognition of the radically innovative nature of Stein's writing practices is apparent in the titles of some of the early books on her: *Gertrude Stein: Form and Intelligibility* (Rosalind S. Miller); *The Development of Abstractionism in the Writings of Gertrude Stein* (Michael J. Hoffman, 1965); *A Primer for the Gradual Understanding of Gertrude Stein* (Robert Bartlet Haas, ed., 1971). Stein's style marked such departures from conventional (and even other modernist) writings that the academic world was left with no adequate terminology or critical tools to determine continuities and divergences.

A good deal of Stein scholarship from the earliest times focused on parallels her writing bears with painting, beyond the essential spatiality of the visual art. My own doctoral dissertation, "Gertrude Stein's Fiction: Painting as Design and Process" (Calicut University, 1993) examined the ways in which Stein approximates the methods of painting both in the design of her individual works and the evolving process of her narrative communication. Stein herself declared that Paul Cézanne, the

French painter, was one of the two most important influences on her (the other being Flaubert). There are interesting parallels between the ways in which both Picasso's innovations in painting and Stein's in writing derive from Cézanne's approach to his medium. Evoking outrage or indifference at first, both experimenters went on to be recognized classics later. The reception of Stein's literary output thus needs to be examined in relation to the changing perceptions and ideas that have overseen the emergence and gradual acceptance of the diverse trends in painting, as also the related social, ideological and institutional frameworks that mediate popular taste.

Marianne DeKoven in her book *A Different Language: Gertrude Stein's Experimental Writing* describes Stein's writing as a "different" language, as it disrupts conventional modes of signification and offers alternatives to them. In place of the linear, orderly, and coherent language of conventional use, the mode that Stein substitutes are "incoherent, open-ended, anarchic, irreducibly multiple, often focused on what Roland Barthes calls the 'magic of the signifier'" (xiii-xiv). Since the writing that this mode opposes is one that comes from a predominantly male oriented tradition, Stein's writing in effect becomes anti-patriarchal, asserting the feminist spirit long repressed by tradition. Since this writing disrupts coherence and closure and opens the possibility of a plurality of meanings, it assumes characteristics of postmodernist writing. Linguistic experimentation leads on to experiments in literary form and the blurring of generic distinctions. The critical response to Stein in recent times thus brings together several critical approaches and issues relating to psychology, philosophy, gender, culture, and the nature of language itself.

With the range of literary forms handled by Stein and the variety of styles experimented with, studies on these writings illustrated new possibilities in twentieth century criticism, and were instrumental in setting new patterns. A significant section of Stein scholarship examines how Stein's writing has enriched and redefined literary forms (*Exact Resemblance to Exact Resemblance: The Literary Portraiture of Gertrude Stein* by

Wendy Steiner, 1978; *Gertrude Stein: Autobiography and the Problem of Narration* by Shirley C. Neuman, 1979; *Gertrude Stein's Theatre of the Absolute* by Betsy Ryan, 1984, etc.). One major focus in recent studies on Stein, whether as the sole subject or otherwise, is primarily on ways in which Stein's writings yield to, or help illustrate, issues of theory, gender, politics, and genre (*The Turning Word: American Literary Modernism and Continental Theory* by Joseph N. Riddel, 1996; *Gender and Genre in Gertrude Stein* by Franziska Gygax, 1998; *Mapping the Private Geography: Autobiography, Identity, and America* by Gerri Reeves, 2001). Among recent contributions to Stein scholarship, *Gertrude Stein: The Language that Rises: 1923-1934* by Ulla E. Dydo (2003) gives a detailed analysis of the nature and implications of Stein's obscure writing of the period. Stein criticism has come to be increasingly marked by crossing of disciplines and inclusiveness of approaches. This plurality of approaches has been a striking feature of Stein studies since the Eighties, and a significant part of American literary scholarship.

Going far beyond mimesis, painting at the beginning of the twentieth century involved, and illustrated, a new understanding about the nature and function of art. The Armory Show, which brought America into closer contact with contemporary European art, challenged and changed the definition of art and the academic and popular attitude to it. The extent to which the growing familiarity with the equivalents in painting, of Stein's experiments, has helped her writing in course of time to appear less inaccessible, needs to be examined in detail. While the study of parallels and influences helps in the better understanding of the author, a closer study of popular taste is essential for assessing the significance of her contribution, and her critical recognition. Stein's critical reception thus needs to be examined in relation to the changing perceptions and ideas that have overseen the emergence and gradual acceptance of the diverse trends in painting.

## List of Works Cited and Consulted

Altieri, Charles. "Picasso's Collages and the Force of Cubism." *Kenyon Review* 6:2 (Spring 1984): 8-33.

Crunden, Robert M. *American Salons: Encounters with European Modernism, 1885-1917*. New York: Oxford UP, 1993.

Daix, Pierre. *Cubists and Cubism*. New York: Rizzoli International, 1982.

DeKoven, Marianne. *A Different Language: Gertrude Stein's Experimental Writing*. Madison: U. of Wisconsin P, 1983.

Golding, John. "Cubism." In Stangos: 50-78.

Haas, Robert Bartlett, ed. *A Primer for the Gradual Understanding of Gertrude Stein*. Los Angeles: Black Arrow Press, 1973.

Hoffman, Michael J. *The Development of Abstractionism in the Writings of Gertrude Stein*. Philadelphia: U of Pennsylvania P, 1965.

Katz, Leon. "Matisse, Picasso and Gertrude Stein." In *Museum of Modern Art*. 51-63.

Kellner, Bruce. *A Gertrude Stein Companion: Content with the Example*. New York: Greenwood Press, 1988.

Kern, Stephen. *The Culture of Time and Space*. Cambridge: Harvard U P, 1983.

*Museum of Modern Art. Four Americans in Paris: The Collection of Gertrude Stein and Her Family*. New York, 1970.

Shattuck, Roger. *The Banquet Years: The Origins of the Avant Garde in France: 1885 to World War 1*. New York: Vintage, 1968.

Stangos, Nikos, ed. *Concepts of Modern Art*. London: Thames and Hudson, 1985.

Stein, Gertrude. *The Making of Americans*. New York: Harcourt: Brace and World, 1962.

Tallack, Douglas. *Twentieth Century America: The Intellectual and Cultural Context*. London: Longman, 1991.

Walker, Jayne L. *The Making of a Modernist: Gertrude Stein from 'Three Lives' to 'Tender Buttons*.' Amherst: U of Massachusetts P, 1984.

# Trauma, Re(-)membering, and Reconciliation: On Maya Lin's Vietnam Veterans Memorial

**Te-hsing Shan**
**Institute of European and American Studies, Academia Sinica, Taiwan**

> History is the subject of a structure whose site is not homogeneous, empty time, but time filled by the presence of the now.
>
> Walter Benjamin

> The purpose of this memorial is to separate the issue of the sacrifices of the veterans from the U.S. policy in the war, thereby creating a venue for reconciliation.
>
> National Park Service, U.S. Department of the Interior

> I consider the monuments to be true hybrids, existing between art and architecture, they have a specific need or function, yet their function is truly symbolic.
>
> Maya Lin

## Background: "Where Have All the Soldiers Gone?"

Fought between 1957 and 1975, the Vietnam War (or, "the American War" from the perspective of the Vietnamese) has exerted lasting and indelible effects on the American psyche. In addition to a heavy financial price of more than US$200 billion, the Vietnam War also had a devastating human toll. Whereas it is extremely difficult to calculate exactly how many people on both sides were killed or wounded in the war, more than 50,000 Americans were killed in action, more than 300,000 were wounded, and many remain missing to this day. No wonder it has been regarded as one of the most tragic chapters in the history of the United States and *the* most traumatic American experience in the second half of the twentieth century, particularly for those who were personally involved in the war.

Coming back from the Vietnam War, many veterans found themselves unwelcome and ostracized in a society strongly critical of the war they fought in. As Kim Servart Theriault points out, "The aftermath of the Vietnam era was traumatic and can be characterized through marginalization, confusion, and loss" (422). The idea of constructing the Vietnam Veterans Memorial (hereafter abbreviated as "VVM") came from Jan Scruggs, who served in Vietnam from 1969 to 1970 as an infantry corporal. After seeing the movie *The Deer Hunter* and the strong impact the war had on its veterans, Scruggs decided to set up a memorial for the Vietnam veterans. Together with Robert Doubek and John Wheeler—both lawyers and veterans—they founded the Vietnam Veterans Memorial Fund, Inc. (hereafter abbreviated as the "VVMF") in 1979, a non-profit charitable organization aiming at establishing a "memorial to acknowledge and recognize the service and sacrifice of all who served in Vietnam." There were four criteria for the design of this memorial as outlined by the group:

1. be reflective and contemplative in character;
2. harmonize with its surroundings;
3. contain the names of those who had died in the conflict or who were still missing;
4. make no political statement about the war.[1]

It can be clearly seen from these criteria that the original idea of the VVM was to highlight the reflective, contemplative, natural, and personal aspects, avoiding the complex and still controversial debate over the war.

How should one face this devastating war? How should one recall this unique trauma known as the Vietnam War? How can the past be represented not only collectively, but also individually? How can bygone traumas be represented to help create a more hopeful and peaceful future? What roles do gender and ethnicity play in remembering and reconciling the past? These are vital questions which were bundled with the aforementioned four criteria and these questions emerged when

Maya Ying Lin (Lin Yin in Chinese *pinyin*), a 21-year-old second-generation Asian American female undergraduate, won the national design competition for the VVM.

Born in Athens, Ohio, USA, October 5, 1959, Lin's parents were Chinese intellectuals who came to the United States in the late 1940s when the Communist Party took over Mainland China. Her father, Henry Huan Lin, a ceramist, was once the Dean of Fine Arts at Ohio University, and her mother, Julia Chang Lin, was a professor of literature.[2] Growing up in this liberal and artistic environment, Maya Lin developed her love for art very early and decided to study architecture since it simultaneously combines art and mathematics. She received her B.A. and M.A. from the School of Architecture, Yale University, in 1981 and 1986, respectively, but it was in her senior year as an architecture student in 1980 that Lin entered a national design competition for the VVM to be built in Washington, D.C. Each design submitted was given a number to ensure anonymity. The design by this young Chinese American student was chosen by the jury from pieces submitted by more than 1400 competitors—some of them well-established artists and architects. While this honor came as a pleasant surprise for the then 21-year-old college student, the ensuing controversy was less so. It was with her perseverance and "strong clear vision"[3] that she personally responded to the various challenges and attacks (some of them focusing on her gender and ethnicity) and oversaw the whole construction process until the VVM (also known as "the Wall") was formally dedicated and officially opened to the public on November 11, 1982.

Despite the heated controversy it aroused in the earlier stages, Lin's design not only has stood the test of time, but also has become one of the most popular, revered, appreciated, and "touching" public memorials in the United States—"touching" not only emotionally, but also physically, as this intimate design allows visitors to actually touch the names of the killed and the missing in the War.[4] And it indeed fulfills what Lin's idea about a memorial should be: "honest about the reality of war, about the loss of life in war, and about remembering those who served and especially those who died" (4:09).

**Trauma, Remembrance, and Identity**

In *Unclaimed Experience: Trauma, Narrative, and History*, Cathy Caruth points out the transformation of the meaning of the word "trauma" in the West: "the Greek *trauma*, or 'wound,' originally refer[s] to an injury inflicted on a body. In its later usage, particularly in the medical and psychiatric literature, and most centrally in Freud's text, the term *trauma* is understood as a wound inflicted not upon the body but upon the mind" (3). Because of this inward turn, Caruth defines trauma as "the response to an unexpected or overwhelming violent event or events that are not fully grasped as they occur, but return later in repeated flashbacks, nightmares, and other repetitive phenomena" (91). This is in agreement with Freud's description of trauma as "the response to a sudden or unexpected threat of death that happens too soon to be fully known and is then endlessly repeated in reenactments and nightmares that attempt to relive, but in fact only miss again, the original event" (139 n.2).

Whereas Caruth's definition of trauma is generally acceptable, her explanation of traumatic experience stresses its paradoxical nature in terms of belatedness and incomprehensibility: "The repetitions of the traumatic event . . . suggest a larger relation to the event that extends beyond what can simply be seen or what can be known, and is inextricably tied up with the belatedness and incomprehensibility that remain at the heart of this repetitive seeing" (92). In *Writing History, Writing Trauma*, Dominick LaCapra also emphasizes the characteristic belatedness and incomprehensibility of trauma, since "[t]rauma is a disruptive experience that disarticulates the self and creates holes in existence; it has belated effects that are controlled only with difficulty and perhaps never fully mastered" (41). He mentions elsewhere that "[t]rauma indicates a shattering break or cesura in experience which has belated effects" (186).

What is of special significance is Caruth's argument that while a traumatic event is often incomprehensible, it is not totally impenetrable. She argues that through "the notion of trauma . . . we can understand that a rethinking of reference is aimed not at eliminating history but at resituating it in our understanding, that is, at precisely permitting *history* to arise where *immediate understanding* may not" (11). In other words, to better understand the once incomprehensible traumatic event, we must resort to history by "resituating it in our understanding." History, then, is not only not beyond recollection, but is not even past. Instead of "letting bygones be bygones," we must view, or rather, re-view the past from the present perspective so as to grasp and re-claim the meaning of a traumatic event which was denied us when it first occurred.

The idea of representing a trauma is very important to LaCapra, who thinks that "[w]riting trauma would be one of those telling aftereffects in what I termed traumatic and post-traumatic writing (or *signifying practice in general*" (186, emphasis added). LaCapra thus elaborates on this signifying practice and its significance:

> It involves processes of acting out, working over, and to some extent working through in analyzing and "giving voice" to the past—processes of coming to terms with traumatic "experiences," limit events, and their symptomatic effects that achieve articulation in different combinations and hybridized forms. (186)

Moreover, it must be pointed out that the significance of remembering an event and dealing with a trauma is not limited to the past or our understanding of the past. It is related to the way we define ourselves in the present and what we want to become in the future. As Andreas Huyssen indicates, "Remembrance shapes our links to the past, and the ways we remember define us in the present. As individuals and societies, we need the past to construct and anchor our identities and to nurture a vision of the future" (249). In short, how we remember the past relates to how we see ourselves now and how we conceive our future self, just as the effort to remember and understand a past event serves to help identify ourselves.

Then, how do we deal with a collective trauma like the Vietnam War and, in doing, anchor ourselves in the past, present, and future? In what follows I will argue that the construction of the VVM is a concrete way to confront that collective traumatic experience in the American psyche and that the controversy surrounding the VVM construction process embodied the American people's strenuous attempt to understand, reconcile, and transcend that formerly repressed and incomprehensible trauma.

## Design, Intention and Debate

*OED* defines a "memorial" as "something by which the memory of a person, thing, or event is preserved, as a monumental erection, a custom or an observance." Arthur Danto also has this to say about the function of monuments and memorials: "we erect monuments so that we shall always remember, and build memorials so that we shall never forget" (152). The VVM, as its name indicates, aims at preserving the memory of the veterans who served in the Vietnam War. According to the official website of the VVM, "This is not a war Memorial but a Memorial to those who served in the war, both living and dead." In order to achieve this aim, the VVMF formulated the aforementioned four criteria as a guideline for how to remember and represent this national trauma through a tangible national memorial. In October 1980, the VVMF announced this news not only to invite interested designers, but also to arouse the attention of the American people in general. Warm responses came from all over the country. A jury appointed by the VVMF anonymously judged the 1421 design entries submitted and finally chose Entry Number 1026 as the winner on May 1, 1981.[5] What the designer and the jury did not expect was the ensuing controversy over this design. Before delving into that controversy, however, let us first look at the design itself and the designer's concept.

The design itself meets all the criteria set by VVMF, though it goes against the conventional conception of a memorial as "a monumental erection." First of all, it was conceived to be harmonious with the overall plan of Constitution Gardens, though in a way running counter to more traditional memorials. As Lin recalls, when she first came to the site, "I had a simple impulse to cut into the earth." She continues, "I imagined taking a knife and cutting into the earth, opening it up, an initial violence and pain that in time would heal" (4: 10). Instead of an abrupt erection from the earth, it was deliberately designed as something down-to-earth, or rather, something down-into-the-earth; some people have even described the VVM as an open wound on the earth allowing visitors a chance to view or touch the gash. If one moves along the VVM from one end to the other, the long slope makes pilgrim-like visitors descend gradually to the center of the memorial and rise again, a process full of symbolic and spiritual significance. Secondly, the polished black granite, of which the VVM was made, reflects not only the natural surroundings, but also the visitors themselves who come to pay homage to the Vietnam veterans a lot of the visitors are the Vietnam veterans themselves or their families, friends, and loved ones. The mirror-like surface, with the names of thousands of veterans who died or are still missing, allows the visitors not only to see the names but also to see themselves seeing. This is "reflective and contemplative in character," indeed.[6] Moreover, so far as the location and direction are concerned, the Wall seems to simultaneously reach out its "arms" eastward to the Washington Monument and westward to the Lincoln Memorial, thus situating itself squarely within the glorious pages of American history. In short, this unconventional design unites human, historical, natural, and spiritual dimensions.

To John R. Gillis, the VVM, "with its wall of names, is generally agreed to represent a turning point in the history of public memory, a decisive departure from the anonymity of the Tomb of the Unknown Soldier and a growing acknowledgment that everyone now deserves equal recognition at all times in wholly accessible places" (13). However, this status is not acquired without contestation. As John Bodnar points out, "a storm of controversy erupted" after the VVM was unveiled in 1981. He summarizes the controversy as follows:

> One side argued that the design lacked a sense of patriotism and glory. These critics felt that the memorial emphasized death and mourning to a disproportionate extent and was nothing but a "black gash of shame" to the nation. Defenders of the design, however, thought the memorial met their powerful need to express empathy for fallen soldiers, often comrades they had known, and to recognize all who suffered. Their commemorative impulse did not originate in any drive to honor the nation-state. (74)[7]

In addition, Mock's documentary *Maya Lin—A Strong Clear Vision* not only chronicles the designer's career from undergraduate student to established artist, but also provides a graphic record of the whole controversy. Apart from the issue of glory, heroism, and patriotism, other issues such as ethnicity, gender, and age were also raised. Since the Vietnam War was fought in Asia, and North Vietnam was allied with Communist China, the designer's identity as a Chinese American was called into question. Similarly, some people doubted whether a female artist was able to undertake this supposedly "masculine" work of designing a memorial dedicated to the veterans of the most traumatic war fought by the USA in the second half of the twentieth century. There was also doubt whether a young and inexperienced college student was able to understand the significance of the memorial to such an extent as to represent it in an artistic way. Despite the heated debate during the process and the compromise that two statues and a flagpole were added near the VVM, time has proven that the VVM is one of the most special, intimate, touching, accessible, and favorite memorials that has ever been designed in the US. It is Lin's artistic, humane, and humanitarian vision as well as her strong determination which carried this design through the heated controversy, which, in my opinion, signifies the American people's effort to come to terms with a trauma of incomprehensible proportions.

## Trauma, Representation, and Reflection

In what follows I will treat the VVM as an attempt to address an incomprehensible trauma in such a way that people can face it squarely and, thus, come to reconcile it with their past and future. In spite of or, rather, because of its controversy, the process was participatory and the result was healing and reconciliatory to a great extent.

As mentioned above, both Caruth and LaCapra regard belatedness and incomprehensibility as two characteristics of trauma. LaCapra also addresses trauma in terms of affect and representation:

> Trauma brings about a dissociation of affect and representation: one disorientingly feels that one cannot represent; one numbingly represents what one cannot feel. Working through trauma involves the effort to articulate or rearticulate affect and representation in a manner that may never transcend, but may to some viable extent counteract, a reenactment, or acting out, of that disabling dissociation. (42)

Viewed from this perspective, the conception and construction of the VVM and the controversy involved can be seen as "working through trauma." Significantly, it was Scruggs, a Vietnam veteran himself, who initiated the idea of setting up a memorial in recognition of the contribution of those who served in Vietnam. The VVMF was founded in April 1979, several years after the end of the Vietnam War. Although somewhat belated, this plan marked the beginning of concerted efforts to face the collective trauma, to articulate and represent it, and to reconnect affect and representation.

The announcement of the competition for the design was significant in several respects. Recognizing that the US government would not initiate this kind of memorial because of the controversial nature of this war and the breach it created among Americans, this memorial project itself stood for an alternative and civil endeavor motivated by the Vietnam veterans themselves to construct something in memory of those who died or are missing in the War. And the anonymous competition was an egalitarian way of ensuring that all those who submitted their designs were given a fair and equal opportunity, and the competition would not be monopolized by famous designers or big companies. In other words, the Vietnam veterans themselves took the initiative to represent themselves and, by making this plan public, not only invited artists and architects to take part in this competition, but also encouraged American citizens to participate and not to leave a past trauma, however tragic it might be, buried and unnoticed. This act clearly demonstrated the agency and subjectivity of the Vietnam veterans, who in their courage and willingness to face their traumatic past, called for the participation of artists and their countrymen to face this public memory and collective trauma known as the Vietnam War.

No design can satisfy all people, of course. However, the controversy immediately after the jury's announcement of the result of the competition was unusually strong. Among those who were against Lin's design, some disliked the black color, saying that it symbolized death and mourning, while others complained that the design itself was like a wound on the ground; some thought that it did not express the spirit of heroism and patriotism that war memorials were conventionally charged with conveying; still others took exceptions to the designer's gender and/or ethnicity (the derogatory expression "gook" was applied to her). All these became part of the strong opposition to Lin's design, and sometimes against even the designer personally.

However, Lin and the jury stood firm. In my view, the controversy served to further the whole process of articulating, representing, and reconciling in the face of this previously buried and, thus, nebulous trauma. In other words, both sides of the debate joined together in making sense of that particular trauma by expressing their feelings and thoughts on *how* to represent it and *why*. It is through this participatory process that the VVM became not only a site of memory or a site of contestation in which different emotions (be it frustration, dissatisfaction, anger, despair, etc.) found an outlet, but also a means for exchange—no matter how heated and quarrelsome these exchanges might be. The participation in and exchange of emotions and ideas from various perspectives were an effective way of confronting a past trauma, articulating a collective memory, and making sense of and coming to terms with various things associated with the greatest loss of American lives in the second half of the twentieth century. To facilitate national healing, the process was necessary and indispensable. Because of this vehement exchange of ideas, some compromise had been made. As the VVM stands now, it is composed of three parts, "the Wall" (as designed by Lin), the three servicemen statue and flagpole, and the women in service to the Vietnam War statue, two additions with a traditional appeal to heroism and patriotism. Despite being somewhat different from Lin's original design, the Wall is still the most touching and spectacular section of the entire Memorial.

What characterizes this site of memory is that it radically transforms people's idea of a memorial as something to be looked upon and admired from afar. In fact, Lin's design allows visitors to gain access to and really touch the names of the deceased and missing Vietnam veterans. For those whose family members, friends, and loved ones were lost in the war especially, the names themselves hold power and serve to cast emotional spells upon them, so to speak. This accessibility, or rather, "touchability," provides real immediacy and intimacy. In addition to the public aspect of a national memorial, by etching individual names into the black granite, Lin's design highlights a personal dimension as well.

The polished granite is an instrument of reflection in both a literal and metaphorical sense. The polished granite with carved names allows the visitors both to see the names and to see themselves mourning the dead or the missing in a beautiful setting. This granite wall, then, not only reflects the images of the visitors and the things brought to the Memorial by them,[8] but also provides a chance to ponder and reflect upon the various meanings embodied by the Wall. While objectively reflecting the images of its visitors, the Wall provides a chance for visitors to contemplate their own feelings of sadness and loss. In a sense, what and how much the visitors bring back from the Wall depends on what and how much they bring to it. Theriault compares the Wall to a screen, for "what people see or do not see in The Wall is their own projection" (429). The Wall stands there quietly, reflecting.

Furthermore, Lin's special design for the Wall as something carved into the earth serves an important function. As visitors move along the Wall from either end, they descend step by step and the Wall rises as they proceed until it is more than ten feet tall at the center. At that point, the Wall seems to shelter the visitors with a sense of quietude, serenity, and peacefulness. As they ascend, the Wall seems to become shorter with each of their steps until the visitors emerge out of its shadow. This passage of descent and ascent also metaphorically reflects the emotional and spiritual movement of the visitors. That is to say, as the visitors descend by degrees along the Wall, and see, and even touch the names etched on the black granite, their emotion will inevitably be affected by their journey. The path of the Wall serves to draw out their personal emotions and thoughts, and as a result, a certain degree of purgation and catharsis is attained. The further movement to the other end of the Wall marks a rise, both emotionally and spiritually. So, the visit to the VVM serves as some kind of a spiritual journey as the visitors tend to leave the Wall with a certain degree of relief, reflection, and, hopefully, reconciliation after confronting their own images reflected upon the names of the dead and missing.

It might seem to be somewhat naïve to draw this kind of optimistic conclusion that responses to the Wall are uniformly positive. For, as Hass points out, "The Wall elicits a physical response. It has inspired visitors to represent their own grief, loss, rage, and despair" (21). However, as I have attempted to argue, to be able to represent and articulate one's emotions in the face of trauma is itself an important step towards penetrating the former's incomprehensibility. This is precisely the "fundamental goal" of Lin's design, "to be honest with death, since we must accept that loss in order to begin to overcome it. The pain of the loss will always be there, it will always hurt, but we must acknowledge the death in order to move on" (Lin 4: 10). Two examples will suffice to illuminate this idea. The first is Hass's study of the things carried to the Wall. In her attempt to study the relationship between the VVM and American memory via these left objects, she skilfully demonstrates people's responses to Lin's design. According to Hass, even before the VVM was completed, people brought objects to the Wall and "by 1993 the collection included well over 250,000 objects of every shape, size, and description" (23). Incredibly numerous and diversified as they are, "[t]he range of the objects in the collection is a testament not only to how intensely the war is still felt but also to the continuing need to negotiate its memory." Although most of those who left things at the Wall did not leave their names, the continuous visits and objects left testify to the fact that there is residual pain and an on-going negotiation with one of the most traumatic experiences in American history. Separately, these objects "make their own particular memorials. Yet together they are a noisy, insistent response to the problem of the memory of all Vietnam veterans" (24).

My second example is the literary works appearing in the literary section of the VVM website. As of January 2005, there are about 140 pieces, mostly poems, written by those who visited the Wall. These works not only describe the physical presence of the Wall, but also express the emotions and thoughts of those who are, in effect, leaving their literary objects at the Wall. Unlike the bearers of objects, the producers of these literary works sign their names, and these signed pieces on the website reflect the authors' efforts to represent the Wall and to make sense of its deeper significance.[9]

In short, the mirror-like wall and the names on it offer a chance for the visitors to simultaneously face the dead, the missing (whose memory and contemplation constitute an indispensable part of one's self), and themselves. This contemplation and self-reflection are vital for the healing process not only on a personal level, but also on a national and even human level. The very fact that Lin is a female, an Asian, and a young person (only a student when she took part in the national competition), instead of forming obstacles to people's understanding of the VVM and its significance, turns out to symbolize the broader participation of people in the healing of the nation regardless of sexual, ethnic, and age boundaries. The Wall and the various responses it elicits thus remind people of the American spirit, which honors a nation "of the people, by the people, and for the people."

## Trauma, Re(-)membering, and Reconciliation

This paper aims to argue that there is no escaping history and no evading trauma. In order to lay the souls of the dead and the living at rest, it is necessary to face history and trauma squarely. The significance of the VVM is that it offers a site for the American people to personally address the most traumatic chapter of their history in the second half of the twentieth century. It is only through *con*-fronting (viz. facing together) the past that people might be better able to view the past as it was and thus see themselves more clearly. It is of special significance that Vietnam veterans took the initiative to face this collective American memory, and Lin's design provides an artifact, which is touching and reflecting in both literary and metaphorical senses. This touching and reflecting wall gives the surviving veterans and the visitors an opportunity to pay homage to the deceased and the missing and to reflect upon the past and, hopefully, to bring forth a more reflective and peaceful future. The controversy during the construction period, though vehement and sometimes even hostile, is indispensable for this collective effort to confront the past and reflects the different ways people choose to face a belated yet incomprehensible trauma. This debate is an important part of the participatory, reflective, reconciliatory, and healing process. And the resultant three-section VVM is a compromise, which tries to incorporate the emotional needs, artistic demands, and cultural imaginaries of different people. The fact that the Wall has been subject to "revisions and compromise" shows that "[t]he multitude of meanings inscribed in The Wall reflect larger cultural issues as basic as right and wrong, good and bad, and as complicated as gender inequity, racism, constructions of identity, masculinities, and cultural, social, and political memory" (Theriault 421). Visiting the VVM and moving along the Wall allows people to go down the slope gradually, get close to the names of those lost in the war, and journey upward to the other end of the Wall. It is through this personal emotional arousal and the down- and up-ward movement that people express and sublimate their emotions and reconcile their memories.

The whole design and its aftermath show that public memory is at its core contested and participatory. The fact that VVM has drastically changed people's view of memorials and that it has become one of the most popular memorials in the US demonstrates that it offers a site of memory and reflection where past wounds can be confronted directly, accepted, coped with, and healed to a certain extent. The Wall brings together the names of the deceased and the missing together with those people reading and touching these names. Through this reflecting Wall, the seen and the seeing, the dead and the living, the past and the present, the human and the natural are brought together. People not only remember things about that tragic war, but also re-member, viz., becoming once again members of the community. Through this memorial, much of the breach due to the war has been somewhat reconciled and the community re(-)membered. In front of Lin's simple, direct, reflecting, and powerful design, the past trauma and collective memory are to be viewed, felt, and reflected upon over and over again. As an interface, the VVM connects a traumatic past and a (reflecting) present, and, hopefully, will bring in a better future.

## NOTES

1. For related information, see the official website of the VVM at http://thewall-usa.com/information.
2. Hui-yin Lin, Maya Lin's aunt, and her husband were internationally known architects in China.

3. This phrase is taken from the title of Frieda Lee Mock's documentary "Maya Lin—A Strong Clear Vision," which chronicles Lin's career from an architecture student at Yale to a well-known artist. This film won the 1995 Academy Award for Best Documentary.
4. There are 58,245 names as of 2004 and, among them, about 1200 were listed as missing (mostly as MIA's and POW's). See the official VVM website.
5. As Doubek recalls in the documentary *A Strong Clear Vision*, the jury was "made up of two architects, two landscape architects, two sculptors, and one humanist."
6. As Lin herself remarks, she chose the black granite as "an interface, between our world and the quieter, darker, more peaceful world beyond. I chose black granite in order to make the surface reflective and peaceful. I never looked at the memorial as a wall, an object, but as an edge to the earth, an opened side. The mirrored effect would double the size of the park, creating two worlds, one we are a part of and one we cannot enter" (4; 10-11).
7. For details, see Jan C. Scruggs and Joel Swerdlow's *To Heal a Nation: The Vietnam Veterans Memorial* and Kristin Ann Hass's *Carried to the Wall: American Memory and the Vietnam Veterans Memorial*.
8. For a detailed analysis of the things carried to the Wall and their significance, see Hass's *Carried to the Wall*.
9. See http://thewall-usa.com/literary/index.html. A lot of the pieces bear "the Wall" either as their full titles, or part of their titles. Therefore, it might be interesting to compare the poems named "The Wall" written by Wolfgang Hummel, Kaye B. McCoy, Julius Marvin Hart, Jr., and Tom Cordle, respectively

## List of Works Cited and Consulted

Bodnar, John. "Public Memory in an American City: Commemoration in Cleveland." *Commemorations: The Politics of National Identity*. Ed. John Gills.74-89.

Caruth, Cathy. *Unclaimed Experience: Trauma, Narrative, and History*. Baltimore and London: Johns Hopkins, 1996.

Danto, Arthur. "The Vietnam Veterans Memorial." *The Nation* 31 (Aug. 1985): 152-55.

Gillis, John R., ed. *Commemorations: The Politics of National Identity*. Princeton, NJ: Princeton UP, 1994.

Hass, Kristin Ann. *Carried to the Wall: American Memory and the Vietnam Veterans Memorial.* Los Angeles and Berkeley: U of California P, 1998.

Huyssen, Andreas. *Twilight Memories: Marking Time in a Culture of Amnesia.* New York and London: Routledge, 1995.

LaCapra, Dominick. *Writing History, Writing Trauma.* Baltimore and London: Johns Hopkins, 2001.

Lin, Maya. *Boundaries.* New York and London: Simon & Schuster, 2000.

Mock, Freida Lee, dir. *Maya Lin: A Strong Clear Vision.* 1995.

Scruggs, Jan C., and Joel Swerdlow. *To Heal a Nation: The Vietnam Veterans Memorial.* New York: Harper and Row, 1985.

Theriault, Kim Servart. "Re-membering Vietnam; War, Trauma, and 'Scarring Over' after 'The Wall.'" *Journal of American Culture* 26.4 (Dec. 2003): 421-31.

*The Vietnam Veterans Memorial.* 5 January 2005 <http://thewall-usa.com/>.

# Cities from the Dead: Wrestling with the Past in Early Black Engagements with Gettysburg

**Debashish Lahiri**
**Lal Baba College**
**Belurmath, Howrah**

No visitor, claims Jim Weeks, can help but notice the seemingly schizophrenic nature of the Gettysburg battlefield. On the heights immediately south of town, where the Army of the Potomac once formed the center of its line of battle, soldiers' graves now compete for space alongside motels, T-shirt stands, and snack bars. It is a paradigm repeated in countless ways across the Gettysburg landscape, an apparent struggle between commemoration and carnival. Yet, to view Gettysburg as a contest between the sacred and the commercial is to misunderstand both the origin and the development of this uniquely American attraction. The relationship is not adversarial but symbiotic. Gettysburg never was at odds with the marketplace, which instead played a major role in 'constructing and deconstructing the shrine' (Weeks 7).

This essay proposes to delve into some aspects of the complexities of memory and identity politics at play among the early tourists to Gettysburg, especially the blacks. It shall also argue that practices of remembrance at the site were necessarily politicized along racial lines, evidenced by the ways individuals and groups 'performed' memory in the physical space of the site. This essay also tries to consider just whose history and what memory is presented and interpreted at such sites like Gettysburg. The concept of memory employed here is intricately tied to a textured understanding of authenticity. Using the theoretical work of Dean MacCannell on staged authenticity in tourist sites, the specific structure of the early Black commemoration and reclamation of history, through tourist forays, is examined.

In August 1899, two Philadelphians sponsored a watermelon-eating contest at a park in Pennsylvania. Offering a prize of $2.50 "to the coloured gentleman" who could devour a watermelon in the shortest possible time, the hosts recruited eight black males. A large crowd gathered around the line of contestants, each of whom received a Georgia watermelon cut into slices. According to a newspaper account, the competitors who tore into the melons "were in bliss" because "they were eating their own favorite fruit, with a prize in view." In just four minutes a Virginian named George Smockes finished his last slice to claim the prize. "Some of the spectators laughed at the funny spectacle until they cried," the paper reported. Such racially demeaning amusement was hardly unusual around the turn of the twentieth century. At great fairs and amusement parks, symbols of the era's new commercial leisure, "coon dunks," or hitting the "coon" with a baseball, watermelon-eating contests, or performing "darkeys" were common. In a nascent mass culture, new white-collar and working-class Americans of diverse European backgrounds were bonded by a feeling of white superiority through racially demeaning entertainment (*Gettysburg Star & Sentinel*, Aug. 15, 1899).

The watermelon-eating contest cited above occurred at Gettysburg, a site sacred in American memory. By 1899 veterans had transformed the scene of slaughter into a genteel memorial park that served as the nation's meeting ground for Blue-Gray reconciliation. Although foreign papers such as the *British Northern Whig* commented that "the tablets at Gettysburg commemorate one of the most significant events of the present century, the death of slavery and the dawn of civil liberty," this recognition was rare in American observations about the battle's significance. The Civil War's seminal issue and continuing racial challenges were overlooked in the interest of national unity at the "Mecca of Reconciliation," especially at Gettysburg's monumental fiftieth anniversary reunion. Although first-person accounts describe black veterans attending the spectacle, the ceremonies and official pronouncements disregarded racial matters altogether (Blight 4-5).

Slavery and its legacy not only were ignored at Gettysburg's sacred memorial performances, solemn gatherings, parades, or speeches, but were also separated from the war's memory by the festivities held there. Like other shrines, Gettysburg has served as an oasis for expressing social extremes of veneration and play. Play, defined here as release from work and responsibility through amusement, existed at the shrine in both traditional and modern forms until the traditional disappeared after the turn of the century. In the late nineteenth and early twentieth centuries, both black and white visitors to Gettysburg brought the spontaneous, communal revelry characteristic of traditional or premodern play, while impresarios of modern commercial culture operated a variety of controlled, rational diversions (Blight 5). Memory is organic and continually revised through new experience, so play at a site of memory can affect the thing being remembered as powerfully as commemorative rituals. This part of my essay argues that both premodern and modern forms of play at Gettysburg have served commemorative purposes that contributed to the exclusion of African Americans from the war's larger meaning.

Historically the Gettysburg neighborhood offered a chilly cultural climate for engaging racial issues. Gettysburg's own black community lived on the edge of town in substandard conditions. The town's Democratic paper continually stirred racial animosity for townspeople who showed little sympathy for black equality. No hostelries welcomed black tourists, and not until well after the turn of the twentieth century did a boardinghouse open expressly for African Americans. Antics of visiting black groups received detailed coverage and censure in the local press, and black tourists also served as a source of amusement for whites.[1] Sometimes white organizations using the sacred ground could be downright hostile to African Americans. When National Guardsmen from Virginia and Maryland encamped with black U.S. Regulars on the battlefield in 1910, several racial incidents erupted. In the ugliest episode a Virginian became enraged when a black trooper sat at the same bar in the Hotel Gettysburg. A brawl ensued that spilled into the square and continued until mounted guards arrived. When a Virginia militia band struck up "Dixie" at the camp on the Fourth of July, a "mighty shout arose" and "the air penetrated to all parts of the camp." In 1925 ten thousand Ku Klux Klan members dressed in colorful capes conducted a rally on monument-covered Oak Ridge in "a sea of red, white, and blue." Klansmen had pasted "On to Gettysburg" stickers to their trucks and cars, "a splendid advertisement for Gettysburg," in the opinion of the *Gettysburg Times* (Gallman 149).

Nevertheless, this town situated on the border between former slave and free states became the nation's chief site for remembering the Civil War. Because a modern, industrializing nation fought the Civil War, the conflict's memory unfolded in part as a leisure commodity for an expanding commercial culture. Nowhere has the market for Civil War memory found a fuller expression than at Gettysburg. Memory at Gettysburg was and continues to be a current event, floated by the latest communication technologies and marketing techniques. Immediately after the battle, boosters began transforming the crimson fields into a tourist site, aided by photographers, artists, and publishers whose commercial representations of the battle enhanced Gettysburg's sacredness. Hosting continual dedications, parades, and other rituals, Gettysburg became the "representative battleground of the Civil War." According to one guidebook, it is "the most consecrated ground this world contains." Veterans erected so many monuments that the battlefield looked like "a vast cemetery" to visitors (Blight 384).

Yet Gettysburg increasingly served as more than a sacred site of memory after a second railroad line eased access from eastern population centers in 1884. To encourage plebeians to ride the rails to Gettysburg, the Gettysburg & Harrisburg Railroad not only slashed fares but constructed Round Top Park, an amusement area between the Round Tops and Devil's Den that appealed to working-class tastes. For all the solemnity of the battlefield's funeral grandeur, commercial enterprises and the crowds they attracted gave Gettysburg a festive air. The juxtaposition of a park for merrymaking alongside a park designed to evoke a sense of debt owed to past sacrifice accounted for the shrine's broad-based appeal. Concentrating play space and sacred space in one location, Gettysburg was a special site for acting out the boundaries of human behavior, one that shared the characteristics of a medieval shrine. It offered tourists the pilgrim experience of temporarily abandoning routine and restraint for extraordinary sights and pleasure. A trip to the Civil War's popular shrine enabled visitors to engage in liminal behavior that pushed the boundaries of ordinary respectability. Although Gettysburg exuded authoritarian symbolism, its contradictions as a shrine permitted escape from authority. Presenting unparalleled opportunities to combine remembrance with release, Gettysburg particularly attracted black and white veterans and black excursionists who could cut loose while ostensibly engaging in the serious business of veneration.

Although African Americans may have been ignored in commemorative activities at Gettysburg, African Americans did not ignore the shrine. In fact, if we look at another parallel context of Black 'roots' tourism that emerged prominently in the middle of the twentieth century, the Gold Coast in Africa, corresponding to modern day Ghana, we will find an edifying word which was also a key concept in the African-American 'roots' tourist's project of recapitulating history in creative ways to increase agency in the present for his community. The word in question is of Akan origin, 'Sankofa', meaning 'one must return to the past in order to move forward'. The absence of African Americans in park records suggests their exclusion from society, but an examination of black and white newspaper articles, squibs, and advertisements during the age of rail reveals a rich story of African American excursions to Gettysburg. Only a brief train ride separated Gettysburg from Baltimore, the nineteenth-century "black capital" that was home to 80,000 blacks by 1900. From 1880, when the first excursion of "coloured waiters" disembarked, and especially after Round Top Park's construction until the start of World War I, black excursionists from Baltimore arrived at Gettysburg frequently during the season. The Baltimore African American elite, reflecting black leadership elsewhere, encouraged uplift through white middle-class virtues, as the path to black advancement. From pulpit, press, and school-room, black elites (perhaps two percent of the black population) urged African Americans to display industry, self-control, and refinement.

Black Baltimore featured a number of strong reform organizations dedicated to elevating blacks to a middle-class standard that would, they reasoned, overcome racial and legal obstacles impeding black progress. While black elites disparaged lowbrow entertainment that challenged their agenda, they approved of genteel leisure promoting uplift. A bevy of black benevolent organizations sponsored edifying activities as well as lyceums and schools for self-improvement. Yet in Baltimore, where free blacks and slaves had commingled, traditional pastimes associated with slave life persisted. As a result, the African American elite in the late nineteenth century were often alarmed at the blend of traditional and commercial leisure (Gaines xiii-xv). Among the suitably respectable and edifying leisure activities, thus, were the excursions to sites like Gettysburg, aimed at communal involvement in the process of reclamation of history.

Although no black troops fought at Gettysburg, the shrine possessed special significance for Baltimore's black Grand Army of the Republic (GAR) posts. These organizations of black Civil War veterans hosted the largest Baltimore black excursions to Round Top Park. Although the date of celebrating slave emancipation varied widely among African Americans according to region, the black posts sponsored an annual Gettysburg excursion in September commemorating the 1862 Emancipation Proclamation. Like the GAR nationwide, Baltimore's black Lincoln, Guy, and Logan posts had grown remarkably large in the late 1880s. For two decades beginning in the 1890s, the outing that sometimes drew more than 7,000 blacks to

Gettysburg raised funds for veterans' widows and orphans. The date in September differed from year to year, but as at the nation's new amusement parks, the railroad opened Round Top Park to black people on a Monday in September, an "off day," to avoid racial mixing (Wiggins xi-xix).[2]

Excursions allowed black organizations to raise money from modern commercial leisure activities, yet the journey allowed excursionists to enjoy traditional pastimes. Inappropriate behavior by black excursionists, as reported in the white press, exacerbated racial differences. Mindful of demonstrating black worthiness, dignity, and morality, black leadership expressed ambivalence about celebrations and excursions in Baltimore's sober *Afro-American* and *Ledger* (merged as the *African-American Ledger* in 1900). On the one hand, elites realized that annual celebrations of emancipation could prove effective "to impress its lessons on the rising generation," as the paper commented in 1901. And with their embrace of refinement as a path to progress, black leaders believed that excursions to scenic areas might be an elevating tool for the race. Baltimore's black community, in fact, funded a "Free Excursion Society" that subsidized excursions for poor women and children. But on the other hand, excursions featuring celebrations could threaten achievement of middle-class respectability. Again and again the black papers condemned excursions as a waste of valuable resources and celebrations as excuses for license. What emerges from such reactions is the fact that these excursions were steadily being treated in quite conscious and premeditated ways as pilgrimages aimed at the recovery of a certain view of the past, as an attempt to make sense of the past.[3] John Lennon and Malcom Foley have discussed the importance of pilgrimage as an organizing principle for survivor groups, still coping with the impact of significant violence and upheaval, as experienced by the blacks.

While incidents related to the Gettysburg excursions bore witness to concerns of the African American elite, success of the black GAR emancipation day outings ensured their continuation. The parties ranked as the largest ever to arrive in Gettysburg and were described by the *Baltimore Sun* to be the largest ever run out of Baltimore. For example, the 1903 excursion to Round Top Park brought seventy-four coaches arriving over a four-hour period. "There was a continuous mass of coloured humanity from the Western Maryland Station to the Public Square," according to the *Gettysburg Star and Sentinel*.

As for commemorative activity approved by the black elites, accounts mention only that excursionists toured the battlefield in hacks or strolled around the monuments. Most apparently spent the day at Round Top Park, and many filtered into town to patronize bars. While occasionally the Gettysburg press labeled the excursionists a "jolly bunch" or "a happy, reveling crowd," more often than not accounts reported "a scene of general debauch" and tantalizing headlines like "Gettysburg Witnesses Annual Orgy." A phrase such as "many were filled with booze and their antics and language were reprehensible" was representative of descriptions in the Gettysburg papers. As long as the revelers confined themselves to Round Top Park they escaped harsh censure, but when their merrymaking edged into the town it shocked the conservative citizenry. Between 1909 and 1915 the papers reported such affronts to propriety as drunkenness, razor fights, brawls, vile language, pick-pocketing, public urination, shootouts, gambling, and alcohol-related accidents. Particularly repulsive to white sensibilities were the "disgraceful scenes" acted out by black women, who got drunk, engaged in hatpin fights, and provided liquor to children (*Adams County News*, Sept. 18, 1909).[4]

White Gettysburg citizens prone to racism were not the only ones to express concern over the excursionists' antics. Baltimore's black elites repeatedly abhorred the "rowdyism" and "very shameful and mortifying nature" of excursionist conduct, fully aware of its harmful effect on the race as well as race relations. "Allowing something for the usual exaggerating account of what takes place on a colored excursion, when the account is written up for the white press," the *Afro-American Ledger* commented in 1916, "it is quite true that many excursionists feel that an outing is a signal for all kinds of 'shines,' and it is not an enjoyable occasion unless they 'let themselves go'" (*Afro-American Ledger*, Sept. 2, 1916). To be sure, only a tiny percentage of the black thousands who descended on Gettysburg were responsible for the most egregious excesses. Still, excursionists focused the celebration on revelry and imbibing. Following years of experience with the holiday, a Gettysburg paper commented after town bars were closed to excursionists in 1916 that "a celebration of Emancipation Day without some good spirits is no celebration at all, in the minds of not a few of the celebrators" (*Adams County News*, Sept. 12, 1914).

But it was precisely the license to celebrate, validated by Gettysburg's stature as a shrine tolerating behavioral extremes, that made it an attractive destination for excursionists. Memory served a central function in the validation of these excursion projects for the black elites. Like heritage, memory is a somewhat intangible commodity and a social construction that mediates individuals' experiences, actions and expectations. It is offered to the tourist for consumption and it is the thing that tourists themselves enact and perform in order to authenticate and make meaningful their experiences at the site. Unfortunately, because neither records of the black posts nor other documentation by participants can be located, it is not possible to determine the expressive significance of the emancipation excursions. The range of behavior the shrine permitted and its inflated reputation apparently allowed the black community to invest the excursions with several meanings. For black veterans sponsoring the excursions, Gettysburg provided a symbolic location not only to commemorate emancipation but also to remember the war as a time when black men claimed their manhood. Otherwise, the veterans might just as well have sponsored emancipation excursions to closer and better-appointed locations. Memory thus became instrumental in the creation of a shared racial historical consciousness for tourists bent on sifting through the past and connecting what they found with their lived experiences of contemporary racial formation. For black elites the shrine represented an important stage on which African Americans might display decorum that would support their argument for expanding rights. For excursionists, however, Gettysburg's capacity to tolerate extremes offered possibilities for commemoration at odds with the edification black elites expected.

In addition to its function as a shrine, Gettysburg appears to have presented an alluring arena for black excursionists to celebrate emancipation because of its distance from Baltimore. Although growing increasingly archaic as industrialization spread, African American celebrations of freedom across the South typically featured libation, exuberance, and carnality. As William Wiggins argues in *O Freedom!* Afro-American Emancipation Celebrations, freedom celebrations originated in the agricultural calendar's slave Christmas (Wiggins xi). Although its date varied according to region, the freedom celebration's ancestry rested in the Christmas carnival custom of premodern Europe that allowed a topsy-turvy world of frolic and license to prevail temporarily. Although violence among slaves often resulted, slave owners encouraged the annual Christmas release from drudgery as a safety valve for the slave system. Owners believed that if they furnished alcohol and suspended daily routine for the holiday, they would appear to their slaves benevolent and deserving of continued loyalty. Moreover, as Frederick Douglass realized, this temporary inversion tricked black people into confusing "a dose of vicious dissipation" with freedom. After this faux liberty sunk them to the depths of degradation, Douglass argued, they happily returned to subservient status, thankful for their master's paternalism. The *Afro-American Ledger* applied Douglass's hypothesis to free blacks living in industrialized communities (Afro-American Ledger, Sept. 2, 1916). The paper observed that while the consumer spree, for leisure or display goods, offered a temporary release, it robbed blacks of money, time, and dignity and in the end only served to reaffirm the racial hierarchy (Douglass 85).

Although such roistering persisted in the rural postwar South, it was censured by black elites eager to abandon slavery's stain and adopt elevating manners that would counter white racism. Paradoxically, it appears that an excursion to Gettysburg allowed the continued practice of familiar holiday forms within the structure of commercial leisure and away from the reproachful gaze of elites. The Gettysburg battlefield's importance for excursionists rested not in its symbolic significance as a struggle that ensured emancipation but in a literal freedom from social pressure urging self-denial, restraint, and self-discipline. Emancipation celebration represented an atavistic form of Christmas revelry that served as a release valve for the slave system; but blacks may have used Gettysburg as a release valve from their own cultural authority. At Gettysburg working-class blacks could escape the city and break the behavioral boundaries that black elites hoped to impose. Following embarrassing incidents in 1916, the *Afro-American Ledger* lamented, "The fact that they are in a strange town, where they do not meet the reproving glances of friends they respect, seems to relieve them of all responsibilities to be self-respecting and decent" (*Afro-American Ledger*, Sept. 2, 1916).

What Americans needed to remember about the Civil War, wrote Union veteran and advocate of black rights Albion W. Tourgee in 1884, "is not the battles, the marches, the conflicts, not the courage, the suffering, the blood, but only the causes that underlay the struggle and the results that followed from it" (Qtd. Blight 220). Tourgee was fighting a losing battle. In fact the changes in the ways that whites and blacks in the North and South remembered the war and understood its meaning during the half century after the conflict were already tending towards the mythically deictic and the celebratory occlusion of memory. For Tourgee, as for millions of other Northern whites initially and for almost all African Americans, the causes of the war were slavery and the South's determination to preserve it; the results were a new birth of freedom in a reunited nation and a new charter of equal rights in the Fourteenth and Fifteenth Amendments to the Constitution.

By 1913, however, at the fiftieth anniversary commemoration of Gettysburg, which attracted five thousand ageing veterans and many more spectators, Governor William

Hodges Mann of Virginia expressed a view that had come to be shared by nearly all Americans except blacks and a small minority of Yankees. "We are not here," intoned Mann, "to discuss what caused the war (of 1861-65), but to talk over the events of the battle here as man to man" (Qtd. Blight 9). The custodians of Confederate memory had won their postwar battle to celebrate the South's Lost Cause as a valiant crusade for constitutional liberties and states' rights that were overwhelmed only by brute force. Slavery had little to do with causing the war, in this version of history, and reconciliation of the two sections that had fought a "brothers' war" was a more important consequence than the abolition of slavery. In 1888, only four years after his plea for a memory of causes and consequences, Tourgee conceded defeat. In the "field of American fiction today," he wrote, "the Confederate soldier is the popular hero. Our literature has become not only Southern in type, but distinctly Confederate in sympathy" (Blight 220).

Flush with victory in 1865 and determined to secure 'the fruits of victory' by planting Yankee institutions and values in the conquered South and empowering white Unionists and black freemen in the domain once ruled by the planter aristocracy, the Northern people within a generation had yielded the field to the guardians of Confederate memory. There was an ongoing tension between healing and justice during the postwar years. Three visions of the war's meaning competed in a variety of forums: a reconciliationist vision, an emancipationist vision, and a white supremacist vision. With seeming inevitability, the reconciliationist and white supremacist visions merged to prevail over the emancipationist vision. The aging boys in blue and gray shook hands across the bloody chasm in a gush of sentimental concord that left no room for the black men in Blue who had fought for the freedom and equal rights of their people. This view of the War and Reconstruction prevailed in the North as well as the South. The Gettysburg reunion took place as a national ritual in which the ghost of slavery, the very questions of cause and consequence, might be exorcised once and for all and an epic conflict among whites elevated into "national mythology" (Blight 390).

Blacks were ignored in Gettysburg commemoration to facilitate the reconciliation between the North and the South, but their premodern celebrating did not measure up to the modern standard of commercial culture. This perceived inadequacy helped push them outside Gettysburg's commemorative purview and aided the white monopoly of the memorial. It was precisely the acting out of their archaic form of celebrating within the nascent mass culture that separated the excursionists from white celebrants and African American elites. Gettysburg, like the new amusement parks of the era, had no place for their carnal, exuberant kind of celebrating. The outsider status for black people helped shape Gettysburg as a public space where all whites acting within the boundaries of the new commercial culture were welcome. As a place where whites might mingle as a privileged group sharing pride in white accomplishment and propriety (excepting the occasional tippling trippers), Gettysburg was a unifying force. Yet this status of "Americanness" was predicated on the contrasts with the 'other' who was unable to observe behavioral codes.

Although affiliated with the latest transportation technology and marketing, the black emancipation celebrations represent one of the few examples of premodern leisure at Gettysburg. The excursions provide an intriguing example of customary celebration surviving in spite of its alliance with commercial culture. Coincidentally, the other type of premodern celebration brought to Gettysburg also reinforced racism but was introduced by white veterans. Among the surge of Union veterans that transformed the battlefield into a "vast cemetery" beginning in the 1880s, no single group could claim more credit for enshrining Gettysburg than the Pennsylvania Department of the Grand Army of the Republic. Enjoying rising membership like the GAR nationwide, and by the 1880s a truly multi-racial body, the Pennsylvania GAR seized control of the moribund battlefield memorial association and began to sculpt a park from the battlefield (Vanderslice 210). The GAR itself, thus, became a site for contested performances of recapitulation and reinforcement of racial agency in history by both blacks and whites.

The Pennsylvanians' interest in the battlefield followed their establishment of annual encampments on East Cemetery Hill beginning in 1878. "Here they enjoy themselves as they cannot any other place," the *Gettysburg Compiler* commented in 1886. But Gettysburg meant more than a week's outing for Pennsylvania veterans. Through play and rituals the encampments served as periodic therapy to readjust memories and to adapt psychologically to a world vastly different from the one left behind at Appomattox. Dress parades and ceremonies enabled veterans dehumanized by the monotony of the factory or economically besieged on the farm to boost their self-esteem. Playful reenactment of wartime scenarios tamed painful memories. Camp life associated with boredom and homesickness, for example, could now be transformed into fun through recreational activities, pranks, picnics, and drinking.[5] Between play and ritual, wartime memories of terror, foreboding, or ennui could be relooped to deliver what most veterans initially had enlisted for—glory, adventure, and fun.

Playlike ritual could rework the present as well as the past. The concept of memory is very powerful in such acts as the human function of '*re-membering*', that is, putting back together, restoring the body, making whole the body politic. As a bodily practice, the memory performed at these sites serves a temporal spatial function by incorporating the awareness of sight, sound, smell, touch and taste to experience fully the spatial arrangement of the memorial grounds. Though commercial forms of play buy release from work and responsibility, traditional play allows for temporary inversion of the status quo. As illustrated earlier, emancipation celebrations at Round Top Park temporarily created a festive world of license and carnality for African Americans. Similarly, white Pennsylvania veterans employed traditional play to suspend the status quo and mock authority, thereby also staging competing performances of authenticity. Hailing chiefly from Philadelphia, members of several GAR posts formed cliques they labeled “Lambs,” “Razors,” “Hawks,” and “Goats,” a reference to the monikers of Philadelphia clubs that mounted antimilitia protest parades in the antebellum era. Many clique members were, in fact, pre-war militiamen, and their GAR posts suspiciously displayed similar discipline problems. By the 1880s the groups had adopted simple but distinctive uniforms and, as the encampments’ unofficial entertainers, provided “a source of endless fun” for spectators and other veterans, according to the *Gettysburg Compiler*. The cliques delighted thousands of spectators packing Gettysburg’s streets and East Cemetery Hill through antics that poked fun at cultural, civic, and military authorities (*Gettysburg Compiler*, June 20, 1893).

At every Gettysburg summer encampment from 1878 to 1894, the groups staged burlesque parades and plays based on Philadelphia tradition that originated with English colonists. Similar in origin to the slave Christmas, burlesque parades borrowed on premodern Christmas traditions involving costumed, sometimes transvestite, “fantasticals” and “callithumpians” who temporarily inverted the social order. During encampments, ceremonies intended to solemnify often were undermined by the “Lambs,” “Razors,” and similar Pennsylvania GAR groups who combined archaic Christmas custom and street protest. Appearing “grotesquely dressed [and] rigged out in all the colours of the rainbow, surmounted by every conceivable species of headgear,” their most characteristic antic involved comic imitation of a formal GAR parade or mincing behind one with horns and noisemakers. Occasionally they added props such as a “Jumbo” elephant float, a pet lamb to head their procession, or goats pulling miniature cannon. In time the veterans added a kazoo band to parody the military brass bands accompanying GAR parades. “Just recall our old Christmas eves,” one veteran noted, “when, equipped with tin horns, parties of men paraded Chestnut and Eighth Streets, creating an almost infernal din with their instruments of torture to weak nerves, and you have a correct idea of what we realized for almost an hour” (Davis 36-38).

Staged performances enabled the groups to specify what they only suggested in parades. Performers mixed burlesque with parody of memorial activities. Almost every summer the veterans staged a mock court-martial and execution for an absurd infraction, after which a "burial detail" carried away the "body."[6] Crowds delighted in speeches filled with double talk ridiculing the pompous, bombastic oratory that characterized familiar memorial rituals. Such burlesque suggested to performers and audience alike that the formal apparatus of remembering the war, from the GAR to the battlefield itself, should perhaps not be taken so seriously.

Yet the veterans also performed racially inspired burlesque as part of their repertoire. For example, in 1880 the "fantasticals" executed "an old African woman" in a staged performance before a large crowd, including state officials and national GAR commanders. Condemned in a mock court-martial for selling water as whiskey, the prisoner's execution mimicked the way Sepoys were dispatched by the British in India. The Proceedings of the annual encampment reported that "the boys went through this performance with undisturbed gravity, while the spectators were constantly convulsed with laughter" (Davis 106). For observers at the time the skit possessed multiple meanings, among them reference to incidents that occurred during the war or in Philadelphia before the war. But on other occasions during the Gettysburg encampments, the veterans donned derogatory racial disguises to depict performing "darkey musicians" or black-face officers.

In his seminal book, *The Tourist: A New Theory of the Leisure Class*, Dean MacCannell has theorized the ways in which the quest for authenticity is a guiding principle of the tourist experience, especially as those tourists negotiate the spatial logic of the site concerned. MacCannell divides the tourist setting into 'front' and 'back' regions: "the front is the meeting place of hosts and guests or customers and service persons, and the back is the place where the members of the home team retire between performances to relax and prepare" (92). In other words, the front region is the space that is presented to the public, as on a stage where actors perform, and the back region is the space hidden behind the stage, where special knowledge is dispensed in occult secrecy. This spatial analysis of the staging of memory in tourist activities aimed at verisimilar, theatrical reenactments is particularly relevant to the Afro-American communal negotiations with the memory of Gettysburg as a repository of a certain kind of history and memory. "For the study of tourist settings, *front* and *back* [may]," writes MacCannell, "be treated as ideal poles of a continuum, poles linked by a series of front regions decorated to appear as back regions, and back regions set up to accommodate outsiders . . . the quest for authenticity is marked off in stages in the passage from front to back" (99). The African-American crowds that thronged at the memorial grounds of Gettysburg and staged their mock executions, court-martials, parades and campaigns, wrestled in the 'front' as MacCannell posits it, believing that it was the 'back', meaning the very core of historical legitimacy that they were trying to prise away from the dominant white community that refused to allow them even a toe-hold on the raft of history plying the tides of the nation's temporal march to the future. Thus authenticity for the black elites consisted in a slow movement from the physical, geographical and exterior acts of presence, visibility and performance to more mnemonic and communal experiences of having a hand on the shoulder of national history, a grip enabling enough to restrain the movement of that discourse to attempts at elision and occlusion of the role of the black community in its being and becoming. This explains, perhaps, their tolerance of the frankly provocative and admittedly rowdy nature of some memorialization attempts, as we have seen.

Racially loaded burlesque may have expressed disagreement with GAR authority over racial matters as much as it did racist sentiment. Before the war young Philadelphians from working-class neighborhoods employed transvestitism, blackface, and masking to maintain racial, ethnic, and gender order in their neighborhoods. Whites prevented blacks from participating in parades, sometimes assaulting those who tried. It may have been the GAR that provoked the cliques to resuscitate prewar play aimed at African Americans. The GAR had taken an unprecedented step among nineteenth-century organizations by integrating its membership. Racially mixed posts were unusual in Pennsylvania, but the GAR nonetheless offered full equality to black veterans as "comrades in arms." Furthermore, GAR elites sometimes referred to racial equality as a goal worthy of the war's sacrifices. And while whites may have been able to restrain black parades on the streets in the antebellum era, black veterans marched in Philadelphia's centennial and bicentennial parades. It may have been these dramatic postwar racial changes that white Philadelphia veterans found threatening. Burlesque served as a way to counterpoise what these veterans felt was a menacing trend perpetuated by elites, the threat of black equality and a perversion of the war's memory. In other words, these Philadelphia veterans used Gettysburg to express disagreements with the status quo. Gettysburg provided them an opportunity to reaffirm the racial hierarchy through what appeared to be folderol (Gannon 169-70).

For all the craziness and ridicule the mummers brought to a town that lived off a shrine, there is no evidence that anyone in Gettysburg or in the GAR hierarchy objected to it. On the contrary, Gettysburg papers indicated that townspeople eagerly anticipated the burlesque antics, and GAR officers occasionally even participated. Possibly, like premodern gentry or slave masters, GAR leadership found in such revelry a harmless release that ensured stability the rest of the year. Neither is there evidence that anyone objected to using the nation's "Mecca" one of its most revered sites, East Cemetery Hill, as the stage for this burlesque. The inferences for these humorous performances staged before thousands of people are inescapable. Even if not aimed at Gettysburg directly, by mocking the rituals that solemnized the place they reduced Gettysburg to manageable size. By emphasizing the humorous, vulgar, and grotesque, the burlesque knocked down the sacred and its oppressive burden. In the process these performances dragged down promises of greater social equality. Perhaps the enthusiasm of performers and audiences indicate exhaustion with the era's pace of change as well as its intense memorialization. Although both black excursionists and white veterans used play to subvert authority, one of the obvious differences is that crowds laughed along with veterans, while crowds either laughed at or disapproved of black antics.

If it is true, as Victor Turner has argued, that celebration can "sound off" better than rituals, then Gettysburg can be seen in a new light. Play, according to Turner, is less constrained than ritual and can therefore comment on a broader range of social issues. For all its appearance of foolery, then, play is serious business that does not mask unpleasant realities hidden by ritual. To the student of leisure, what is remarkable about black and white veterans' behavior is that it documents both the use of premodern play to remember the Civil War and the survival of traditional celebration at a modern site of memory. In effect, a modern site of memory enabled these groups to prolong a form of celebration that was dying in the new commercial culture. Play offered both groups an opportunity to control the memory of the event remembered. One group could selectively recall lustful celebrations that had disappeared in the new commercial culture. The other remembered the prewar order in the streets. For both, Gettysburg provided a temporary but regular escape from class authority and an inversion of the social order. Memory of the Civil War provided a pretext for traditional celebration that ironically served to perpetuate racism at a shrine previously dedicated to equality (Turner 29).

Trends in commercial play at Gettysburg served African Americans no better than traditional play. Throughout the twentieth century and long after the end of racially demeaning amusements and segregated facilities, the marketplace became another form of authority that separated them from the Civil War's legacy. A host of factors contributed to the disappearance of black visitors, including Gettysburg's inhospitality, the decline of Baltimore's black GAR posts, and the closing of Round Top Park. They also vanished because the automobile replaced train travel as the chief form of tourist conveyance.

Even though cars and outings were common during the interwar period, the automobile did not represent a fundamentally democratic instrument of leisure that all Americans could afford. As a result, autos replaced train travel that had been accessible to nearly everyone and ended the communal experience some groups expected. During the Cold War, Gettysburg became a shrine for white middle-class families who bonded around family automobile touring and the embracing of national memory (Brown 210).

Even in the twenty-first century commercial leisure has continued to discourage African Americans from pilgrimages to Gettysburg. In the final decades of the last century, Gettysburg became a "heritage" attraction that stages a tangible and entertaining past for a segmented market of specialized leisure consumers. Heritage activities such as recreating the "authentic" environment of 1863 and "authentically" reenacting the battle are a new form of play at Gettysburg supported by several different groups of consumers. Yet by only restoring select slices of the original event, heritage has aided the transformation of Gettysburg into a rescripted memory where slavery is absent in a sanitized landscape. The more visitors rely on reproduction of the battle's tangible elements to understand the Civil War, the more historical meaning is excluded from the shrine (Lowenthal 3-6).

With current visitors disproportionately white and male, questions surface about Gettysburg in a nation with a rapidly growing minority population. Academics, African American leaders, and Gettysburg National Military Park (GNMP) administrators have expressed concern about broadening Gettysburg's constituency. The GNMP has taken steps to focus more on the "new birth of freedom" inherent in the Gettysburg Address through the downtown Wills House and a new visitors' center. But dogmatism about "authenticity" has prompted some enthusiasts to term displays about slavery and freedom "politically correct spin." Moreover, just as the play of visiting blacks once affronted whites, the authenticity white people today consider acceptable play seems inappropriate to minorities. After all, reenacting not only puts play above politics, but also intentionally reinvokes a reality devoid of progress in race relations that was, ironically, precipitated by the Civil War. And incarnating Lost Cause mythology through pageantry mocks ground made sacred as a birthplace of freedom. In 1999, for example, an African American history professor describing his walk over the battlefield in the *New York Times* wrote of his "emotional detachment." While he fully appreciated the significance of Gettysburg to African Americans, on Little Round Top he came upon two re-enactors assuming their Confederate identities for tourists. They themselves were simply tourists role-playing men who long fought to save slavery from destruction on that very spot. "I wanted to scream at them," the black visitor wrote, but instead he trekked back along Cemetery Ridge, wondering how it came to be that he "still felt like an unwanted guest on this spot" (Ballard 2).

Gettysburg is an ongoing project with no final meaning, an American shrine in a continuous state of becoming. Gettysburg always has reflected the current needs of its consumers, and the heritage vision is simply the latest stage. However, heritage has only encouraged forgetfulness of Gettysburg's historical meaning as a battle to create a more egalitarian society. Although Gettysburg never dealt with racial issues effectively, a century ago thousands of African Americans visited Gettysburg for annual emancipation day celebrations. Visitors could escape or protest the authority of everyday life through play, whereas only a narrow kind of heritage play, of interest only to heritage consumers, is permitted today. The current focus on authenticity has discounted the importance of race in the causes and legacies of the Civil War, making African Americans feel less welcome at the shrine and in the nation's memory. To paraphrase Hamlet, the disjunction between historical meaning and authenticity has thrown a segment of American history out of joint. Indeed, Gettysburg will realize its potential only when it finds a place for this wider meaning in its continuing creation.

# NOTES

1. White locals and tourists, for example, enjoyed chuckling over black jittering and cakewalks at Round Top Park, located at the southern end of the battlefield. Some black excursionists, such as a 300-pound woman or a wizened man alleged to be a century old, were ogled by townspeople and tourists as if they were freaks.
2. Estimating in 1899 that blacks had squandered millions on excursions, the *Ledger* stated, "Added to this enormous amount is the cost for string bands and regalia, to say nothing of the many fights, police court scrapes, broken limbs, and the character of girls who have been ruined on these excursions, together with the demoralizing effect in general." In the view of black progressives, excursions chained blacks under the guise of freedom. Baltimore's Àfrican Methodist Episcopal ministers in 1905 resolved that "excursions heretofore given for and by our people have not been conducive to their moral improvement" and urged abstention (*Ledger*, April 23, 1898).
3. Every conveyance in town was pressed into service, the trolley used every inch of standing room, and several well-lathered horses died under the strain. Estimating that the excursion cost $10,000, the *Afro-American Ledger* pointed to the foolishness of a GAR charity that returned perhaps 10 percent to the black community. "Can we afford such extravagance as to spend ten thousand dollars for one day's pleasure? We think not," the *Ledger* declared (*Gettysburg Compiler*, Sept. 16, 1902).
4. "It is a pitiful and humiliating scene," lamented the *Adams County News*, "to see a drunken man giving an exhibition of what is more becoming to a four-legged animal, but to see a drunken woman planted in the middle of Center Square half clad and wallering [sic] in the mud, is not pitiful, but about the most disgusting exhibition that any person would care look upon" (*Adams County News*, Sept. 18, 1909).
5. Beginning in 1881 the Pennsylvania GAR staged volcanic sham battles that drew thousands of spectators to the encampment. Reintroducing the Civil War as benign pyrotechnics, opposing "Union" and "Confederate" forces engaged to the tune of martial music in dusk flared by hundreds of Roman candles, rockets, small cannon, and firecrackers. According to the veterans' *Grand Army Scout & Soldier's Mail*, at the 1884 battle "the old soldiers among

the spectators all agreed that the skirmish seemed very natural and like old times" (*Grand Army Scout & Soldier's Mail*, 4).

6. At one performance the "Lambs" erected a "monument" to a leader "immortally wounded by a malt shot" while a veteran in drag played the deceased's widow (*Gettysburg Star & Sentinel*, Aug. 1, 1878). Fort Mill, S.C., is the kind of place neighboring Charlotte N.C. that its National Football League club Carolina Panthers probably would like to forget. Even the most savvy public relations machine would find it difficult to put a positive spin on the 'faithful slave' monument that stands in the town's park. Erected by the local cotton mill owner in the 1890s, the monument is an obelisk with carved panels near the base commemorating field slaves and 'mammies' who stayed with their masters during the Civil War. It is one of a series of Confederate monuments in the town. Others honor the Confederate soldier, Confederate women and Indians who fought for the Confederacy.

## List of Works Cited and Consulted


Blight, David W. *Race and Reunion: The Civil War in American Memory*. Cambridge, Massachusets: Harvard University Press, 2001.

Brown, Dona. *Inventing New England: Regional Tourism in the Nineteenth Century*. Washington, D.C.: Smithsonian Institution Press, 1995.

Davis, Susan G. *Parades and Power: Street Theatre in Nineteenth-Century Philadelphia*. Philadelphia: Temple University Press, 1986.

Douglass, Frederick. *Narrative of the Life of Frederick Douglass, an American Slave: Written by Himself.* New York: Signet, 1968.

Gallman, J. Matthew and Susan Baker. "Gettysburg's Gettysburg: What the Battle Did to the Borough." *The Gettysburg Nobody Knows*, ed. Gabor S. Boritt. New York: Oxford University Press, 1997.

Gaines, Kevin. *Uplifting the Race: Black Leadership, Politics, and Culture in the Twentieth Century*. Chapel Hill: University of North Carolina Press, 1996.

Gannon, Barbara A. "Sites of Memory, Sites of Glory: African-American Grand Army Posts in Pennsylvania." *Making and Remaking Pennsylvania's Civil War*. Ed. William A. Blair and

William Pencak. University Park: Pennsylvania State University Press, 2001.

Lennon, John and Malcolm Foley. *Dark Tourism: The Attraction of Death and Disaster*. New York: Continuum, 2000.

Lowenthal, David. *Possessed by the Past: The Heritage Crusade and the Spoils of History*. New York: Free Press, 1996.

MacCannell, Dean. *The Tourist: A New Theory of the Leisure Class.* Berkeley: University of California Press, 1999.

Turner, Victor. Introduction. *Celebration: Studies in Festivity and Ritual*. Ed. Victor Turner. Washington D.C.: Smithsonian Institution Press, 1982.

Vanderslice, John M. *Gettysburg: A History of the Gettysburg Battlefield Memorial Association, with an Account of the Battle.* Philadelphia: The Association, 1897.

Weeks, Jim. "Gettysburg: Memory, Market, and an American Shrine." Ph.D. diss. Pennsylvania State University, 2001.

Wiggins, William *O Freedom! Afro-American Emancipation Celebrations*. Knoxville: University of Tennessee Press, 1987.

## Journals and Newspapers Cited

*Gettysburg Star & Sentinel.*
*Adams County News.*
*Gettysburg Compiler.*
*African-American Ledger.*

# The Shattering of American Values in Vietnam War Literature

**Kamaluddin Ahmed**
**University of Chittagong, Bangladesh**

> There lies at the root of such judgment, rather, the idea that existence has another and much more worthy purpose, for which, and not for happiness, reason is quite properly intended, and which must, therefore, be regarded as the supreme condition to which the private purpose of men must, for the most part, defer. (Kant 194-213)

Kant here argues for the existence of supreme moral law, which exists as the sole extension of reason; he contends that the only purpose of reason is to define and create moral ethics, and thus the conclusion that any action is "moral" must be reached solely through reason itself. This idea, that the reason dictates morals, has been one of the most influential philosophical ideas in western thought. It influenced strongly the great political theorists, including Locke and Voltaire, and was hailed as the New Ethics for the Enlightenment. Indirectly, it can be said to have influenced strongly the two great revolutions (French and American), both of which resulted in nations, which held that reason was the highest goal of humanity, and that morality could be defined by rational means.

But what happens when reason is taken away? What if there is no rationality, no empirical data, and no logical progression of facts? What if nothing makes sense? What would happen to morality? These are the questions brought forward by the Vietnam War. The War was a huge setback to the rationalism of the past, and shook America to its roots, because it challenged one of the very foundations on which this country was founded: the idea that there was a rational, moral law. America had to completely rethink its ideals; the Americans saw a side of themselves that they had previously thought extinguished by their vast reason and subsequent moral superiority. They found that, much to their surprise, they were capable of atrocities that defied all rational attempts at explanation. This paper will attempt to explore this phenomenon.

Several explorations of this phenomenon can be found in the narratives that grew out of the Vietnam conflict. The intention of these narratives is more than merely "to explain the war"; their intention is not only to describe the reality of war, but also to suggest something to the reader to convey a message in an instructive way. That is to say, the war novel has a moral intention. We find in these war novels that the soldiers went through a period of indoctrination, in which they were taught the "rational" way to fight a war; they were then put into jungles in which all of their rules of engagement ceased to apply. What the soldiers were told was incompatible with what they saw, fragmenting their need and desire to define morality from their ability to do so. This resulted in an overall collapse of the idea of morality itself; it made justifiable many of their atrocities committed during the war, and caused complications that are still being dealt with, or ignored, today.

The indoctrination of soldiers is one of the most carefully thought out and scientific of the military's activities. It is imperative that soldiers act as one, that they follow orders, that they perform without question in duty to their country. In following orders the soldiers are engaged in making moral judgments about the conflicting ethical principles to which people adhere. Philip Caputo's *A Rumor of War* best illustrates this when Caputo states:

> The purpose of drill was to instill discipline and teamwork, two of the Corps' cardinal virtues. And by the third week we had learned to obey orders instantly and in unison, without thinking. Each platoon had been transformed from a group of individuals into one thing: a machine of which we were merely parts. (10)

Caputo continues to describe how the soldiers were put through extreme hardships, weakening their physical and mental resistance to make them more adaptable and impressionable to the propaganda by which they were bombarded everyday.

> Throughout, we were subject to intense indoctrination, which seemed to borrow from communist brainwashing techniques. We had to chant slogans while running: "Hut-two-three-four, I love the Marine Corps." And before meals: "Sir, the United States Marines, since 1775, the most invincible fighting force in the history of man. Guong ho! Guong ho! Guong ho! Pray for War!" (12)

The soldiers were also told heroic, half-true legends about the amazing exploits of the military of the past, creating heroes and gods out of the soldiers of World War II and World War I and the Spanish-American war, and then telling the soldiers that these legends were real soldiers, real Americans, real men. Subsequently, everyone would do everything to be those men. War was honorable. War was glorious. War was Good, with a capital G.

Once convinced of the bravery of war and justness of American military involvement, they were then taught the right way in which to make war. There were rules that they were taught. When the enemy did this, they did that. When they did that, the enemy did this, so that they could then do that. There were plans, there were protocols, and there were Standard Operating Procedures. You did not mutilate their dead; else the enemy mutilates yours. You treated POWs with, if not kindness, at least a sense of human rights. Civilians were civilians, and off limits. Trust your officers; trust your men. War was bloody, but it was civilised. It was rational. It had to be, because their reason for fighting was that they were more right than they were, and to be more right, they had to be more reasonable, more rational. They were enlightened.

All of this changed when the soldiers were inserted into the bush. Another Vietnam War novelist James Webb captures the initial shock of combat in *Fields of Fire*:

> The next day, as he was walking to an indoctrination class with another Lieutenant, the base was rocketed. He sprinted to a dry ditch and dove in, feeling like a true combat veteran. One rocket landed perhaps fifty meters away, directly on top of a tent, and he began composing in his own mind how he would put that into a letter to someone. And then he climbed out of the ditch and almost stepped on the severed hand of a man who had been inside the tent . . . and it wasn't fun anymore. (51)

Suddenly, the supreme logic they had been so well taught no longer applied. The soldiers found that there was no traditional "enemy." There was the NVA, but who were they? There were the Vietcong, but who were they? It was impossible to define who the soldiers were fighting, and the more they fought, the more NVA and VC there seemed to be. They did not use US tactics; they did not play by US rules. They used women and children as decoys, or sent them on suicide missions. They sniped American soldiers. They used booby traps. They used hit-and-run guerrilla tactics. They just ate away at our troops, and there was nothing they could do about it.

The soldiers were subjected to unspeakable horrors; atrocities, which their indoctrination told them, were impossible. Caputo describes some of these horrors:

> One of the 1st battalion's radio operators was captured by an enemy patrol, tied up, beaten with clubs, and executed. His body was found floating in the Song Toy Loan three days after his capture, with the ropes still around his hands and a bullet hole in the back of his head. Four other marines from another regiment were captured and later discovered in a common grave, also tied up and with their skulls blasted open by an executioner's bullets. (228)

The horrors incurred by the NVA and the Vietcong were magnified by the extreme hardships of the soldiers in the bush. The paranoia of night patrols, the misery of long marches, disease, and long periods of boredom punctuated by moments of sheer terror created an environment of misery that few would be able to appreciate. The pressures of these hardships often resulted in sudden release from the soldiers: "with the mud, heat, leeches, and chewing thorns, and the risk of a wounded VC lobbing a grenade from his hiding place, the mood of the platoon grew savage." (Caputo 118)

Morality, then, became impossible to define. Unlike Graham Greene in *The Quiet American*, most American writers deny the possibility of moral responsibility in a war as problematic as Vietnam. "We all had roughly the same position on the war," Michael Herr writes in his war memoirs: "we were in it, and that was a position" (226). Tim O'Brien arrives at more or less the same "position" in his memoir *If I Die in a Combat Zone* (1973). Though convinced the war was "wrong" for various reasons that "could be murmured like the Psalms on a cold-moon Vietnam night," O'Brien went to war because he feared "censure, embarrassment, the end of everything that had happened in my life, the end of it all" (O'Brien, *If I Die* 133, 22). Likewise the protagonist of O'Brien's excellent novel, *Going After Cacciato* (1978), goes to war knowing that "the moral climate was imperfect." Pfc. Paul Berlin overcomes his moral objections, as he says at one point in the novel, out of "the dread of abandoning all that I hold dear. I am afraid of exile." (O'Brien 322)

However, Philip Caputo's *A Rumor of War* provides the detailed dismissal of the many moral objections to the war. Writing about his own experience in Vietnam, Caputo admits that he and the other Americans lost their "humanity" in an inhuman war, but then asks, "who was to speak of rules and ethics in war that had none?" (230). Caputo argues that "everything rotted and corroded quickly over there: bodies, boot leather, canvas, metal, morals" (229). For twenty years of terrorism and fratricide had obliterated most reference points from the country's moral map long before we arrived" (xvi); Caputo thereby rationalizes what he refers to as the "brutish state" into which he and his fellow soldiers sank. By blaming the Vietnamese 'and their debauched moral landscape, Caputo conveniently denies his own responsibility for the brutality he admits participating in.

Everything the soldiers had been taught, everything they had been indoctrinated to believe, crumbled before their eyes. There were no logical expected outcomes; there were no ways to predict the enemy. There were no plans, there were no protocols, and there were no Standard Operating Procedures. Their dead were mutilated, their prisoners systematically executed. Civilians could not be trusted; anyone could be a Vietcong. War was certainly bloody, but it was not civilized. It was not rational. If it was not rational, then it could not be fought rationally. If it could not be fought rationally, reason was useless. If reason was useless, so was morality. If morality was useless, then they could not be right. If they were not right, then why were they fighting?

Thus decayed the moral fabric of the American soldier. Nothing made sense anymore. Caputo captures the essence of the problem in this way:

> According to those "rules of agreement," it was morally right to shoot an unarmed Vietnamese who was running, but wrong to shoot one who was standing or walking; it was wrong to shoot an enemy prisoner at close range, but right for a sniper at a long range to kill an enemy soldier who was no more able than a prisoner to defend himself; it was wrong for infantryman to destroy a village with white-phosphorus grenades, but right for a fighter pilot to drop napalm on it. Ethics seemed to be matter of distance and technology . . . that was the strategy, the best our best military could come up with; organized butchery. But organized or not, butchery was butchery, so who was to speak of rules and ethics in war. (229-30)

There was no reason to be moral any more; no reason to "treat humanity . . . always at the same time as an end and never simply as a means" (Kant 210). The soldiers simply had no need to follow codes or ethics, because their enemies followed none, and following them could get them killed. At the same time, the atrocities they witnessed eroded their very desire to seek out morality; if an atrocity has been committed, who would not want to pay back the perpetrators of it?

> We paid the enemy back, sometimes with interest. It was common knowledge that quite a few captured VC never made it back to prison camps; they were reported as "shot and killed while trying to escape." Some line companies did not even bother taking

> prisoners; they simply killed every VC they saw, and a number of Vietnamese who were only suspects. The latter were usually counted among enemy dead, under the unwritten rule "if he's dead and Vietnamese, he's VC." (229)

This in turn allowed American soldiers to justify horrible atrocities on their own part. A captain in James Webb's *Fields of Fire* says:

> I'll tell you how I feel. Best friends murdered like that. For God's sake, there's been enough tragedy without compounding it. If they did kill the people, they'll have to live with it. It was a mistake. They're kids. They're fucked up and confused. You said it yourself: nothing makes sense out here. (339-40)

Thus, the American had become exactly that which they thought they were fighting—a force of inhuman, terrible power capable of barbarity that they thought they had overcome through the virtue of their reason. They lost their right to fight, because they were fighting for nothing. They turned their back on the very reason that they held so dear to their core values. They essentially rationalized their inhumanity, and perpetrated that inhumanity on not only those they fought, but also on those they sought to protect, and not only those they sought to protect, but on themselves as well.

Caputo's specious logic on the denial of his own responsibility for the brutality can best be seen in the final section of his narrative, appropriately entitled "In Death's Gray Land." There Caputo describes an incident that occurred late in his tour of duty, for which he and two others were brought before a court-martial. As a first lieutenant, Caputo ordered two men to go into a village at night and "get" two suspected Vietcong. Caputo recalls his instructions as: "you get those goddam VC. Snatch'em up and bring'em back here, but if they give you any problem, kill'em" (317). Following his instructions, Caputo's men kill the two suspects, who turn out not to be Vietcong after all, and the three Americans find themselves facing court-martial on charges that Caputo labels "absurd." In his response to those charges, Caputo again attempts to justify his own conduct, this time by blaming the war itself:

> The deaths of Le Dung and Le Du could not be divorced from the nature and conduct of the war. As I had come to see it, America could not intervene in a people's war without killing some of the people. But to raise these points in explanation or extenuation would be to raise a host of ambiguous moral questions. It could even raise the question of the morality of American intervention in Vietnam. (323)

The killings were "inevitable," Caputo argues. Thus he exempts himself from moral responsibility, as if an immoral war excuses immoral individual conduct. But if individuals cannot be held accountable for their own actions, then who can? Caputo never answers this question.

It is important to understand that the men who fought are not to blame; the society that sent them to fight is. Vietnam is an indictment of America, not of the Vietnam Veteran. It is not even the fault singularly of the politicians and power brokers that issued the first orders to go to Vietnam. The war was a moral atrocity, and it was everyone's. All of America lost its innocence in Vietnam. Caputo mainly concerns himself with the timeless theme of innocence savaged and destroyed on the battlefield. The most succinct statement of this theme appears in the "Epilogue" of *A Rumor of War.* The narrator-correspondent Phil Caputo observes from a circling helicopter the hasty and chaotic American evacuation of Saigon on 29 April 1975, the day prior to the fall of the city to the North Vietnamese:

> My mind shot back a decade, to that day we marched into Vietnam, swaggering, confident, and full of idealism. We had believed we were there for a high moral purpose. But somehow our idealism was lost, our morals corrupted, and the purpose forgotten. (328)

The "we" of the quote refers to Lieutenant Caputo and the members of the 9th Expeditionary Brigade arriving in Vietnam in March 1965. But, on another significant level, the "we" refers to Americans in general as the first combat units entered the war.

The American learned a lesson in Vietnam, a lesson captured by novels such as *A Rumor of War* and *Fields of Fire*—a lesson that they would never forget. There are stories of individuals' loss of innocence and coming of age in a war that politically was America's first defeat and left the country scarred. As Caputo describes his own innocent yearning for adventure, the inspiration of Kennedy's Camelot, the strong belief in an international role as protector from communism and defender of democracy, he is also presenting an example of American innocence prior to the Vietnam War. Such innocence initially cracked with President Kennedy's assassination but shattered in the political and military turmoil of Vietnam. Karnow, in describing the Vietnam Veterans Memorial in Washington, comments on this end of national innocence:

> They [names of dead] bear witness to the end of America's absolute confidence in its moral exclusivity, its military invincibility, its manifest destiny. They are the price, paid in blood, and sorrow, for America's awakening to maturity, to the recognition of its limitations. With the young men who died in Vietnam died the dream of an "American century." (9)

With the death of the dream of an "American century" the Americans learned that war is not glorious, not glamorous, not good, but irrational and immoral. They learned that they could not sacrifice their morals in the name of their ideals. They also learned that they have not attained enlightenment of any kind; they are as capable of atrocity as anyone else. American values did not die in Vietnam; Vietnam is just their greatest injunction against those values. It is the greatest of a history of atrocities into which their ideas about their own superiority have led them. It is a reminder that when they lose sight of the fact that they are not morally superior to the rest of the world, they lose sight of their very rationality, and thus their moral worth. America should not forget the insanity of war as Zalin Grant argues in "Vietnam as Fable": Caputo "pleaded that the insanity of the war . . . made him do it, and the critics generously agreed" (Grant 24). Caputo fails to take into account that sense of the other on which morality depends. To be sure, the military and the "political witch doctors like John F. Kennedy" (Caputo's phrase) should be held morally responsible for the abyss of Vietnam. Beyond a doubt, the policies of government and military officials led to the repeated atrocities that plagued the war, as Caputo alleges. But those who actually carried out the executions of the women and children at My Lai, for example, certainly share that moral responsibility. To argue otherwise is sheer sophistry.

## List of Works Cited and Consulted


Caputo, Philip. *A Rumor of War*. New York: Henry Holt, 1996.

Frankena, William K. *Ethics*. Englewood Cliffs, N.J: Prentice-Hall, 1963.

Grant, Zalin. "Vietnam as Fable." *The New Republic.* March 25, 1978.

Greene, Graham. *The Quiet American*. Harmondsworth: Penguin, 1955.

Herr, Michael. *Dispatches*. New York: Alfred A Knopf, 1977.

Kant, Immanuel. "The Foundations of Ethics." *Moral Philosophy: A Reader*. Ed. Louis Pojman. Indianapolis: Hackett, 1998.

Karnow, Stanely. *Vietnam: History*. New York: Viking, 1983.

O'Brien, Tim. *Going After Cacciato*. New York. Dell, 1978.

_____. *If I Die in a Combat Zone. Box Me up and Ship Me Home*. New York: Laurel, 1973.

Webb, James. *Fields of Fire*. New York: Bantam, 1978.

# On Locating Landmarks in Recent American Literature: Thoughts on Some Native American Short Stories

**Nila Das**
**University of Kalyani, West Bengal**

Let me begin on a personal note. In a snowy morning some three years back, while knocking around the collection of American literature at the University of Iowa library, I had chanced upon a 1998 collection of contemporary Native American short stories. The book had a catching title, as a Native American book usually has, with a tribal air about it, *Earth Song Sky Spirit.* What had drawn me to the book, however, was not the title as such, or the names of the storywriters, many being familiar to me, thanks to the U.S. Information Service and the international book market. My prime attraction has been the very tuning of Professor Trafzer's introductory essay. The essay began: "In a dream I first met an Indian elder. . . . The old man walked with me . . . pointing out places he thought important for me to know. . . . As we walked along, the old man spotted a leafy green plant. 'Oh, you will like this,' he exclaimed, 'this is good root'. . . . The elder . . . began to unearth the root with his hands, and as he did, he sang his song, a song of thanksgiving to the earth, and to the plant. He sang a song praising the Creator" (2). This was an American university professor recapitulate his dream of a Native elder, the image of America's suppressed and forgotten past, with all reverence, involvement, and care.

On another occasion I have been equally amazed reading the Hispanic American novelist Rudolfo Anaya's views on the myths in American literature, many of which do not originate in his own cultural tradition. "The mythos of the people and the writings speak to the underlying philosophical assumptions which form the particular world view of culture. . . . In real sense, the mythologies of the Americans are the only mythologies of all of us, whether we are newly arrived or whether we have been here for centuries" (*Society and Values*. 2000:46) Racially discriminating America spoke to me in a language I have not been accustomed to associating it with.

Professor Trafzer's dream reminded me of some basic truths of literature often unrecognized in the current crossfire of literary theories and discourse. Yet these truths go in creating and recognizing landmarks in literature. A creative writer with his/her artistic insight is the "elder," who initiates the audience to the areas of human experience important for all to know. In a sense, literature is a process of unearthing the roots that make a culture what it is. A creative writer brings to light the life ways, life views, the value and belief systems, the ideas and dreams of a community, a country, a civilization. Literature in all its forms is a song of creation, a mode of thanksgiving to the earth.

A good many practising U.S. creative writers attach much significance to literature as a route to re-define American culture, and to re-discover what being an American is or should be like in the present U.S. situation. "Each voice is valid and valuable. And the more open we are in listening to these diverse voices, the more enriched and enlarged our own lives will be," says Amy Ling, another reputed Asian American novelist. "The mainstream of American literature is being re-defined. It's no longer a literature of "the other," or the margins. It is reflecting more who we are as Americans. People writing in this new tradition are at . . . cross roads of culture. They are part of it and also slightly out of it. It's a unique position, perspective and time," writes Cristina Garcia, the Cuban American novelist (*Society and Values* 45-46). Taken together, these voices and many of the kind increasingly arising from the very heart of America, though largely from the marginalized communities, beacon a turning point in the approach of the U.S. creative writers themselves to American literature and culture. The creative writers are "the elders" who initiate the audience to views important to know.

One may legitimately doubt if the majority U.S. audience have their mind set to accepting the notion of "total heritage" Bharati Mukherjee speaks about, or if they can reach out to the "diverse voices" the way Amy Ling recommends. It is well known that for all the drum beating of the "mosaic" of America's pluralistic society and culture the process of "Othering" that the U.S. history started with, continues in insidious forms when not overt. Even in the U.S. academia the persistent canon war in literature sustains the process on grounds other than aesthetic. Till date not merely the mainstream communities, the extremely self-conscious marginalized ones too have been keen on defining and defending their identity, visibility, power and stature in terms of distance, difference, opposition, exclusion rather than through reciprocal relationships that actually pattern a "cultural mosaic" as socially wholesome and aesthetically whole. How long and how far the parameters of ethnic/racial difference, distance, distinction will hold good with the third, fourth, fifth generation Americans coming to the frontline with their shared life ways, and to a large extent life views, is another matter. Or rather it is the most significant matter in the present context.

It is said that it takes generations to make, absorb, sustain the value and belief systems that mark a civilization. The U.S. civilization, to apply the term the U.S. academics are fascinated with, is a civilization in the making. It is being created by people who belong to the young U.S. republic (the republic is not always and necessarily identical with the people though), but carry inside them the age-old cultural traditions of varied communities and regions that continually rub up against one another, yet accommodate one another, and get fused with one another to give rise to particular meanings and forms identified as distinctly American. Socio-cultural adaptations, imbrications, cross-fertilizations happen slowly, often unnoticed. Making of a culture/civilization is not an out and out elective "pick and mix" device. The effort yields cultural fragments and hybrids, not a rich cultural tradition. The truth is culture/civilization involves a constant movement onward. One cannot move unless one has the back foot firm on the ground. One's own cultural heritage is the firm ground that one has. The new perspective the recent U.S. creative writers speak about, and reflect in their literature is geared to re-fertilizing America's cultural ground.

Without being a fanatic over a territorially exclusive culture, it can be stated in the context that one's cultural heritage is rooted in one's relation to the land. Attachment to the land is attachment to the people inhabiting the land. That creates a sense of heritage across generations. As Geary Hobson, the Native American poet, says: "Heritage is people. People are the earth. In remembering these relationships—to the people, the past, the land—we renew in strength our continuance as a people" (*Society and Values*: 41). The poet may have said this in relation to the Native American people, but it is relevant to all the U.S. communities and groups. As a matter of fact, even though Americans of different communities/groups attribute meanings to the land in their own ways, and read its history in different terms, all of them are conscious that it is the land that has brought them to it. The land has a vital impact in shaping and reshaping their life ways and mental maps. In his book on cultural geography Mike Crang emphasizes that people are defined by where they live, and in turn define it. In the recent American cultural context defining the land, or relating oneself to the land and to its people implies not merely knowing the "Others," or letting the "Others" be, but knowing into the" Others."

This reminds me of some lines of a poem by the Japanese American poet, Joan Miyamoto. A *sansei* girl defines her identity in relation to the land she was born, and is growing up in

> People kept asking me
> What are you?
> And I would always answer I'm an American
> They'd say
> No, what nationality?
> I'm an American

That's where I was born
Flashing hot inside when I'd tell them what they wanted to know
Japanese. . . .
Oh I've been to Japan. (Iwasaki 1971: 98-99)

Even when she accepts the tag Japanese have given her, she is all too aware of her distance with Japan. Her psychic estrangement from her Japanese cultural roots shows signs of her dislocation from a large section of her community in the States, the first generation immigrants who are more Japanese than American, and the radicals who wear their racial distance as a distinction. A daughter of the American soil, the unnamed *sansei* girl feels at home being American, past her skin color, and the shape of her eyes. The land is her heritage, and that is all that matters.

Published in the early seventies, the poem is a wayside flower too fragile to draw the attention of literary highway riders. Yet, sometimes the wayside flowers act as landmarks, if the traveler has the eyes to see. For the last few decades there has been no dearth of literary wayside flowers coming up from different corners of America's socio-cultural landscape. The literary pieces, branded marginal, bear the message of the *sansei* girl of the poem in varied modes and idioms. It is said that a literary landmark mirrors in gist a culture in its onward flow. The marginal texts mirror the flow in their own ways, as they signal a new direction towards responding to America's multi-cultural/cross-cultural situation, so long written in literature mostly in terms of anger, agony, clash, exclusion, confusion, despair. Henry James once remarked that it takes a lot of history to produce the flowering of literature. It certainly takes a lot of history, including the ideational and cultural, for an author to make a literary landmark, and for the audience to accept it.

## II

I began the discussion with reference to Professor Trafzer's reverent response to Native American tales, and Professor Anaya's to the American mythologies. If not too exceptional, the response of both the academics from different U.S. communities reflects the long-awaited turning point in the audience orientation to American literature and culture. Let us read two recent Native American short stories in tune with the new approach. The random choice is self-explanatory. Both the stories focus on the Anglo-Saxon and the non Anglo-Saxon Americas reaching out to one another in amicable terms in spite of the dominant trend of differentiation, confrontation and exclusion.

To the Native Americans, story telling is a mode of preservation and communication of knowledge (Ethos), law (Nomos), cultural history, custom ways, value and belief systems that guide the community across generations. Highlighting the significance of Native American stories and the Native art of story telling/writing Scott Momaday, the first Native American Pulitzer Prize-winning novelist, said: "Telling story is a process in which a man invests and preserves himself in the context of ideas." Many recent Native writers share his view. Gerald Vizenor's "An Edible Menu and a Slow Food Trickster" (1978 *Wordarrows*), the story we begin with, is especially relevant as a story of ideas. The story is set on road, in the typical pattern of a trickster tale. A Euro-American sociologist chance meets a Native American jailbird on parole. The Native American eventually turns out to be his pathfinder, both figuratively and literally.

The story begins, "'Call me Ishmael,' he said, while he escorted a short balding sociologist across Cedar Avenue, 'follow me and you will find the best place to cross the road'." Ishmael is actually a man with no name. Born without certification at an ice fishing house, the brunt of Native American history in the U.S. written large on him, he had been called Noname at his school in the Reservation. "The patriarch of the church" gave him the name Ishmael. "He will be a wild man, his hand will be against every man, and every man's hand against him," said the priest quoting *Genesis,* as he deliberately chose the name of the mythical cultural drop-out for the tribal American child.

Frequently called to task for his deceitful/evil exploits, the norms of assessment different in two cultures, Ishmael had ultimately been sent to prison for life on a false charge of "first degree burglary and rape." The prosecutor won elections in return. In the trickster way, Ishmael had smiled on the travesty of justice. "The subject has not recognized the seriousness of his crime, refuses to accept sound measures," wrote the prison psychologist attending him, in the office note.

In his trickster way again, Ishmael outwitted the prison authorities, escaped, and set sail at sea. "Sailing is freedom, the sea is free. . . . Prison is the scenario," he cried in glee. As anticipated, his freedom did not last long. Re-arrested and on parole, he keeps on deliberately violating the law, even if it amounts to crossing at the middle of the road. "Was the middle of the road, the figurative middle, worth the round trip to prison?" asks the sociologist. "Metaphors are not quantities," replies Ishmael. "The middle weather was fine, but I was slow to learn about scenarios."

Explaining the Native American philosophy of life, Vizenor said in an interview, "Life is not static. Philosophically . . . we should break out of our roots . . . break off invented cultures and repressions." In the story Ishmael refers to the institutionalized ideology dominant in the U.S., by the term scenario, and contrasts it to the Native American ideology he identifies as ritual/ ceremony. "Ideologies become scenarios" he explains, "scenarios are plans for owning and having. Rituals are celebrations." To the Native Americans ideology sets directions to life, as it celebrates, confirms, and transforms from within. One needs a psycho-cultural orientation to imbibe the ideology. Without offering any counter-argument, as expected, the Euro-American sociologist participates in the discourse in tune with the Native speaker, "the rituals celebrate the known and the unknown, even the foreknowable . . . the conscious and the unconscious through time and space. . . . There are no mysteries in the scenarios."

The sociologist wonders at the identity of his companion. "Who are you?" he asks. "Call me Ishmael," comes the answer. The Euro-American refuses to co-relate the Native with the image of the evil-maker that the name signifies. "What are you looking at?" he enquires. "The trickster" replies Ishmael.

> "Where?"
> "In the mirror there"

The mirror reflects Ishmael's own image. Noname finds his true self in the image of the mythical trickster. The Euro-American sociologist too recognizes him as the culture symbol, "You would be the winning hand of a trickster." In Native American belief the trickster is the one who is "neither good nor evil yet he is responsible for both. He possesses no rules moral and social, is at the mercy of his passions, yet through his actions all values come into being" (Paul Rodin 1978, 107). The story ends with the sociologist accepting the trickster as his pathfinder.

Our next story, poet and artist Duanne Niatum's "For Her with No Regrets" (1998, *Earth Song*) is of a different flavor. Situated at the socio-cultural cross-roads that the present generation Americans inhabiting multi-racial, multi-cultural locales live through, it is a love story of Young, a Native American, and Suzanne, a married Jewish American lady. The secret relationship, an "on and off" affair, traps both into "more corners than a chess game." Highly uneasy over Suzanne's marital status, both the lovers find themselves self-critical of their attachment to each other. In course of events Suzanne returns to her husband. "Habit alone makes it scary to leave the roost," she tells Young justifying her decision, though none too happy over it. Both the Native man and the Jewish woman treasure their love for each other with no regrets.

The story is narrated by Young. Virtually the story is a monologue of a highly sensitive man, recapitulating his feelings, thoughts and realizations as he came close to a lady of a different community. "That tribe is as crazy as ours," he fondly remembers the words he had read once in a journal. In racial American terminology, however, Suzanne has been the "Other." A "little siren," a "doll of hysteria," "a comrade of wrong roads," she would make Young "the one left holding a blank page," forewarned the Native community. Young himself had been conscious of the possibility. Left forlorn, he has realized another truth. It has been the tall, slim, Jewish lady, the "Other," with her gipsy hair "of the kind only the wind knows how to form," and eyes "with the blue of a waterfall," who had made him blossom up in body and mind.

The story begins, "Did I hear a key make music out of glass tap, tap, tap? . . .Was I dreaming what? Then the cadence of those unforgettable words told me this was no dream. 'Wake up, wake up. . . . I am bringing you the morning." The voice has been Suzanne's, but in reality long lost. The cadence remains in Young's mind. The lines read like a poem. The entire story, Young's waking dream, is a lyric poem in prose, composed with all the tenderness of a lover's remembrance.

Young recapitulates how Suzanne had attracted him being the "Other, though all along the story he does not highlight the points of difference in her ethnic ways and patterns of thought, remaining silent on his own as well as on Suzanne's responses/ reactions in this regard. In their love story the difference did not count. To both of them the moments together had been "a ritual of surprise." "We applauded the band that played our secret nature. We were near the end of the song when she whispered . . . 'I believe in you, I believe in me. I believe in us. Honest'." Young reciprocated her feelings. Closeness of human relationship had made them "soul mates."

Young's thoughts move back to his ancestors. "Our ancestors . . . had taught us how to make a life out of nightmares. The grandfathers and grandmothers who speak in flames sing endlessly to us of how scars bind together . . . as much as tenderness." The continued value system, his cultural heritage, has taught Young to enrich life in relation to the "Other," knowing into the "Other," being together with the "Other." He remembers the last note Suzanne had pinned to his door prior to her departure, "Even though we cannot be together, our past and our dreams remain." Young knows "Time the medicine man, in charge of us all" will heal up the loss, but Suzanne will remain in his mind for ever, re-vitalizing him, bringing mornings in his hours of darkness.

One is reminded of Paula Allen's Ephanie in the well-known novel, *The Woman who Owned the Shadows* (1983), in the context. Native American Ephanie deliberately keeps herself distanced from the social and cultural mores of her Japanese American husband, breaks off with him on ground that they do not share each other's thoughts and dreams, yet finds even the memory of the relationship haunting her. It is a permanent scar in her life. Niatum's Young and Allen's Ephanie, for all their temperamental difference, offer scope of an in-depth study of America's response to the multi-ethnic, multi-cultural situation.

The story ends with Young proposing a toast to Suzanne. His words are half prayer, half poetry, "May her cup be full when this memory raises her sweet bird of a hand to the stars and the moon we had followed so many nights, to catch the last glimpse of those exiles . . . whom only darkness will remember or name." The calm of mind reflected in his tone indicates that the exile in Young has returned home, if "home" is one's harmony with oneself.

Do these wayside flowers in the colorful floriculture of recent American literature make landmarks? It is for the audience both in the U.S. and outside to say.

### List of Works Cited and Consulted

Allen Paula Gunn. *The Woman who Owned the Shadows*. San Francisco: Spinsters/Aunt Lute, 1983.

Bruchac Joseph. *Survival This Way: Interviews with American Indian Poets.* Tuscan: U of Arizona Press, 1987.

"Contemporary U.S. Literature: A Multi-cultural Perspective." *U.S. Society and Value*. Electronic Journal. U.S. Embassy: New Delhi. August 2000.

Crang Mike. *Cultural Geography.* Routledge, 1998.

Iwasaki Bruce. "Responses and Changes for the Asian in America: A Survey of Asian American Literature." *Roots: An Asian American Reader*, ed. Ami Tachiki. Los Angeles, California: UCLA Asian American Studies Centre, 1971.

Trafzer, Clifford E., ed. *Earth Song Sky Spirit: Short Stories of the Contemporary Native American Experience.* New York: Doubleday, 1993.

Vizenor Gerald. *Wordarrows: Indians and Whites in the New Fur Trade*. University of Minnesota Press, 1978.

# Landmarks in Native American Literature: A Study of *House Made of Dawn*, *Ceremony*, and *The Death of Jim Loney*

**Brajesh Sawhney**
**Kurukshetra University, Kurukshetra**

> We are the land. To the best of my understanding, that is the fundamental idea embedded in Native American life and culture in the Southwest. More than remembered, the earth is the mind of the people as we are the mind of the earth. The land is not really the place (separate from ourselves) where we act out the drama of our isolate destinies. It is not a means of survival, a setting for our affairs, a resource on which we draw in order to keep our own act functioning. It is not the ever-present "Other" which supplies us with a sense of "I." It is rather a part of our being, dynamic, significant, real. It is ourself, in as real a sense as such notions as "ego," "libido" or social network, in a sense more real than any conceptualization or abstraction about the nature of human being can ever be. . . . Nor is this relationship one of mere "affinity" for the Earth. It is not a matter of being "close to nature." The relationship is more one of identity, in the mathematical sense, than of affinity. The Earth is, in a very real sense, the same as ourself (or selves), and it is this primary point that is made in the fiction and poetry of the Native American writers of the Southwest. (Allen 191)

The present paper is a study of three American novels published within the past quarter of the twentieth century: N. Scott Momaday's *House Made of Dawn* (1968), Leslie Marmon Silko's *Ceremony* (1977), and James Welch's *The Death of Jim Loney* (1979). Each of these novels occupies a very important place among the texts that established the Native American literature as part of the American literature canon. But, to identify them as Native American works would be to marginalize them. Using such a label would mean categorizing literature according to its ethnic qualifications. The present paper will explore the ways in which these three novels can be seen as representative examples of recent American fiction without applying ethnocentric criteria. This is possible because, in these three works, the common referent that serves to characterize, approximate, and validate identity is a physical landscape/ landmark rather than a social fabric.

The theoretical formulations of the deconstructionist approach during the 1980s resulted in willingness among the conformists of literary academia to review the traditional canon of American literature. And their efforts to redefine or expand the literary cannon led them to one or another of these three works. Although the search for longer "representative" Native American texts written in English began with these texts, it did not end there. All three of these writers have gone on to publish novels that are perhaps more mature or even more "representative" of a strongly emerging Native American tradition. And a great deal of Native American writing by young Native authors can also be considered as "representative" of a strong emerging tradition. The writings prior to these three works also cannot be ignored; they have made an important contribution in times when native writing was in nascent stage. Still these three novels have come to be generally regarded as unquestionably most important Native American texts. It is for this reason that I am focusing on these three texts.

The question of identifying the Nativity of an author has been a contentious topic among scholars and writers. It would be beyond the scope of the present paper to deal with such an extensive and controversial topic.[1] But the three novels chosen for study have been written by Native American writers who have established tribal affiliations. Moreover, all three works feature a Native character, foreground Native settings that include Indian reservations, and embody distinctly Native American tropes in form of tribal ceremonies, rituals, oral histories, as told to stories and traditional wisdom or epistemology. A non-Native reader, who is trained in Euro-American tradition with certain codified cultural assumptions, finds these textures as culturally exotic. His training in a non-Native culture obstructs a free play between him and the Native American text. Greg Sarris has rightly observed in this regard,

> In any event, what all these scholars do not seem to see is that while purportedly defending Indians and enlightening others about them, they replicate in practice that which characterizes not only some non-Indian editor's manners of dealing with Indians but also that of an entire European and Euro-American populace of which these scholars and editors are a part. The Indians are absent or they are strategically removed from the territory, made safe, intelligible on the colonizer's terms. (78)

Students and teachers have obviously found difficulty in reading such texts in the classroom situation. And the most apparent obstruction in their understanding is, to use Hirsch's term, their cultural illiteracy. Many readers presume that since the "subtext" in these works is culturally unfamiliar to them, the text itself will be closed to all but fairly sophisticate Native readers. As a result, much of the interpretative criticism available on these works is designed to facilitate an easy entry of the non-Indian reader to these texts. Such interpretative works provide meanings, though the surface meanings only, of the culturally specific ceremonies, rituals, myths, legends and oral traditions to the non-Native reader.

It does not imply that the efforts of the scholars who facilitate the readers with explanations of tribal culture and tradition are worthless. It would be pointless to discount the usefulness of such scholarship for any reader trying to gain entry to these works. However, there are certain tropes in the text, which are specific to Native cultures. The effort on the part of non-native reader to engage with the text as a means of testing his intellectual stamina would prove counter productive. The aboriginal texts seem even more inaccessible to non-Native readers who fail to understand their own "otherness" while approaching such texts.

This paper proposes to analyze and demonstrate the usefulness of a slightly different way of understanding and evaluating such texts. It derives from the proposition, generally encoded in many Native American cultural traditions themselves that place—in the sense of a real geophysical entity—matters. "Life" is a "property" of the land as well as of the life forms occupying it. As a cultural pretext, this concept fundamentally shapes both the individual creative visions of the writers of these texts and the collective visions of the Native cultural traditions represented in these novels.

The issue of engagement between the mainstream and "marginalized" literatures has dominated literary studies in the United States since 1980s. Theoretical propositions of the poststructuralists and deconstructionists have foregrounded marginalized literature: Native American writings, Chicano writings, Asian American literature and Afro-American literature. But the writings of scholars like Cathy N. Davidson has called for a reevaluation of the past binaries and divisions between mainstream and marginalized literature. In a book entitled *No More Separate Spheres* (2002) Davidson has hinted at the new direction in literary criticism that has a more hybridized approach to literature, calling for an approach that can include the fruitful complications that arise out of a hybridized approach to issues of race, sexuality, class, region, religion, and occupation. In this light, the study of teaching and reading "current literature" in which concurrent "currents" compose "current literature" can preserve the fruitful complications that arise from creative interactions between various streams of literature. Thus, it is not a matter of center and margins now, but rather of concurrent streams of development. Taken all together, the course of postwar prose, consisting of all such currents, may still be usefully conceptualized as a mainstream, with sub-currents, fed by branches that tend to enrich the mainstream at their confluences. It will be worthwhile to try to locate these three novels in that conceptual mainstream.

The American literary tradition, like the European tradition out of which it primarily evolved, had become characteristically postmodern in temperament by the 1960s. Although there has been little agreement among scholars about what that term means, it still persists and has evolved into a variety of forms. In a way it acknowledges the influential power of twentieth-century existential thought in postwar literature. Irving Howe identified and defined the postmodern temperament phenomenon in terms of "collapse of social consensus." It was, according to him, a result of the general loss of faith in the institutions of Western civilization. This loss was triggered by the intellectual recognition that all such institutions were finally arbitrary and by the shattering social dislocations brought about by World War II. John Barth, in his *Atlantic* article "The Literature of Exhaustion," called attention to "literary self-reflexivity"—of "novels which imitate the form of the Novel, by an author who imitates the role of Author"—as one of the most characteristic qualities of postmodern fiction. Thematic concepts as antirealism, the antihero, and the impenetrable surfaceness of the phenomenological world are recognized as some other important features of postmodern American novel. All such attempts depend for their logical integrity on the basic proposition, popularized in the postwar years under the rubric Existentialism, that the human condition disallows any discovery of meaning or value because the human entity is fundamentally estranged from the world as "Other." Underlying the postmodern temperament is this recurrent conviction that alienation *is* the human condition and that consequently *all* statements of meaningful relationship between the individual and anything/everything else are, necessarily, fictions.

In the mid-60s, and prior to publishing the *Atlantic* manifesto, Barth—in that decade generally considered one of the foremost of the American postmodernist writers as well as one of its most articulate spokespersons—had this to say about his own creative vision:

> If you are a novelist of a certain type of temperament, then what you really want to do is re-invent the world. God wasn't too bad a novelist, except he was a Realist. Some of the things he did are right nice: the idea that ontogeny recapitulates phylogeny is a

> masterstroke; if you thought that up you'd be proud of yourself. But a certain kind of sensibility can be made very uncomfortable by the recognition of the *arbitrariness* of physical facts and the inability to accept their *finality*. Take France, for example: France is shaped like a teapot, and Italy is shaped like a boot. Well, okay. But the idea that that's the only way it's ever going to be, that they'll never be shaped like anything else—that can get to you after a while. . . . And it seems to me that this emotion, which is a kind of metaphysical emotion, goes almost to the heart of what art is, at least some kinds of art, and this impulse to imagine alternatives to the world can become a driving impulse for writers. (Enck, "John Barth" 8)

At about the same time, John Hawkes spoke of the "need to preserve the truth of the fractured picture" and of the correlative freedom to create the "imaginary landscapes" (Enck, "John Hawkes" 148-49) the disturbingly Daliesque distortions of Italian and English countrysides of *The Cannibal* and *The Lime Twig*, or the more overtly "otherworldly" milieu implicit in the title of an early collection of stories, *Lunar Landscapes*—that function appropriately as settings for such truths. Taken near to its extreme, we get the characteristically anti-realistic fiction of Richard Brautigan, whose nameless antiheroic protagonist finds himself near the end of *Trout Fishing in America* in the Cleveland Wrecking Yard still searching for "America, often only a place in the mind" (72), or of Thomas Pynchon, whose *Oedipa Maas* either discovers or invents the recognition that "there either was some Trystero beyond the appearance of America, or there was just America and if there was just America then it seemed the only way she could continue, and manage to be at all relevant to it, was as an alien, unfurrowed, assumed full circle into some paranoia" (182).

As several critics have noted, postmodern American fiction, generally speaking, is a "literature of illness,"[2] and the illness from which such protagonists suffer is essentially the illness of alienation, of estrangement—a sickness for which there is no cure, given the tenets of existential thinking, only the sedative of fiction-making. Or as Kurt Vonnegut puts it in a chapter of *Cat's*

*Cradle* titled "A Medical Opinion on the Effect of a Writers' Strike":

> "When a man becomes a writer, I think he takes on a sacred obligation to produce beauty and enlightenment and comfort at top speed."
> "I just can't help thinking what a real shaking up it would give people if, all of a sudden, there were no new books, new plays, new histories, new poems. . . ."
> "And how proud would you be when people started dying like flies?" I demanded.
> I turned to Castle the Elder. "Sir, how does a man die when he's deprived of the consolations of literature?"
> "In one of two ways," he said, "petrescence of the heart or atrophy of the nervous system. . . . For the love of God, *both* of you, *please* keep writing!" (189)

The American Indian works mentioned above also address this postmodern disease. To the extent that we can speak of a postmodern disease as having become a central concern of the American literary tradition, and to the extent that a self-conscious state of alienation is the signature of the postmodern protagonist, these three novels fit neatly into the flow of the American literary mainstream. Each of these novels opens with its protagonist suffering from acute alienation, physically as well as spiritually sickened in the postwar era. Existentially speaking, all three protagonists awake into a state of consciousness every bit as culturally and psychologically estranged as, say, Barth's Todd Andrews or Pynchon's Oedipa Maas. The difference is that while the canonized postmodern protagonist goes on either to propagate the disease or to succumb to it, the protagonists of these three novels (as in many other postwar American Indian texts) acquire the blessing of a cure. The antidote to alienation and its consequences in these works is (to push this metaphor to its limit) a rather old-fashioned-looking but still potent vaccine: geographical realism.[3]

It is worth pointing out here that one (though by no means the only) symptom of the disease reflected in this "literature of illness" is the sense of the arbitrariness and hence meaninglessness of the physical world, of the inappropriateness of real landscapes as metaphors for what these writers and/or their protagonists recognize, or come to recognize, as the human condition.[4] By and large, postmodernism rejects the possibility of an intrinsically healing relationship between the individual and the world prior to some act of attenuation or distortion of that environment through an operation of imagination. This is where the novels treated in this study diverge from the postmodern mainstream—or, seen another way, where these novels come to constitute a major contribution to that mainstream. As fictions, these texts take as an inviolable referent a physical landscape, one that exists prior to the fiction and then comes to exist (the way referents can be said to "exist") within the fiction as well. For both the writer creating the fiction and the fictional protagonist discovering or creating a viable identity, the physical landscape functions in these works as a dependable constant: the land as a place provides them with a referential framework that lies, undistorted by the imaginative operations of either the writers or their protagonists, "outside" the postmodern temperament but, as things develop in each of these fictions, as the basis for recentering of self-consciousness as well.

From the cultural perspective of most American readers, these three novels may look like a new realism. Perhaps more accurately, what we're seeing is a renaissance of a species of literary realism gradually abandoned in the course of the Euro-American literary tradition's evolution but faithfully maintained for centuries in American Indian creative consciousness. By 1959 Howe could argue persuasively, that social consensus was the true referent of both modernism and realism in the Euro-American literary tradition; in 1959, it was also being maintained by Native storytellers (albeit rarely enough in print) that cultural identities, like individual identities, emerge not from class struggle but rather from the land.

While it is true enough that the protagonists of these novels are culturally estranged (Tayo and Loney are "halfbreeds," Abel a "mixed breed"), the cure for the disease of alienation in their cases depends on their willingness and ability to enter (or, more precisely, in the cases of Abel and Tayo, re-enter) into identity with the landscape, the place where the event of their lives happens to have taken and to be taking place. The process of identification with place allows these protagonists to enter also into identity with whatever tribal traditions—encoded in stories and ceremony—happen also to have come about in these places. A degree of reidentification with some Native cultural tradition plays an important part in the healing process of these protagonists,[5] but in the pattern of these fictions as in their Keresan, Towan, and Blackfeet, and Gros Ventre epistemological contexts, stories grow out of the land just the way other forms of life do. Or to put the matter into existential terms, the "existence" of the land precedes the "essences" (cultural and personal identities, and the stories about those identities) that come into being there. Acquisition of a "realistic" vision of the landscape is, in these works, a prerequisite to the acquisition of a verifiable cultural identity. This is the premise that these Native fictions have in common, and this is the premise that at once controls the distinctly "Native" texture of these works and sets these works apart from much of the rest of the postwar American corpus.

A powerful respect for place, in the sense of a particular real landscape, is characteristic of much of what we categorize, as Native story—both fiction and poetry—is not novel. And yet, such claims about the shaping power of landscapes upon the literary imagination, made by writers and leading critics of American Indian literature alike, have rarely been demonstrated methodically in critical writings about that literature. Generally speaking, literary criticism resists the notion that the land has a life of its own and tends instead to proceed as though vitality were a quality imposed on the land by human imagination but not vice-versa. This sort of preemption of significance, or privileging of human imagination, is one of the dangerous shortcomings of the Euroamerican humanistic tradition in general and of a conventional humanistic approach to this literature in particular: presupposing and then magnifying the shaping power of people in these stories limits our ability to recover the *pre*-human context of the human condition in these stories.

This is not to say that the humanistic impulse is not an integral element of American Indian fiction. Clearly it is. The test of humanity in these works, though, is the land itself rather than any ideology: the protagonists of these fictions prove their humanity not by conquering the land or by living in spite of it, but rather by finding ways—sometimes "traditional," sometimes "innovative," and sometimes a creative blend of the two—to live *with* the land, holding and being held by the life that precedes and survives the life of any individual, as well as the life of any culture.

About the "*sense* of place," a phrase that privileges the process of human identification *with* the place that informs American Indian cultures, I have nothing new to say. Dozens of competent critics—Paula Gunn Allen, Keith Basso, William Oandasan, Larry Evers, and others—have done that already. I wish only to draw attention back to the particular landscapes—the geophysical landscapes that precede and at least partially determine the social or cultural ones that serve not only as the "settings" of these fictions but also as principal "characters" in them. Others have shown, and will continue to show, how the process of recovery for the protagonists of these novels can be understood as a process of acquiring an appropriate cultural literacy—a process of learning or re-learning, living or re-living, the stories and lifeways of the People (be they Keresan, Towan, Kiowa, Navajo, Blackfeet, or Gros Ventre) and thereby identifying themselves with a particular cultural milieu. My intention is to show how a key element of "cultural literacy," in these works specifically and perhaps by extension in American Indian cultural contexts generally, is an intimate knowledge of a particular landscape. As Basso has demonstrated for the case of the White Mountain Apache, this kind of knowledge is encoded in the stories of many Native cultures and is available in that form to the tribally literate; but of course very few of us are literate if the referent is White Mountain Apache or Keresan/Laguna or Towan/Jemez or Blackfeet/Gros Ventre oral and written traditions. These fictions provide culturally non-Native readers with landscapes that function as pre-verbal, pre-conceptual, pre-cultural frames of reference, frames that shape the creative vision and language of these texts in much the same way the language and vision characteristic of the respective tribal traditions must have been shaped. Reproduced "realistically," the landscapes of these texts are themselves living texts and can be "read" in any language.

## NOTES

1. For a detailed discussion of this topic see Jace Weaver's *That the People Might Live: Native American Literature and Native American Community* (New York: OUP, 1997).
2. I am indebted here to Scarberry-García for a phrase used by in her Introduction to *Landmarks of Healing: A Study of* House Made of Dawn (Albuquerque: Univ. of New Mexico Press, 1990), in which she notes that (in addition to the postwar writers and works I have already mentioned) "many contemporary American novels, such as those by Bellow, Kesey, and Updike, are unfulfilled 'narratives of illness.'"
3. In his Foreword to Scarberry-García's *Landmarks of Healing: A Study of* House Made of Dawn, Wiget makes a very similar point:

    > Like other contemporary Euroamerican literary traditions, much Native American writing acknowledges alienation and cynicism as the starting point for fiction. Native American writing, however, is attracting more and more readers, precisely because much of it does not accept the brokenness of the present world as an immutable condition of things, but invokes deeper patterns of order and meaning, often rooted in the themes and images of tribal oral traditions, as a means of restoring wholeness. (xi)

    Wiget contends that these "deeper patterns of order" are encoded in Navajo healing ceremonies—that is, in socioculturally specific pretexts. My point is that such ceremonies themselves take particular geographies as *their* pretexts. In the cases of these three novels, the land validates both the novel as text and the ceremonies as texts.

4. Critics have made this connection in the cases of individual writers. For instance, in *City of Words*, a brilliant survey of American fiction 1945-70, the British critic Tony Tanner makes a similar observation about Barth's early fictions *The Floating Opera* and *The End of the Road.*
5. As I suggested earlier, this act of cultural (re-)identification is often taken to be the quintessential event of the novel—a bias that has ironically kept much Native literature marginalized, since this approach requires the reader to be familiar enough with the cultural tradition to understand how it validates the experience of the protagonist.

## List of Works Cited and Consulted

Allen, Paula Gunn. "Iyani: It goes this way." *The Remembered Earth: An Anthology of Contemporary Native American Literature.* Ed. Geary Hobson. Albuquerque: Red Earth Press, 1979.

Davidson, Cathy N., and Jessamyn Hatcher, ed. *No More Separate Spheres! A Next Wave American Studies Reader.* Durham, NC: Duke Univ. Press, 2002.

Enck, John J. "John Barth: An Interview." *Contemporary Literature* 6.1 (Spring 1965).

_____. "John Hawkes: An Interview." *Contemporary Literature* 6.1 (Spring 1965).

Momaday, N. Scott. *House Made of Dawn.* New York: Harper & Row, 1968.

Sarris, Greg. *Keeping Slug Woman Alive: A Holistic Approach to Native American Texts.* Berkeley: Univ. of California Press, 1993.

Scarberry-García. *Landmarks of Healing: A Study of* House Made of Dawn. Albuquerque: Univ. of New Mexico Press, 1990.

Silko, Leslie Marmon. *Ceremony.* New York: Viking, 1977.

Vonnegut, Kurt. *Cat's Cradle.* 1963. New York: Dell Laurel, 1988.

Weaver, Jace. *That the People Might Live: Native American Literature and Native American Community.* New York: OUP, 1997.

Welch, James. *The Death of Jim Loney.* New York: Harper & Row, 1979.

# Present Past, and Absent Future: (Re)Creating a Lost Identity and Native American Fiction

**Punyashree Panda**
**Silicon Institute of Technology, Bhubaneswar**

What makes a Text a landmark in the literary history of a Nation? Is it merely the repetition and continuation of a particular form or style? Does it function merely with the motif of documenting the contemporary time and trends? And what is it that would qualify a text to claim landmark position in the literary history of the United States? If we assume that a literary text acquires the position of a Landmark Text when it works at the dual levels of popular recognition and aesthetic innovation and all the while keeps with the tradition and values of the community it represents, then N. Scott Momaday started a new era and a new world order by winning the 1969 Pulitzer Prize for fiction. The "Others of the World," as fashionable critical terminology calls the Native Communities of the world, are no more silent. Searching for a place beyond the western concepts of theory and literary canon, Native American authors like Momaday and Leslie Marmon Silko have brought the pride back to the tribes by telling us their side of the story and thus reestablishing their own collective identities as a race and culture.

The rise of the postcolonial voices across the globe in hues and colours as varied as the communities and peoples who have raised them has redefined and unsettled all previous isms. The potent anti-colonial insurrections of the last hundred years have raised doubts and questions for the collective global future: What does Postcolonialism mean for the "colonizer" and the "colonized"? Is it used and misused merely with the motif of reproducing structures of domination (racism, sexism, homophobia etc) within the third world? Or does it on the other hand, signify the first world's anxiety about its own decentred status? Why is it that the 'marginal' are trying to make their voices heard: voices, which range from the hyphenated communities of the First world to the lost tribes of the First Nations? The focus of my paper is the search for a national/ cultural identity in such difficult times. I would like to argue that any statement of identity is an assertion of difference and an exhibition of community pride, pride that lets these existing and conceived communities live with dignity.

Drawing heavily upon the Laguna tradition of storytelling and by her sensuous use of language, Silko, in her novel *Ceremony* explores the mindscapes of Tayo, the protagonist who as a World War II veteran, is desperately trying to reconnect with the land and its people as well as the Lost World—the community, its life, and rituals included. N. Scott Momaday's ground-breaking novel *House Made of Dawn* as a multilayered text deals not merely with Abel's confused struggle to reappropriate his individual past but also with the Kiowa author's search for a collective history, the hunt for a 'home'. Rejecting the dual choices of assimilation or destruction offered to them by the colonizing powers, these authors, in their roles as representatives of their respective communities, also become aware of their own "ethnic consciousness" through the process of writing.

Leslie Marmon Silko's *Ceremony*, along with being an authoritative text of the Land and the People, is also highly illustrative of the Native traditions of orality, thanks to its fractured memories, story-like quality, and the cyclical nature of family legacies. Silko's style in this novel is to repeat phrases, thoughts, and actions over and over, wrapping one story unto the next. The stories are so unique to the culture and traditions of the Laguna that it foregrounds the pain within. Each of the stories has its own pain, its own lessons. Sometimes she lets us know the end of the story, sometimes one can only guess. She paints a picture of the White Man as a sadistic, self-centred and more importantly, self-destructive force who has crushed the spirit of her people. Even worse, the White Man has violated Mother Earth, because to hurt the Earth is to destroy oneself. To quote:

> The people had been taught to despise themselves because they were left with barren land and dry rivers. But they were wrong. It was the white people who were suffering, as thieves do, never able to forget that their pride was wrapped in something stolen, something that had never been, and could never be, theirs. (204)

The damage thus caused to those who have been colonized is documented by Silko through her focus on how one individual has been affected, and just as the novel chooses to focus on certain effects and issues of colonization, so I choose to focus on those of a lost identity, language, history and culture. As David L. Moore suggests, in Silko's novel *Ceremony*, Laguna myths weave allegorically through the personal and cultural healing of Tayo, a mixed-blood Laguna Pueblo veteran of World War II. America's perception of and relationship with Native Americans are detailed through the half-Caucasian, half Native American protagonist of Silko's novel Tayo, and his experiences of biculturalism.

Having returned from the horrific scenes of World War II, Tayo suffers from a strange illness and a terribly devastating memory. Torn between the White and the Native world, Tayo must come out of his nightmares to live a life of belonging. And his cure lies, as family and friends suggest, not in the "white walls" of the Army hospital, but in the age-old ceremonies of the community. He must witness the convergence of life and truly understand the cyclical nature of his emotions and the events that he has experienced. The history and the wisdom of the people is expressed through stories and beliefs: "What she said: the only cure I know is a good ceremony, that's what she said" (3).

Like the author, the protagonist, Tayo, is also a mixed-blood from an influential family in the community, which "meant being different from, and not fully accepted by either the full-bloods or the whites." Searching for the identity that has been long lost, Tayo seeks answers from the community and for the community. Tayo suffers because he does not 'know'. His illness results from the separation of the ancient unity of person, ceremony and land and he will be cured only when he recognizes this unity. Hereupon, I am reminded of Momaday's *The Way to Rainy Mountain* in which he writes about the impact land can have on individual personality:

> All things in the plain are isolate; there is no confusion of objects in the eye, but one hill or one man. To look upon that landscape in the early morning, with the sun at your back, is to lose the sense of proportion. Your imagination comes to life, and this, you think, is where Creation was begun. (5)

Using the Native tradition of storytelling and oral tradition, Silko further emphasizes the role of land in her cultural lineage. To quote:

> they had seen what the white people had made from the stolen land. It was the story of the white shell beads all over again, the white shell beads, stolen from a grave and found by a man as he walked along a trail one day. . . . He could not eat, and he could not work. He lost touch with the life he had lived before the day he found the beads. (169)

A very integral aspect of Silko's *Ceremony* is her belief in words and language as powerful weapons of time—past, present, and future. She believes that English, the language of the colonizer, makes the people powerless. Ceremonies are sacred and ceremonies use a language of their own. The Navajo and Laguna ceremonies described in the novel use words in the form of chants and songs to extract and utilize the power of these words. To quote:

> He stood up. He knew the people had a song for the sunrise.
> Sunrise!
> We come at sunrise.
> to greet you.
> We call you
> at sunrise.
> Father of the clouds

> You are beautiful
> at sunrise.
> Sunrise!
>
> He repeated the words as he remembered them, not sure if they were the right ones. But feeling they were right, feeling the instant of the dawn was an event which in a single moment gathered all things together—the last stars, the mountains tops, the clouds, and the winds celebrating this coming. . . . He ended the prayer with "Sunrise" because he knew the Dawn People began and ended all their words with sunrise. (182)

The connection Silko made between land and human identity is a crucial thread, prominent throughout her novel and in doing so he fosters a sense of harmony with the Mother earth. The land, at the center of the spider's web, thus came to be associated with human identity. Land, as a creation of the imagination of the Thought Woman is again connected with the explanation given by the old people to a consequence of the white people's destroying the earth for uranium mining. In an interview with *Suntracks*, James Ruppert quotes Silko:

> People tell those stories about you and your family or about others and they begin to create your identity. In a sense, you are told who you are, or you know who you are by the stories that are told about you.

On a paradoxical level, in *Ceremony*, the blood "Cousin-brother" Tayo reenacts a contemporary variant of the old twin myths, reasserting the need for idiosyncratic pairing a full blood who imitates and dies for whites. Furthermore, the paradox is also established in the fact that these marginals, the neglected people of the land, are used up and thrown away after a time of crisis. They are drafted to fight for the country that stole their land, yet they are expected to be patriotic, loyal, and willing to die for America. Such discrimination may lead one to doubt how just the "land of the free" is in terms of their treatment of Native Americans.

> an old white woman rolled down her window and said "God bless you, God bless you," but it was the uniform, not them she blessed. (41)

The trail of tears serves as a constant, historical reminder of the mistakes the American government has made. Conversely, as James Ruppert puts it, when Silko has Tayo realize that the path back to harmony with the Land and Laguna culture requires that Tayo live again in the multiple present moment and that he must rely on the Laguna language, whose grammar subtly implies a world where the past and future coexist. Linguistically always in the present, she voices a perception of time and linguistic distinctions that do not arise out of traditional Laguna culture.

> He knew then why the old times could only speak of yesterday and tomorrow in terms of the present moment: the only certainty: and this present sense of being was qualified with bare hints of yesterday or tomorrow. (192)

The celestial laughter Silko calls forth by her ceremony shows that the Native Indian civilization is living and has the potential to transform Anglo-culture. The path Tayo takes to return from his showdown with Emo to the Pueblo is apparently designed to accommodate the further transformation of Tayo's individual life into a fuller representation of the life of the People. The consciousness that returns to the Pueblo after Tayo undergoes the ceremonies with the help of old Betonie, then, is a shared one. Tayo and also Ts'eh, Josiah, Rocky and others are in a sense, coming "home." As Lavonne Ruoff has argued, Silko emphasizes the need to return to the Keres rituals and oral tradition of the past in order to rediscover the basis for one's cultural identity. "Only when this is done is one prepared to deal with the problems of the present. . . . Silko demonstrates that the rituals and traditions have survived all attempts to eradicate them and that the seeds for the resurgence of their power lie in the memories and creativeness of her people" (Ruoff 15). In a striking metaphor, the text also speaks of Tayo's tongue having become "dry and dead, the carcass of a tiny rodent." A power of words as well as body seeks recovery, opines A. Robert Lee.

Using the half-Mexican, half Laguna Betonie's wisdom of the world and the age-old traditions of the land, Tayo comes to a path of recovery. Within the context of this larger pattern of redemptive/regenerative rediscovery of the people's power (when rightly and delicately aligned with the old ways) to make things happen, we can see. Tayo is functioning as a sort of eponymous representative of the people; his ceremony, when successfully completed, will bring the People, as well as himself as a delegate of the people, back into graceful balance with the external world. To do so, Tayo must go and actively seek out the force, align his own identity with it, and then bring his own renewed identity back to the community. To quote from David L Moore, "Relational identity is both the structure and the substance of his ceremonial role, whereby Tayo takes the responsibility for the relational dynamics of his won will, the rain, the land, the people." This mythic ecology, which revives Tayo and which Tayo revives, is not a static structure. From Betonie's description of necessary changes in the ceremonies, we can see it as a complex of changeable differences united merely by the mutual context, which they form.

> He cried the relief he felt at finally seeing the pattern, the way all the stories fit together—the old stories, the war stories, their stories—to become the story that was still being told. He was not crazy; he had never been crazy. He had only seen and heard then world as it always was: no boundaries, only transitions through all distances and time. (258)

An equally engrossing tale of the search for identity, N. Scott Momaday's widely appreciated novel *House Made of Dawn* is the story of a Kiowa Indian boy's search for self. Momaday has not merely appropriated the cause of his People through his writing in this novel but also presented and brought forth never-before known myths and legends of the Kiowa community. On a deeper level, he has attempted to appropriate the follies of history, to resurrect the mutilated race and show the pride of the community to the world.

Momaday's masterpiece and one of the most appreciated novels in Native American Literature, *House Made of Dawn* is the story of Abel, an illegitimate son of a Tanoan Mother and an unknown father, probably a Navajo. On his return from World

War II, Abel is already lost in the lanes of alcoholism and the path ahead does not at all seem easy. Abel, unlike as some critics have argued, is not merely a Noble Red Victim of the heinous forces of America but a representative of the individual's search for identity and the community's search for the lost pride.

As Silko's *Ceremony* brings forth the solution in finding out the age-old witchery as the cause of all destruction and misunderstanding among the Natives and Whites, Momaday's *House Made of Dawn*, while dependent on, as well as inspired by, the traditional sources of myths, legends and stories, also talks about the American ideals of life. A very close reference to another American text of great importance, Arthur Miller's *Death of a Salesman*, is found in this novel:

> But Milly believed in tests, questions and answers, words on paper. She was a lot like Ben. She believed in Honour, Industry, the Second Chance, The Brotherhood of Man, the American Dream, and him—Abel; she believed in him. (107)

Is this the Ben of Miller's *Death of a Salesman*, the personification of the American Dream?

Coming back to the focal point of my discussion, Abel's mysterious ways are perhaps best explained by his sense of confusion, to be a part of the White World or to go back to a life in the lap of the community. Dealing with the history of a dislocated Kiowa, Abel, caught in the wake of World War II between a contemporary Los Angeles and tribal memories, Momaday's *House Made of Dawn* serves as a representative text of a shocked, hallucinatory, wordless individual on the surface and a community within.

According to Norman R. Cary, the concept of "Othering" comes into play when the other's cultural discourse is perceived as empty, valueless or inferior, a rationalization that facilitates the projection onto the Other of the discourse of one's own culture and values. Indigenous religions were regarded as idolatrous, devilish or at best preparatory to the superior revelation of Christianity. This serves as a great cause for rebellion against the colonizer for he was now trying to take away the People's lifeline, their spirits, their stories and their traditions, and thus all that was left with the community.

> It was as if, conscious of having come so close to extinction, they had got a keener sense of humility than their benefactors, and paradoxically a greater sense of pride. . . . They had acquired a tragic sense, which gave to them as a race so much dignity and bearing. (16)

Language and nationality are the central determinants of a living culture. And when language dies, it leads to the death of a Nation. Though writing in the colonizer's language, i.e. English, Momaday is conscious of his own heritage and takes up his case in the novel by talking about patterns in the language.

> They have a lot of words, and you know they mean something, but you don't know what, and your own words are no good because they're not the same; they are different, and they are the only words used to it. (158)

Again when Abel laments his distances from the people, he is saddened by the thought that he is unable to understand his grandmother's prayers:

> I did not always understand her prayers; I believe they were made of an older language than of ordinary speech. There was something inherently sad in the sound, some slight hesitation upon the syllables of sorrow. (133)

Despite all the tortures the community is subjected to by the whites, the author believes that as "In the word there was the beginning," so the White Man will "Perish by the word" because he has disregarded the power of words.

Abel, the insider outsider, the returned war veteran, experiences a loss of whatever clear sense of identity he had as a young man and thus as per the standards of society, fails to come to terms with life. As observed by James Ruppert, he is torn between two worlds and defeated by the social forces that push him to war, to jail and to relocation in the city .The story is striking in its message as it works on the twin levels of reflecting on the Native American tradition in the context of both the social as well as the individual.

Momaday is of the view that the spirit informs the memory and the one memory is that of the land. Land is an important element in Momaday's novel as it is in Silko's *Ceremony.* It is the land which gives some sense of identity to the war-returned and alienated Abel. As Barbara Strelke very aptly suggests, "While he walks the land, Abel recalls incidents from his past. These remembrances from fragment of Abel's identity, fragments which he can not piece together to make a whole."

The process of alienation takes place early in an Indian child's life, half-breed or full blood, Tayo or Abel, when s/he is sent to school. They are taught little of their culture and history. All education does to the Indian child is to make her/him a loser, at home and at school. If the child does not behave, speak and think like a white, middle-class child or tries to resist it, s/he becomes a failure at school. And if the Indian pupil does assimilate, s/he is bound to become a failure as an Indian. Whatever the case, s/he loses. This problem is also dealt with much detail in *Ceremony* as well as *House Made of Dawn*.

The idea of a Native Consciousness to regenerate the lost pride among the people is also an agenda in Momaday's work. And in doing so, he plays with words to foreground the 'reality' of his people taking them out of the walls of fiction and making them more real. He does not claim his people to be uncontaminated creatures from a different and far-off world. While agreeing that the people have their own follies, Momaday makes it a point to ascertain the 'uniqueness' of his tribe and his people, and this is what Abel, the protagonist, also searches for:

> Their invaders were a long time in conquering them; and now, after four centuries of Christianity, they still pray in Tanoan to the old deities of the earth and sky and make their living from the things that are and have always been within their reach; while in the discrimination of pride they acquire from their conquerors only the luxury of example. They have assumed the names and gestures of their enemies, but have held on to their own, secret souls, and in

> this there is a resistance and an overcoming, a long outwaiting. (58)

As noted by Singh, the dialogue between the ethnic self and the dominant culture is a significant part of the process by which both the individual and the group confront the socio-political challenges in American life. Almost all the Native American characters in *House Made of Dawn* are headed towards spiritual suicide, though Abel serves as the primary example. His confusion about the White Man's world is symbolized by his view of the prison where he spends six years for killing the Albino:

> The walls of his cells were white, or perhaps they were gray or green; he could not remember. After a while he could not imagine any thing beyond the walls except the yard outside, the lavatory and the dining hall or even the walls, really. They were abstractions beyond the reach of his understanding; not in themselves confinement—but symbols of confinement. The essential character of the walls consisted not in their substance, was white, perhaps or gray, or green. (97)

Even amidst all the chaos he finds a reason to live and get back his identity while he does the preburial rituals of his grandfather and that is what we call hope.

If Momaday's magic lies in his form and content interlock and in an end that is not entirely grim as Abel finds himself back in the center of the tribe, Silko's novel, with a beautiful intermingling of prose and poetry in a circular narrative fashion, tells us that the origin of evil is not the White race but an age-old witchery created by the tribes themselves.

Both the novels are connected in the sense that the protagonist in both these stories is a World War II veteran who comes back home to find no home and no sense of security. Tayo believes that his actions have had far-reaching effects for his community and hence he must regain his lost "home." Abel too, feels for his community and tries, even though very subtly, to gain the pride back. Contrary to the views expressed by earlier critics, I believe that though the solution provided at the end of both the novels may not be categorized as altogether bright and beautiful, there is a hope that the stories could continue, that the tradition is alive and would remain so.

I agree with A. Robert Lee when he says that Tayo's Ceremony signifies a restoration, the self against odds reintegrated back into the curative wheel of his People's history, "the old dialect" of the Laguna as the novel calls it. And I find it especially interesting to see where *House Made of Dawn* ends—Abel runs and as he runs, he sings the Navajo prayer song. He finds himself back in his own culture and is no more ashamed of his tribal ancestry.

Ultimately, using the genre of fiction to tell their own stories and writing in the language of the colonizer, i.e. English, Silko and Momaday work as the dual functionaries of mediators to the outside world, White or otherwise, and more importantly, as keepers of their own aboriginal traditions. Underneath all this, they serve another ideological objective: to set the record straight and rewrite history, the contaminated White history. They try to overcome the injustices of the past, diffuse the damage done, and salvage the pride of their culture.

### List of Works Cited and Consulted

Cary, Norman R. "Postcolonial Literature and the Story of Christ." *Postcolonial Literature and the Biblical Call for Justice*. Ed. Susan Van Zanten Gallagher: University Press of Mississippi.

D'haen, Theo. *Shades of Empire: In Colonial and Post-colonial Literatures*. Ed. C.C. Barfoot and Theo D'haen. Rodopi: Amsterdam, Atlanta, GA, 1993.

Lee, A. Robert. "Decolorizing America." *Shades of Empire: In Colonial and Post-colonial Literatures.* Ed. C.C. Barfoot and Theo D'haen.

Miller, Arthur. *Death of a Salesman.* New York: The Viking Press, 1949.

Momaday, N. Scott. *House Made of Dawn.* New York: Harper and Row, 1998.

_____. "The Magic of Words." *Survival This Way: Interviews with American Indian Poets*. Ed. Joseph Bruchak. Tuscon: Suntracks and University of Arizona Press, 1987.

_____. "Man Made of Words." *Literature of the American Studies: Views and Interpretations.* Ed. Abraham Chapmen. New York: New American Library, 1975.

_____. *The Way to Rainy Mountain.* Albuquerque, New Mexico: University of New Mexico Press, 1969.

Moore, David L. "Myth, History and Identity in Silko and Young Bear." *Native American Women's Writing C.1800-1924, An Anthology.* Ed. Keren L. Kilcup. Blackwell, 2000.

Ruppert, James. *Mediation in Contemporary Native American Fiction.* Norman and London: University of Oklahama Press, 1993.

Ruoff, A. Lavonne. "Ritual and Renewal: Keres Traditions in the Short Fiction of Leslie Silko." *MELUS* 5.4 (1997): 2-17.

Silko, Leslie M. *Ceremony*. New York: Viking Press, 1977.

Singh, Amritjit, and Peter Schmidt. "US Studies and Postcolonial Theory." *Post-colonial Theories and the United States*. Ed. Amarjit Singh and Peter Schmidt. Jackson: University Press of Mississippi, 2000.

Strelke, Barbara. "N. Scott Momaday: Racial Memory and Individual Imagination." *Literature of the American Studies: Views and Interpretations*. Ed. Abraham Chapmen.

Velie, Alan R. *Four American Indian Literary Masters: N Scott Momaday, James Welch, Leslie Marmon Silko, and Gerald Vizenor*. Norman: University of Oklahoma Press, 1982.

# The Sound beneath Her Beat: Assigning Landmark Qualities to Salman Rushdie's *The Ground beneath Her Feet*

**Jana Fedtke**
**University of Potsdam, Germany**

In his leading role as Mr. Raj Malhotra in *Baagbaan* (2003), Amitabh Bachchan says, "Lekhak to soch ke saagar mein doobke najaane kaise-kaise moti nikaal lete hain."[1] If you take this statement to mirror the process of writing and its results, it is well possible to consider Salman Rushdie's 1999 novel, *The Ground Beneath Her Feet*, such a gem. Exploring the concept of the *global city* and arriving at the formation of a *globalized human psyche* that unites people who do not belong or conform, the novel not only embraces globalization; it also acknowledges its limitations, and thus enables Salman Rushdie to develop a challenging theory in what I will call the *post-global condition of human melodies*, or in other words, 'the sound beneath her (that is, the city's, and by extension the world's and the human psyche's) beat'.

Why Salman Rushdie, and why *The Ground beneath Her Feet*? The novel's wittiness, entertaining qualities, and language games, but particularly the project of coming to terms with globalization that Rushdie undertakes in *The Ground Beneath Her Feet,* make the text an outstanding example of American literature. It forms a book that appeared at the right time, in the right place, on the right topic, and makes it worth including this writer of South Asian origin in the supposed canon of US fictions.

The text is essentially concerned with the love story of world-famous singers Vina Apsara and Ormus Cama, as told through the photographer eyes of their friend Umeed 'Rai' Merchant.[2] Having left Bombay and their past behind, the duo (also known as VTO[3]) soar to superstardom in the US and—through the mechanisms of *cultural globalization* and consumption—equally across the globe. After Vina dies in an earthquake in Mexico and Ormus is killed by a deranged fan, Umeed is left to tell the tale. This short and somewhat understated summary reluctantly but necessarily omits many of the details present in the 600-page text that is full of descriptions, anecdotes, songs, puns, and last but not least, digressions. Using the postmodern tools of fragmented narration, intertextuality, parody, and self-reflexivity, *The Ground Beneath Her Feet* encapsulates a vastly ranging list of topics from myth and history, via love and music, to popular culture and commercialization. This paper will, however, focus on the representation of the city Bombay (specifically *not* referred to as Mumbai here, for reasons well-known[4]) as a postmodern site of reflection within the context of globalization.

Bombay is foregrounded in the first half of *The Ground Beneath Her Feet*. The city is not simply the setting but "a net, a web" (Concilio 129) that brings the protagonists together and traces their development over time. While Rushdie seems to follow the modernist tradition of metropolitan literature, Nilufer Bharucha has aptly shown that the author simultaneously "transcends realistic boundaries" ("Imagined Worlds" 54) and establishes Bombay as well as London and New York City as both "real and imagined" cities that resist representation as simple mimesis. Bombay forms a character in its own right. The narrator remembers the city of his childhood fondly complete with hints of nostalgia, and refers to it in gestures of anthropomorphization. One of the first characteristics attributed to Bombay is concerned with its linguistic diversity, where people speak "five languages badly and no language well" (*TGBHF* 5). Umeed literally embraces this polyphony of voices: "Our acronymic name for it was Hug-me. Hindi Urdu Gujarati Marathi English" (ibid). He also enthusiastically recalls "the tumultuous sensation of the city: the scents of channa and bhel . .

. ; the shouting voices . . . and the quarrel of traffic . . . and the electricity of a society at a point of transformation" (43). Hinting at the reasons for his departure, the narrator establishes Bombay as a rival to his parents' love of the metropolis, "the daughter they never had" (80).

As an imagined entity, a construct, the Bombay in *The Ground Beneath Her Feet* can be quite literally read as a text. Carmen Concilio has traced the movements of the protagonists through the urban landscape from the suburbs of Juhu and Bandra down to the historic Fort area and Malabar Hill (136). Reading the movements and taking the addresses as full stops in the story, she establishes the novel's precise symmetric structure,[5] which creates oppositions between Ormus and Rai (Malabar Hill / West and Cuffe Parade / East) as well as Rai and Vina (their meeting on Juhu Beach / North) in contrast to Ormus and Vina (their meeting in the record store in the South of the city). Concilio convincingly argues that "the space of the city figuratively mirrors the shape of a page" (137), thus further supporting the argument of the city as text. This holds true at least in those regions of the world in which a page is read from top to bottom and more importantly from left to right.

Rushdie's belief in the city of being eternal and a solid structure when he was a child is echoed in Umeed Merchant's likening of Bombay to Rome (79), "the Eternal City" built on seven hills, while Bombay was built on seven islands. The city "rival[s] the capital of a western colonial empire" (Concilio 142). Yet, its foundations have begun to shake with the arrival of fundamentalist groups that threaten the city's secular and multifaceted character. It is this Bombay that neither Rushdie nor the narrator is interested in anymore. While Umeed's father, V.V. Merchant, loved to explore the city's past and his mother, Ameer Merchant, loved to envision its future of skyscrapers that closely resemble New York City's architecture, Umeed himself—though he affectionately remembers and recreates the city—feels imprisoned by it and by his parents: "the whole damn city felt like my mother's womb and I had to go abroad to get myself born" (78). After a passionate farewell speech (256), the narrator frees himself from "Wombay" (103) by going to America, where the second part of the novel is mainly set.

Leading into the realm of the global[6] with its setting moving from Bombay via England and the US to Mexico, *The Ground Beneath Her Feet* presents a critique of "cultural imperialism" and "satirizes the idea of globalization by engaging with notions of uncertainty and duality" (Sanga 7). The narrator recounts myths, slightly changes historical "facts," or suggests, for example, different origins of rock music from what most of the world has been made to believe so far. Rushdie, himself a metaphor of globalism, has Vina and Ormus transcend boundaries through their popular music since "songs could cross all frontiers" (55). The singers' reliance on art as their means of communication and agency is a direct representation of what Rüdiger Kunow, among others, has called an "enabling in-between-ness" (Glage and Kunow 12). According to this definition, borders do not function as constraints. They assert a liberating effect on those who cross them. Thus, in contrast to Homi Bhabha's concept of *hybridity*, there is no synthesis in *transnationalism*. Crossing borders involves a continuous movement of locations as well as identities. Rushdie's characters in *The Ground Beneath Her Feet*, floating across nations and enacting globalization, present a case in point.

In his excellent article entitled "A Globalized Search for Home in Salman Rushdie's *The Ground Beneath Her Feet*," Randy Boyagoda acknowledges Rushdie's "portraits of individuals dislocated from familiar, defined territories yet not necessarily reaffiliated to others" (130). According to the author, these individuals are freed and at the same time "burdened by their lack of formal, nation-based identifications" (130). The fact that Rushdie has Vina and Ormus die in the novel and Rai, the only surviving character, welcomes a return to the stable yet ordinary family life in America is taken by Boyagoda as an indication of a shift in Rushdie's ideas of a globalized world. He argues that Rushdie "accepts, indeed stresses, the belonging so desperately needed in such a setting" (131). This belonging is, in Boyagoda's estimation, "plausible only in the cosmos that is contemporary New York City, and possible only through the very conventional means of immigrating to the United States" (131). While Boyagoda has a point assuming that "Rushdie senses that in-between locations cannot be permanent" (132), I do not agree with his reading of Rushdie's novel as attempting to end the "danger [. . .] to exist without national affiliation" (139). You cannot "*admit* the essential hybridity of a globalized world" (141, emphasis mine), as Boyagoda puts it, while at the same time opting for "conventional domesticity and national belonging" (141). It seems to me that the author confused Rushdie's fiction of the year 1999 and his biography including his subsequent move to the US, which precedes Boyagoda's 2003 article. Boyagoda's arguments equal accusing Rushdie of moving backwards and invoking the outdated binarisms of East (that is, India) as bad and West (that is, the United States) as good, a move that I do not wish to be guilty of.

Instead, I argue in accordance with a concept that I see Rushdie developing in the novel and that I have called the *post-global condition of human melodies*. As early as on page 42, Sir Darius Xerxes Cama, Ormus's father, in his explorations of the mythical past, wonders, "What about *outsideness*? . . . What about people who just don't belong. . . . Anywhere. To anything, to anyone. The physically unattached." He delights at the idea and finally exclaims, "The only people who see the whole picture . . . are the ones who step out of the frame" (43). This positive indication of being different and not belonging is further explored by the narrator Umeed in the theme of a *globalized human psyche*:

> in every generation there are a few souls . . . without affiliation to family or location or nation or race . . . the phenomenon may be as "natural" a manifestation of human nature as its opposite . . . those who value stability . . . have erected a powerful system of stigmas and taboos against rootlessness . . . so that we mostly conform. . . . But the truth leaks out in our dreams . . . we soar, we fly, we flee. . . . In our myths, our arts, our songs, we celebrate the non-belongers, the different ones, the outlaws, the freaks. (74)

This celebration of freedom, non-affiliation, rootlessness, dreams, art, and particularly songs, including its alleged downsides of uncertainty and the much-invoked shaking ground,[7] is the thread that runs through the text and refuses to cease its existence. It is the personal melodies that count, the *sounds beneath* the ground; even if they end in death and destruction. Boyagoda would find evidence against this argument by quoting Rai: "[We were in] a transitional phase in which we might have been *trapped* forever" (Boyagoda 139, his emphasis). Yet, is this statement not to be taken ironically, as so many others of the narrator's remarks? The same accounts for the significance of Umeed's name that Boyagoda alludes to. Hope, yes; but unfulfilled in my view, if domesticity in the US is the result. There might be hope, however, in his daughter, aptly named (and maybe of foreshadowing proportions) Tara, the star. Closing the circle to art and music, and consequently following Vina's and Ormus's path, Tara says about the duo—and this is the concluding sentence of the book, "I thought they were supposed to be *dead*, but in real life they're just going to go on singing" (595).

This paper has looked at how Salman Rushdie's novel *The Ground Beneath Her Feet* engages with, and goes beyond, issues of globalization. In its attempt to map cultural spaces and to foreshadow that which follows colonialism, postcolonialism, and globalization, the novel presents a landmark in American literature. The text questions available models of the global and develops a theory of its own, in what can be called *the post-global condition of human melodies*. This admittedly simple and to a certain degree not very academic-sounding theme, however, finds its roots in the concept of the *globalized human psyche* that does not—and does not want to—belong. It is also deeply indebted to the global myth of music and its powers. As Tara says, "they go on singing"—oyr in an allusion to Ormus's model of real-life star status, Freddy Mercury of *The Queen*: "The Show Must Go On."

# NOTES

1. "Writers are those that plunge deep into the ocean of knowledge and come up with rare gems of literature."
2. For a detailed interpretation of the characters' names, see Anderson, Bharucha, and Pirbhai.
3. "VTO" can have multiple meanings. See Rushdie, *TGBHF* 6-7.
4. See Bharucha, "Bombay to Mumbai: Postcolonial Repossessions and Hegemonies" for an excellent historical overview of the city's development and naming throughout the centuries.
5. For further structural references, see Viktoria Tchernichova, "'The Solutions to the Problems of Art are Always Technical": Some Observations on Textual Topologies." *The Great Work of Making Real: Salman Rushdie's* The Ground Beneath Her Feet. Ed. Elsa Linguanti and Viktoria Tchernichova. Pisa, Italy: ETS, 2003. 165-83.
6. In my discussion of the broad issue of cultural and economic globalization. I have drawn largely from concepts established by Appadurai, Harvey, Jameson, Tomlinson, and last but not least Rushdie himself.
7. There are earthquakes in Bombay, India, and later Mexico; as well as many other instances of people not feeling the ground beneath their feet in this so-called "quake-age."

## List of Works Cited and Consulted

Anderson, Claudia. *Bombay between Reality and Imagination in the Novels of Salman Rushdie, Rohinton Mistry and John Irving.* n.p.: Books on Demand, 2001.

Appadurai, Arjun, ed. *Globalization.* Durham: Duke, 2001.

Bhabha, Homi. *The Location of Culture.* London: Routledge, 1994.

Bharucha, Nilufer E. "Bombay to Mumbai: Postcolonial Repossessions and Hegemonies." *SPAN: Journal of the South Pacific Association for Commonwealth Literature and Language Studies* 45 (1997): 13-36.

_____. "Real and Imagined Worlds: Salman Rushdie as a Writer of the Indian Diaspora." *Flight from Certainty: The Dilemma of Identity and Exile.* Ed. Anne Luyat and Francine Tolron. Amsterdam: Rodopi, 2001. 51-62.

Boyagoda, Randy. "'Three Kings of Disorient': A Globalized Search for Home in *The Ground Beneath Her Feet*." *South Asian Review* 24.1 (2003): 130-43.

Concilio, Carmen. "The City as Text(ure): Bombay in Salman Rushdie's *The Ground beneath Her Feet*." *The Great Work of Making Real: Salman Rushdie's* The Ground Beneath Her Feet. Ed. Elsa Linguanti and Viktoria Tchernichova. Pisa, Italy: ETS, 2003. 129-50.

Glage, Liselotte, and Rüdiger Kunow, ed. *"The Decolonizing Pen": Cultural Diversity and the Transnational Imaginary in Rushdie's Fiction.* Trier: Wissenschaftlicher Verlag, 2001.

Harvey, David. *The Condition of Postmodernity: An Enquiry into the Origins of Cultural Change.* Cambridge: Blackwell, 2000.

Jameson, Fredric, and Masao Miyoshi, ed. *The Cultures of Globalization.* Durham: Duke, 1998.

McClintock, Scott. "Geography of Difference: The Changing Image of Bombay in Salman Rushdie's Fiction." *South Asian Review* 24.1 (2003): 144-60.

Pirbhai, Mariam. "The Paradox of Globalization as an "Untotalizable Totality" in Salman Rushdie's *The Ground Beneath Her Feet*." *International Fiction Review* 28.1-2 (2001): 54-66.

Rushdie, Salman. *The Ground beneath Her Feet.* 1999. New York: Picador, 2000.

_____. "March 1999: Globalization." *Step Across This Line. Collected Nonfiction 1992-2002.* New York: Random, 2002. 267-69.

Sanga, Jaina C. *Salman Rushdie's Postcolonial Metaphors: Migration, Translation, Hybridity, Blasphemy, and Globalization.* Westport, CT: Greenwood, 2001.

Tomlinson, John. *Globalization and Culture.* Cambridge: Polity, 2001.

# Home and the World: Writing from the Liminal Space

**Nandini Bhadra**
**BKM Science College, Valsad**

> Breathes there the man with soul so dead,
> who never to himself hath said,
> "This is my own, my native land!"
>
> (Walter Scott, "Patriotism")

Native land, homeland, motherland, fatherland—which is the "mot juste" (the right word) for describing a place where one lives, earns his/her bread, where one has his/her family, social and cultural life, more appropriately, where one belongs?

"Is home a place? A memory? An ideal? An imagined space?" (192), asks Susan Friedman. The paper attempts an analysis of "home" and the "world" as presented by a couple of writers of Indian origin who have chosen to make America their home. In the diasporic writers' "struggle for a place in the new world," and their longing for the homeland they have left behind, one feels a sense of déjà vu as we have already encountered such 'angst' or 'anhaga' of the exile in Anglo Saxon poems as *The Wanderer* and *The Seafarer*.

> "oft him anhaga are gebideth" (often the exile is plagued by solitude) (160)

So the question of dislocation, relocation, home, assimilation and multiculturalism become the dominant themes of the expatriate writers. Both the America-based writers I have chosen—Jhumpa Lahiri and Amitav Ghosh, bound together by a past, a country, a vocation and a common native tongue, attempt to demystify the myth of the ideal homeland for the immigrant who is continuously living in a space between two cultures, and for whom, 'homeland' is a kind of mental construct.

Jhumpa Lahiri in her debut novel *The Namesake* (2003) showcases the peculiarly lonely lives led by the expatriate Bengali community in the Boston area with their extended family of fellow expatriates who view their everyday experiences through their customs and traditions back home. She also explores the struggles of the second-generation expatriates who, while trying to "fit in," question their identity and sense of belonging. Lahiri here expands on the themes of her short stories *The Interpreter of Maladies* (2000)—the immigrant experience, the clash of cultures, the conflicts of assimilation and most poignantly the 'tangled ties' between generations.

Lahiri's story is much more than exoticising the Indian-American backdrop; she draws the unique dilemmas of her characters with great empathy. Flaubert had said of *Madame Bovary*: "Madame Bovary, cest moi" (xviii). Lahiri seems to be sharing Flaubert's sentiment in her portrayal of characters. *The Namesake* takes the Ganguly family from their tradition-bound life in Calcutta to Massachusetts in America after the arranged marriage of Asoka and Ashima. The ingénue Ashima whose name means borderless is ironically bound to her middle class tradition and hates all things American. We follow her as she struggles alone with the process of childbirth in an unknown land.

> that it was happening so far from home, unmonitored and unobserved by those she loved. . . . But she is terrified to raise a child in a country where she is related to no one, where she knows so little, where life seems so tentative and spare. (38)

When their son is born, the task of naming him betrays the "vexed results of bringing old ways to the new world" and as the letter suggesting the name of the boy by Ashima's grandmother is lost, the parents make-do with the name of 'Gogol' in memory of a catastrophe years ago; and Gogol travels through life in

America suffering the burden of his heritage and his odd antic name.

One can hardly overlook the author's agony as she narrates the exile Ashima's struggle to come to terms with the sudden news of the loss of her father—alone, so far away, "she refuses to picture what she shall see soon enough, her mother's vermilion erased from her part, her brother's thick hair shaved from his head in mourning." (47)

And within a decade of living in America, they had lost almost all their loved ones; "they are both orphaned." (48)

In a realistic manner, Lahiri delineates the life of the diaspora for whom "family members who continue to live seem dead, somehow always invisible, impossible to touch" (49). In a way, the diasporic Bengali community tries to relive the cultural life of the community through the celebration of Durga Puja—which is celebrated on a weekend for convenience's sake.

> The cultural baggage is passed on to the second generation also when Gogol is in third grade, he is sent to a Bengali language and culture lesson every Saturday. It never fails to unsettle them that their children sound just like Americans, expertly conversing in a language that still at times confound them, in accents they are accustomed not to trust. (66)

And when her son Gogol is taken on a field-trip to the cemetery in his art class, the shocked Ashima says, "Death is not a pastime, not a place to make paintings." (70) That death could be used for making art remains an enigma to Ashima.

Lahiri has an extraordinary gift for inhabiting the emotional space of her characters while describing even the most mundane events in the lives of the Indian diaspora. With great authenticity, she narrates the experiences of the Ganguly family as they stay in India for eight months. As they enter through the airport, "there are endless names Gogol and Sonia must remember to say; not uncle this or uncle that, but terms far more specific: mashi and pishi, mama and maima, kaku and jethu, to signify whether they are related on mother's side or father's side, by marriage or by blood." (81) During their visit, they both fall terribly ill and on their return journey to Boston, for Gogol, "relief quickly replaces any lingering sadness." (87)

Strangely enough, their American friends "ask them nothing about where they have been after their return . . . so eight months are put behind them, quickly shed, quickly forgotten, like clothes worn for a special occasion, or for a season that has passed, suddenly cumbersome, irrelevant to their lives." (87) The fact that on trips to India, Gogol's American-accented English is a source of endless amusement to his relatives in India is recalled with humour. Lahiri calls our attention to the difference in attitude between the two generations she writes about. While Ashima can never bring herself to refer to Pemberton Road as home, Gogol effortlessly refers to New Haven—a place where he's just shifted after he turned 18, as home, which enrages Ashima. It is in fact not the home of the past locked in memory and nostalgia, neither the 'imaginary homeland' for which Ashima pines, but the concrete homeland of the assimilated immigrant for whom America is home in more complete ways.

Gogol, now Nikhil, struggles through successive ill-fated relationships; his path is strewn with conflicting loyalties as he comes to accept his father's death. Indeed living with a pet name and a good name in a place where such distinctions do not exist is the greatest confusion of all. And finally he goes on to read the Russian writer Nikolai Gogol's story *The Overcoat*, the book which had literally saved his father many years ago after he had met with an ill-fated accident. He also then learns to appreciate his parents' true bravery, the world they left behind, and the new world they created.

His mother Ashima, after being widowed, decides to divide her time between India and the States. True to the meaning of her name, "she will be without borders, without a home of her own, a resident everywhere and nowhere." (276) While Ashima, a diasporic for 33 years, is about to return to Calcutta, she suddenly feels lonely—permanently alone. On the verge of her departure, she realizes she will "miss the country in which she had grown to know and love her husband. Though his ashes have been scattered into the Ganges, it is here, in this house and in this town, that he will continue to dwell in her mind." (279)

Thus Ashima becomes truly 'unbound', though not 'unhomed' or 'homeless'; she straddles between two homelands, between two cultural spaces and becomes a global, multicultural citizen, establishing a bridge between the two lands she inhabits. Like Bimala in Tagore's *Ghare Baire* (*The Home and the World*) and Paro in Saratchandra's novel *Devdas* she comes out of the "confined space" of her home into the domain of outer world.

Amitav Ghosh's latest novel *The Hungry Tide* (2004) is set against the backdrop of the overwhelming presence of nature in the Sunderbans (the tide country or what he calls *the bhatir desh*). The novel focuses on the micro-culture in the region of the tide country—the islets of the Ganges delta that lie South of Kolkata and just east of West Bengal/ Bangladesh frontier. The sense of 'place' dominates the novel (*Economist* review). Ghosh himself reasserts such a view. "A novel . . . must always be set somewhere, and within the evolution of the narrative, this setting must play a part almost as important as the characters themselves." As Brinda Bose points out: "Ghosh's aesthetics is a fictional embracing of historical/political subtexts and an intellectual exploration of both the major, as well as the marginalized contexts of modern history—nationalism, internationalism, migrancy, memory, nostalgia, etc." (238)

In a recent interview Ghosh defended his choice of fiction over history: "I think the difference between the history fiction writers write is that fiction writers write about the human history. It is about finding the human predicament." It is with this interest of a human historian that Ghosh delves into the inner lives of his characters, characters which straddle cultures, negotiate between two lands divided by both time and space, history and geography and attempts to redefine the present through an understanding of the past.

The novel has a contemporary setting, but history/past is intermittently brought into relationship with the living/present. The story centres on two visitors to the Sunderbans community; Kanai Dutta, a Delhi based businessman who runs a translation agency and Piyali Roy, a cetologist from America of Bengali origin, and their interaction with that community and with each other. Kanai is on his second visit to the Sunderbans to his aunt Nilima, an NGO activist who runs a hospital on one of the islands, to read a journal left by his late uncle Nirmal, an idealist Marxist intellectual who is smitten by the idea of revolution.

The narrative, alternating between Kanai's 'here and now' experiences and his reading of his uncle's journal, brings past and present into a symbiotic encounter. One of Ghosh's most persistent themes in the novel is of the ephemerality of concepts of national and ethnic identity. The multiplicity of names for the Sunderbans-"bhatirdesh" is itself a metaphor for that ephemerality. As the late Nirmal recounts in his journal, "In this place that I had lived for 30 years, the birds were vanishing, the land was being reclaimed by the sea . . . what would it take to submerge the tide country? Not much—a minuscule change in the level of the sea would be enough." (215)

Small wonder then, that a little after the publication of *The Hungry Tide* an event of the proportions of Tsunami could hit a few South Asian countries, destroying many lives, washing homelands for many, pushing continents and islands farther, thus unmapping mapped spaces, erasing borders and boundaries. The Tsunami-struck world is still reeling from the smell of death and destruction as many thousands have lost even the ground beneath their feet. So the post-Tsunami physical evidence of impermanence confirms the theory that we find in Nirmal's journal that the world's continents had existed as a single landmass and not only the continents, even the crust of the earth was in constant motion. So why get exercised over mere geographical boundaries, tying ourselves up in knots over geocentric identities, questions the author in *The Hungry Tide*. From the atomic to the cosmic, nothing displays signs of permanence.

The novel is an impeccably researched work where history and ethnography converge (Ghosh has a doctorate in anthropology). Here, he focuses on a series of cultural features of the tide country's micro community, of its natural ecosystem pitted against human saga which Piya and Fokir and to a certain extent Kanai also try to unravel. However, the major geo-political and historical landmarks of the tide country and its people are reconstructed by Kanai through his uncle's journal.

Nirmal had realized years back that in the "tide country the wheel of time was spinning too fast to be seen." "In other places it took decades, even centuries for a river to change course—it took an epoch for an island to appear. But here in the tide country, transformation is the rule of life." (224)

Further, Nirmal's diary recounts the great storm of 1737 in which "2 dozen ships sank . . . nothing escapes the maw of the tides, everything is ground to fine silt, becomes something else. It was as if the whole tide country was speaking in the voice of the poet,—life is lived in transformation." (225)

Another parallel strand which is interwoven with the main narrative of the novel through Nirmal's journal is the plight of the refugees from Bangladesh, the marginalized "wretched of the earth" who try to settle in the island of Morichjhapi but encounter constant resistance from the government agencies. They call themselves *"bastuhara"* (dispossessed of land). Their agonized question "where do we belong?" touches the idealist revolutionary Nirmal who in fact finds in it the 'deepest uncertainties' of his heart. He grapples with the question of his own identity, "Who was I? Where did I belong? In Kolkata or in the tide country? In India or across the border? In prose or in poetry?" (254) As Nirmal tries to negotiate between the powerless and the powerful, the privileged and the underprivileged, the center and the margin, he is drawn into an in-between space of liminality. However one soon realizes the limits of the liminal space and as the rebellion of the settlers is crushed, Nirmal falls apart, becomes disoriented and ultimately dies. So negotiation becomes one of the dominant discourses of the novel.

That change is the law of nature is what the late Nirmal had proposed to teach the settler students of Morichjhapi—a lesson which dates back to prehistoric times—where history and mythology converge:

> I decided I'd tell them the story of the Greek Goddess who was Ganga's mother. India was far, far away then in another hemisphere. It was attached to Australia and Antarctica . . . there were no Himalayas then, . . . no Jamuna, no Ganga, no Saraswati, no Brahmaputra. (181)

Thus the legacy of history and myth is such that its reverberations are felt years and generations later. Nirmal and Kusum in the earlier generation, and Fokir and Piya at a later time, break through class barriers that bring them together on some level.

Piyali Roy, the cetologist felt an affinity for the marine mammals and studied field biology as it offered her a different kind of life to be on her own, to have "no fixed address, to be far from the familiar," (219) as she was only too aware of the dangers of what Homi Bhabha calls "the fixity of identity." (9)

Her father, a first generation Indian believed that Indians, Bengalis in particular even when abroad always have their eyes turned homewards. He decided not to make that mistake, "to fit in." She, like Fokir, had to go through the burden of growing up without a mother who she feels should never have strayed too far from home. In Seattle "she had no one—no friends, no servants, no job, no life," while her father was the "perfect immigrant—driven, hard-working and successful." (219) Her mother fell through the cracks and died of depression and subsequently cancer.

Piya, despite her Indian origins, knowing neither her mother tongue Bengali, nor Hindi, requires a translator/interpreter and a cultural mediator like Kanai whose service though sometimes inadequate, is somewhat necessary in the wider context of globalization which brings the likes of her to locations as the Sunderbans. The novel's conclusion, though open-ended, moves towards a possibility of communication across cultural barriers. Finally, both Kanai and Piya undertake the task of re-interpretation of their Sunderbans experiences though both have lost their textual evidence (Kanai's uncle's journal and Piya's cetological datasheets). However, they are willing to reconstruct the pieces from memory. Both in a strange way return to the tide country and in fact Kanai shifts his residence to Kolkata so that he can be near "the real India." Piya, though initially shattered by the burden of the guilt of Fokir's death, decides to continue her research in the Sunderbans and to learn Bengali, giving a surprising "preference to the local over her globalised American identity." (220) Meanwhile the possibility of a future union between Kanai and Piya is left open, but for sure their paths will cross once again. In fact, in the last chapter of the novel, "Home, an Epilogue," Piya calls the tide country her "home," "Piya's choice of words surprised Nilima so much that she dropped the spoon she was using to stir the leaves. Did I hear you right? Did you say home?" (400)

*The Hungry Tide* is made up of interwoven strands: Kanai's narrative and Piya's, the present lived by the characters like Nirmala, Moyna and Fokir, and the past of Nirmal's journal "that converge and diverge and reconverge." The novel resists polarities/ binaries which cannot be straitjacketed into categories as insider/outsider, margin/center, local/global, past/present, homed/unhomed, self/other, speech/silence, tradition/modernity, oral narrative/written tradition etc. There is an attempt to negotiate these polarities resulting in "overlapping of the domains of difference." The silences from the voices of the margin towards the end of the novel does not indicate closure, but possibility of a further future resistance.

*The Hungry Tide* has claimed its sacrificial victim in Fokir, but the utopian goal of mutual understanding implied in the novel's recurrent theme of translation seems not an unattainable possibility. Both Piya and Kanai seem to emerge at the end of the novel as new multicultural citizens who can feel equally at home in a place as remote and rural as the tide country. Thus, Ghosh's latest novel opens up new and unexpected arenas, reminding us once again that ethnic, cultural and territorial barriers are mere "shadow lines" and we as global citizens should learn to communicate in new forms 'to think transculturally and build new bridges across that world,' so that with the sanction of dual citizenship by the Manmohan Singh Government, the N.R.I. (non-resident Indian) can now become a true M.R.I. (multi-resident Indian) and learn to develop roots in cultural plurality and establish his identity in a borderless world.

The recent judicial petition to delete the word Sindh from the National Anthem is yet another instance of the issue of possession/dis-possession of homeland. Sindh is much more than a geopolitical entity; it is a people, a culture and a civilization. The universality of Tagore's art lies in his all-embracing vision which is perhaps as deep and wide as Sindhu, which was a sea and not a river. The true spirit of India is its enormity. The two expatriate writers Jhumpa Lahiri and Amitav Ghosh have been able to capture the true essence of India which is borderless, inclusive in culture and cosmic in character which again shows that they have more than one foot and their heart also in the right place, in their homeland India, though they have another home in another land.

## List of Works Cited and Consulted

Apte, Sudheer. Rev. of *The Namesake* by Jhumpa Lahiri, Sept. 7, 2003

Bhabha, Homi K. *The Location of Culture*. New York: Routledge, 1994.

Bose, Brinda. "Footnoting History: The Diasporic Imagination of Amitav Ghosh." Paranjpe, Makarand, ed. *In Diaspora: Theories, Histories, Texts*. New Delhi: Indialog Publications, 2002.

Flaubert, Gustave. *Madame Bovary*. London: Everyman, 1993.

Friedman, Susan. *Tulsa Studies in Women's Literature*, (Fall 2004)

Ghosh, Amitav. *The Hungry Tide*. New York: Harper Collins, 2004.

Kymlicka, Well. *Multicultural Citizenship*. Oxford: Clarendon Press, 1998.

Lahiri, Jhumpa. *The Namesake*. USA: Harper Collins, 2003.

Rollason, Christopher. Rev. of *The Hungry Tide* by Amitav Ghosh, 4 July 2004.

Whitelock, Dorothy. *Sweet's Anglo-Saxon Reader*. Oxford: Clarendon Press, 1975.

Wolfreys, Julian, ed. *Glossalalia*. Edinburgh: Edinburgh U P, 2003.

# Teaching/Reading Maxine Hong Kingston's *Tripmaster Monkey, The Fifth Book of Peace,* and *The Woman Warrior,* in a Time of War and Conflict

**Kuldip Kaur Kuwahara**
**North Carolina Central University, USA**

A twenty-first century work written in a time of tremendous social, political, and cultural upheaval, Maxine Hong Kingston's part-memoir, part-fiction, *The Fifth Book of Peace* (a continuation of the fictional *Tripmaster Monkey*), is a landmark work in American and World Literature. Published in 2003, *The Fifth Book of Peace* poses the question: How can we create community in multi-ethnic America and across world cultures? How can we collapse the Euro-centric focus of "traditional" structures with marginalized African-American, Native American, and "others" to include them in a circle of connectedness, mutual respect, and celebration of the rich, multi-layering of diverse hybrid cultures that collectively shape a distinct American cultural sensibility?

The hero of *Tripmaster Monkey*, Wittman Ah Sing, represents the quintessential American poet, Walt Whitman, whose all-encompassing epic, *Leaves of Grass*, touches every blade of grass in cross-cultural, multi-ethnic America. It goes beyond America to include an East-West cultural consciousness deeply rooted in American Transcendentalism and Eastern mysticism. Kingston's reach includes Whitman, James Joyce, and other transnational and global writers. Hers is an American voice, a call for community in America and a challenge to critics like Frank Chin, who see her as an Asian-American writing "fake" Chinese history for the Euro-American reader. Chin's accusation of Kingston as an "orientalist" both complicates and clarifies her position as an American writer, who, in writing a strong indictment of American society, expands the notion of a "collective unconscious" to interpret more richly the American dream.

From Freud's *Dreams and the Unconscious* to Jung's "Collective Unconscious" is a big leap that can help the reader connect Kingston's *Fifth Book of Peace* with her first book of peace, *The Woman Warrior*. In *The Woman Warrior*, Kingston works with the myth of woman as conqueror, who flashes her sword of victory in triumph as she overcomes challenges of seemingly insurmountable obstacles within mythic and social structures. In doing this, she plays with the masculine/feminine duality to underline the paradox of masculine weakness and feminine strength in Chinese-American cross-cultural contexts. The woman warrior is portrayed as both feminine/weak and feminine/strong, as one who asserts woman power in giving birth; at the same time, she wears masculine attire and armor to disguise perceived feminine fragility set off against Asian-American patriarchal power structures.

The writer as mythmaker, the assertion of power, and conflict of power relations in cross-cultural settings, are among Kingston's themes in *The Woman Warrior*. The strong, feminine woman warrior breaks the silence imposed by patriarchal power with a sword. In doing so, she gives voice to the No-Name Woman with which Kingston's *Memoirs of a Girlhood Among Ghosts* begins. In narrating the dramatic story of her aunt's life and death, Kingston's mother gives shape and meaning to the silence of shame, fear and chaos that eventually lead to the self-destruction of a young mother and her new-born child. Looking back on the years of silence, she begins her narrative in America where the mother tells her daughter:

> "You must not tell anyone," my mother said, "what I am about to tell you. In China your father had a sister who killed herself. She jumped into the family well. We say that your father has all brothers because it is as if she had never been born."

> "In 1924 just a few days after our village celebrated seventeen hurry-up weddings--to make sure that every young man who went 'out' on the road would responsibly come home--your father and his brothers and your grandfather and his brothers and your aunt's new husband sailed for America, the Gold Mountain." (4)

With her husband gone for many years, the aunt was discovered to be pregnant; she was avenged by the villagers the night the baby was to be born:

> On the night the baby was to be born the villagers raided our house. Some were crying. Like a great saw, teeth strung with lights, files of people walked zigzag across our land, tearing the rice. Their lanterns doubled in the disturbed black water, which drained away through the broken bunds. (4)

She concluded her narrative of how she found the aunt and her baby next morning "plugging up the well." Since then, there had been silence, the aunt forgotten and denied as if she had never been born.

Haunted by the story of the No Name Woman, her aunt, Kingston self-consciously asserts at the close of the opening chapter of her memoir, "My aunt haunts me—her ghost drawn to me because now, after fifty years of neglect, I alone devote pages of paper to her" aware that "The Chinese are always frightened of the drowned one, whose weeping ghost, wet hair hanging and skin bloated, waits silently by the water to pull down a substitute" (16). Unafraid, and pen in hand, Kingston sets out as female avenger to affirm the meaning of her aunt's life, and to break the silence with the triumphant flashing of her mythic sword.

Not only does Kingston set out to break the silence of her female ancestor's life, she also explores the significance of talk stories to make sense of life. "In the twenty years since I heard this story, I have not asked for details nor said my aunt's name; I do not knøw it," she writes (16). She had grown up on her mother's stories that tested "strength to establish realities" (5) and the first American generations "had to figure out how the invisible world the emigrants built around our childhoods fits in solid America" (5).

Addressing Chinese-Americans, Kingston challenges them with the question, "Chinese-Americans, when you try to understand what things in you are Chinese, how do you separate what is peculiar to childhood, to poverty, insanities, one family, your mother who marked your growing with stories, from what is Chinese? What is Chinese tradition and what is the movies?" (5-6) The writer brandishes her sword to face and expose the truth to tell her story of growing up female, listening to stories, imagining the "real," trying to separate tradition from fantasy growing up in "solid America" raised by parents who themselves were nurtured and raised in faraway China, rooted in Chinese tradition and taking on new names when their lives changed as immigrants and sojourners in a new land.

An Asian-American writer like Kingston draws on a range of references and socio-cultural sources working at once with several layers of reference challenging the twenty-first century reader to interpret her work with awareness of the need for a hybrid aesthetic. Jung's interpretation of the Collective Unconscious provides an effective tool to approach Kingston's themes and techniques as she deftly knots together autobiography, memoir, and fiction, in an Asian-American cultural context.

Kingston takes the reader on a journey into the interior with its conflicts and anxieties as well as to the outer social world of human connections and contradictions. As Bonnie TuSmith observes:

> In *Woman Warrior* Kingston uses a narrator who has a child's passion for knowing. What is Chinese, and what is American? What is real and what is make-believe? Do the Chinese despise women, or do they see them as potential warriors? Since we have an impressionable protagonist/narrator who feels bombarded by confusing stories in her childhood, this desire for definition is understandable and in character. (49)

It is a process of growing up, listening to stories that contradict and confuse the "real" with the imagined and lead ultimately to an awareness of a Chinese-American cultural consciousness. Kingston explores and triumphantly celebrates the gradual shaping of a collective consciousness between the individual and community through reflections, dreams and mythmaking.

Jung's Collective Unconscious underlines the pattern Kingston sets out to discover. In acknowledging the achievements of Freud, Jung points out that "By evaluating dreams as the most important source of information concerning the unconscious processes, he gave back to mankind a tool that had seemed irretrievably lost" (169). He further asserts that "It may well be said that the contemporary cultural consciousness has not yet absorbed into its general philosophy the idea of the unconscious and all that it means, despite the fact that modern man has been confronted with this idea for more than half a century" (169). Writing her memoir in the twentieth-century, Kingston's woman warrior wields her powerful sword as deftly as her pen to uncover a complex web of conscious and unconscious realities.

In the Chapter titled "White Tigers," Kingston writes about the power of story-telling, "Night after night my mother would talk-story until we fell asleep. I couldn't tell where stories left off and dreams began, her voice the voice of heroines in my sleep" (19). One of these heroines was the warrior, Fa Mu Lan, a girl who took her father's place in battle. Her mother taught her the chant, "the two of us singing about how Fa Mu Lan fought gloriously and returned alive from war to settle in the village" (20). In repeating this story of Fa Mu Lan and teaching her the chant of victory, her mother's story permeated her conscious and unconscious reality prompting her to take on the challenge that "[She] would have to grow up a woman warrior" (20). In her dreaming, listening to stories and myth-making, the warrior-woman-in-training calls out, "I learned to make my mind large, as the universe is large, so that there is room for paradoxes. . . . We would always win, Kuan Kung, the god of war and literature riding before me. I would be told of in fairy tales myself" (38).

The power of writing, that writing gives shape to conscious and unconscious meaning as it heals and makes whole the dreamer and the writer empowering them to create bonds of sympathy with others, is evident in Kingston's writing. Jung's questions, after his break with Freud, are significant in this context. Jung's patients would report their fantasies and dreams to him and he would ask, "What occurs to you in connection with that?" or "How do you mean that, where does that come from, what do you think about it?" (170). All he knew was that dreams "indicated an unusual activation of the unconscious" even as he continued to search for a criterion and arrived at a moment of unusual clarity when he thought, "Now you possess a key to mythology and are free to unlock all the gates of the unconscious psyche" (171). As he worked on the inner world of fantasies, he gradually came to the realization that "delivering himself" to the psyche "was the only way by which I could endure my existence and live it as fully as possible" (192). He concluded:

> I could find contact with the outer world and with people only if I succeeded in showing—and this would demand the most intensive effort—that the contents of psychic experience are real, and real not only as my personal experiences, but as collective experiences which others also have. Later I tried to demonstrate this in my scientific work, and I did all in my power to convey to my intimates a new way of seeing things. I knew that if I did not succeed, I would be condemned to absolute isolation. (194-95)

In *The Woman Warrior*, Kingston moves from the search for the self (personal identity formation) to a collective consciousness, and, by extension, a Collective Unconscious. With a mission to protect and heal her community, the woman warrior (once she has defined herself and become her own person) is the powerful writer and truth-teller who rides into mythic battles with courage and compassion creating order and community. She is not the wife and slave with bound feet but flies free, both loved and loving, spreading her wings; she is vast and awe-inspiring as the dragon, and swift as a tiger. Her mission is to give voice to the No Name Woman, the gypsy women who roam helplessly, and the Moon Orchids who succumb to madness in their failure to affirm the self and connect with community.

Within the story Kingston narrates, are the stories she grew up on, including the strong influence of her mother's talk-stories. As Bonnie TuSmith points out, "In *The Woman Warrior* verbal articulation is necessary to survival. The protagonist shows how acutely she feels this when she tortures the quiet girl" to articulate something (53). "If you don't talk," she exclaims, "you can't have a personality" (53). Towards the conclusion of her *Memoirs of a Girlhood among Ghosts*, Kingston structures the mother-daughter talk-stories in sequence, the daughter's following the mother's: "Here is a story my mother told me, not when I was young, but recently, when I told her I also talk-story. The Beginning is hers, the ending, mine" (207). The mother tells of the songs of Ts'ai Yen, a poetess born in A.D. 175 who was captured by a chieftain during a raid by the Southern Hsiung-nu. Her songs of sadness and anger filled the desert air. The daughter continues the story of how after twelve years among the Southern Hsiung-nu, Ts'ai Yen was ransomed and married to Tung Ssu and that "She brought her songs back from the savage lands, and one of the three that has been passed down to us is "Eighteen Stanzas for a Barbarian Reed Pipe," a song that Chinese sing to their own instruments. It translated well" (209).

*The Woman Warrior: Memoirs of a Girlhood among Ghosts* ends with the music of the flute composed centuries ago by a poetess who reflects on her life's experiences, giving expression to emotions of sadness and anger as Kingston picks up the fictional pattern of talk-story within talk-story; it is this continuity that creates the Collective Unconscious, a pattern the writer seeks in her search for a definition of Chinese-American identity within the larger cultural context of American multi-ethnic consciousness. It is this myth-making ability, in the Jungian sense, that grows into the larger awareness and celebration of community with which *The Woman Warrior* concludes.

*Tripmaster Monkey* and *The Fifth Book of Peace* also conclude on a note of celebration and hope. At Tana and Wittman Ah Sing's wedding celebration in *Tripmaster Monkey*, "To drums and horns, the dragons and lions were dancing, a bunny-hopping conga line that danced out of the house and into the street. Wittman's community was blessing him, whether he liked it or not" (340). Wittman Ah Sing had made up his mind "not to go to Vietnam or to any war. He had staged the War of the Three Kingdoms as heroically as he could, which made him start to understand. . . . Studying the mightiest war epic of all time, Wittman changed-beeen!-into a pacifist" (340).

Exploring the meaning and significance of peace at the conclusion of *The Fifth Book of Peace*, Kingston points out: "The images of peace are ephemeral. The language of peace is subtle. The reasons for peace, the definitions of peace, the very idea of peace have to be invented, and invented again" (402). In a time of conflict and war, Kingston leaves us with the power of the written word. Affirming life's endless possibilities, she asserts, "Children, everybody, here's what to do during war: In a time of destruction, create something. A poem. A parade. A friendship. A community. A place that is the commons. A school. A vow. A moral principle. One peaceful moment" (402).

## List of Works Cited and Consulted

Jung, C.G. *Memories, Dreams, Reflections*. Trans. Richard and Clara Winston. Ed. Aniela Jaffe. New York: Vintage Books, 1989.

Kingston, Maxine Hong. *The Woman Warrior: Memoirs of a Girlhood among Ghosts*. New York: Random House/Vintage Books, 1977.

_____. *Tripmaster Monkey*. New York: Random House/Vintage Books, 1990.

_____. *The Fifth Book of Peace*. New York: Random House/Vintage Books, 2004.

TuSmith, Bonnie. *All My Relatives: Community in Contemporary Ethnic American Literatures*. Ann Arbor: The University of Michigan Press, 1994.